Key Issues in Creative Writing

Edited by

Dianne Donnelly and Graeme Harper

MULTILINGUAL MATTERS
Bristol • Buffalo • Toronto

Library of Congress Cataloging in Publication Data
A catalog record for this book is available from the Library of Congress.
Key Issues in Creative Writing/Edited by Dianne Donnelly and Graeme Harper.
New Writing Viewpoints: 9
Includes bibliographical references.
1. Creative writing--Study and teaching. I. Donnelly, Dianne. II. Harper, Graeme.
PE1404.K47 2012
808'.0420711–dc232012036454

British Library Cataloguing in Publication Data
A catalogue entry for this book is available from the British Library.

ISBN-13: 978-1-84769-847-6 (hbk)
ISBN-13: 978-1-84769-846-9 (pbk)

Multilingual Matters
UK: St Nicholas House, 31–34 High Street, Bristol, BS1 2AW, UK.
USA: UTP, 2250 Military Road, Tonawanda, NY 14150, USA.
Canada: UTP, 5201 Dufferin Street, North York, Ontario M3H 5T8, Canada.

The policy of Multilingual Matters/Channel View Publications is to use papers that are natural, renewable and recyclable products, made from wood grown in sustainable forests. In the manufacturing process of our books, and to further support our policy, preference is given to printers that have FSC and PEFC Chain of Custody certification. The FSC and/or PEFC logos will appear on those books where full certification has been granted to the printer concerned.

Typeset by The Charlesworth Group.
Printed and bound in Great Britain by the MPG Books Group.

Key Issues in Creative Writing

NEW WRITING VIEWPOINTS
Series Editor: Graeme Harper, *Oakland University, Rochester, USA*

The overall aim of this series is to publish books which will ultimately inform teaching and research, but whose primary focus is on the analysis of creative writing practice and theory. There will also be books which deal directly with aspects of creative writing knowledge, with issues of genre, form and style, with the nature and experience of creativity, and with the learning of creative writing. They will all have in common a concern with excellence in application and in understanding, with creative writing practitioners and their work, and with informed analysis of creative writing as process as well as completed artefact.

Full details of all the books in this series and of all our other publications can be found on http://www.multilingual-matters.com, or by writing to Multilingual Matters, St Nicholas House, 31–34 High Street, Bristol, BS1 2AW, UK.

Contents

Acknowledgements   vii

Contributors   ix

Introduction: Key Issues and Global Perspectives in Creative Writing
Dianne Donnelly and Graeme Harper   xiii

Part 1

1   Reshaping Creative Writing: Power and Agency in
the Academy
Dianne Donnelly   3

2   Hey Babe, Take a Walk on the Wild Side – Creative
Writing in Universities
Mimi Thebo   30

3   Creative Writing Habitats
Graeme Harper   48

4   Beyond the Literary: Why Creative Literacy Matters
Steve Healey   61

5   To Fill with Milk: or, The Thing and Itself
Katharine Haake   79

6   Creative Writing Research
Graeme Harper   103

7   Creative Writing Knowledge
Dianne Donnelly   116

Part 2

8   Teaching Toward the Future
Stephanie Vanderslice   137

9   Holding On and Letting Go
Indigo Perry   146

10   Programme Design and the Making of Successful Programmes
        Building a Better Elephant Machine: A Case Study
        in Creative Writing Programme Design
            Nigel McLoughlin   159
        The Future of Graduate Studies in Creative Writing:
        Institutionalizing Literary Writing
            Patrick Bizzaro   169

Conclusion: Investigating Key Issues in Creative Writing
Dianne Donnelly and Graeme Harper   178

Index   181

Acknowledgements

Dianne Donnelly. Collaborating on *Key Issues in Creative Writing* with Graeme Harper, who always seems to have a finger on the pulse of creative writing happenings, has been such a delight – many thanks, Graeme! Much appreciation goes to our contributors, whose thoughtful chapters present diverse and intelligent perspectives. Warm acknowledgments are sent to my friends and colleagues, particularly Joe Moxley and Rita Ciresi. As always, my love and gratitude go to my children Keith and Julia.

Graeme Harper. My warm thanks to Dianne, with whom it has been a very great pleasure to work on this book. A big thanks also to each, and all, of the contributors. It has been fabulous to bring together such a lively international team! Thank you greatly. Finally, love and thanks to Louise and the boys, Myles and Tyler.

We'd both like to send our considerable thanks to Anna Roderick, Tommi Grover and Elinor Robertson at Multilingual Matters. Thank you for your considerable vision, your fabulous support and your wonderful enthusiasm!

Contributors

Patrick Bizzaro

The Future of Graduate Studies in Creative Writing: Institutionalizing Literary Writing

Patrick Bizzaro, PhD, has published nine books and chapbooks of poetry (with another forthcoming in 2013), two critical studies of Fred Chappell's poetry and fiction, a book on the pedagogy of academic creative writing, four textbooks, and around 200 poems in magazines. His articles on Creative Writing Studies and composition have appeared regularly in *College English* and *College Composition and Communication*, and he is coeditor of *Composing Ourselves as Writer-Teacher-Writers* (2012). He has won the Madeline Sadin Award from *NYQ* and the *Four Quarter's* Poetry Prize as well as a Fulbright to visit South Africa during 2012 and nine teaching awards. Additionally, he is a frequent reviewer and critic of his peers' work in magazines like *Asheville Poetry Review*, *North Carolina Literary Review* and *Appalachian Journal*, among others. He is Professor of English at the Indiana University of Pennsylvania.

Dianne Donnelly

Introduction: Key Issues and Global Perspectives in Creative Writing (with Graeme Harper), *Reshaping Creative Writing: Power and Agency in the Academy*, *Creative Writing Knowledge*, and *Conclusion: Investigating Key Issues in Creative Writing* (with Graeme Harper)

Dianne Donnelly, PhD **(Editor)**, is the author of *Establishing Creative Writing Studies as an Academic Discipline* (2011) and the editor of *Does the Writing Workshop Still Work?* (2010). She is a regular contributor to the theory and pedagogy of creative writing and a frequent presenter at CCCC and AWP on creative writing pedagogy. She is on the editorial board for *New Writing: The International Journal for the Practice and Theory of Creative Writing* and *Writing Commons*, referees for the online peer-reviewed journal *TEXT*, and teaches writing at the University of South Florida. Currently, she is at work on a new novel and a collaborative creative writing research project.

Katharine Haake

To Fill with Milk: or, The Thing and Itself

Dr Katharine Haake's books include two works of fabulist fiction from What Books Press, *The Time of Quarantine* (2012), a dystopian novel, and *The Origin of Stars and Other Stories* (2009), a collection of eco fables, and two works of hybrid narrative from the University of Nevada Press, *That Water, Those Rocks* (2003), a novel, and *The Height and Depth of Everything* (2001), stories. Her writing has appeared widely in such literary journals as *One Story, Witness, The Iowa Review, New Letters* and *Crazyhorse*. A regular contributor to scholarship in the theory and pedagogy of creative writing, she is also the author of *What Our Speech Disrupts: Feminism and Creative Writing Studies* (NCTE), and teaches at California State University, Northridge.

Graeme Harper

Introduction: Key Issues and Global Perspectives in Creative Writing (with Dianne Donnelly), *Creative Writing Habitats*, *Creative Writing Research* and *Conclusion: Investigating Key Issues in Creative Writing* (with Dianne Donnelly)

Graeme Harper, DCA, PhD, **(Editor)** is Director of The Honors College and Professor at Oakland University, Michigan. He holds doctoral degrees from the University of East Anglia (UK) and from the University of Technology, Sydney (Australia) – the latter, Australia's first doctoral degree in Creative Writing. He has been a professor or honorary professor in the UK, USA and Australia, and from 2008–2011 was inaugural Chair of the Higher Education Committee of the UK's National Association of Writers in Education (NAWE). His latest works of fiction include *The Invention of Dying* (2012) and *Moon Dance* (2008), under his pseudonym, Brooke Biaz. He has also recently published *Inside Creative Writing* (2012) and *On Creative Writing* (2010). He is Editor-in-Chief of *New Writing: The International Journal for the Practice and Theory of Creative Writing*. His awards have included the National Book Council Award for New Fiction (Australia), among others.

Steve Healey

Beyond the Literary: Why Creative Literacy Matters

Steve Healey, PhD, is the author of two books of poetry, *Earthling* (2004) and *10 Mississippi* (2010), both published by Coffee House Press. His essays and criticism have appeared in magazines such as *The Writer's Chronicle* and *Rain Taxi*. His poems have appeared in anthologies such as *Legitimate Dangers: American Poets of the New Century*, and in many journals, such as *American Poetry Review, Boston Review, Fence* and *Jubilat*. He has an MFA in poetry writing from UMASS/Amherst and a PhD in English from the University of Minnesota. He is an Assistant Professor of English at Minneapolis Community and Technical College.

Nigel McLoughlin

Building a Better Elephant Machine: A Case Study in Creative Writing Programme Design

Nigel McLoughlin, PhD, is Professor of Creativity and Poetics at the University of Gloucestershire. He is a prize-winning poet with five published collections, the latest of which is *Chora: New and Selected Poems* (Templar Poetry, 2009) and he edits *Iota* poetry journal. In 2011, he was awarded a UK National Teaching Fellowship.

Indigo Perry

Holding On and Letting Go

Indigo Perry, PhD, is a lecturer in Professional and Creative Writing within the School of Communication and Creative Arts at Deakin University, Melbourne, Australia. She teaches mainly in the areas of fiction and life-writing. Previously known as Gaylene Perry, her book, *Midnight Water: A Memoir* was shortlisted for Australia's National Biography Award. Currently at work on a novel, she is also engaged in creative writing and creative arts theory and practice and practice-led research. She is on the Executive Committee of the Australian Association of Writing Programs and a referee for the online journal *TEXT*.

Mimi Thebo

Hey Babe, Take a Walk on the Wild Side – Creative Writing in Universities

Mimi Thebo, PhD, is the author of seven books of fiction for children and adults. Her work has been translated into seven languages and signed for beginning deaf readers. Her children's book *Wipe Out* was adapted for film, translated into French and won an award from CRUSE, the children's grief charity. She has been shortlisted for the Lancaster Book Award, the McKitterick Prize and the Ian St James Awards and is also a prize-winning poet. Mimi's work in the academy includes several investigations into the employability of creative writing graduates, and she has widely published and spoken about her innovative curriculum design.

Stephanie Vanderslice
Teaching Toward the Future

Stephanie Vanderslice, MFA, PhD, teaches creative writing at the University of Central Arkansas where she also directs the newly-minted Arkansas Writers MFA Program. Her latest book is *Rethinking Creative Writing in Higher Education.* Her fiction and non-fiction have appeared in numerous journals and edited collections. She is currently at work on a novel.

Introduction: Key Issues and Global Perspectives in Creative Writing

Dianne Donnelly and Graeme Harper

Creative Writing Practice and the Academy

Hazel Smith and Roger T. Dean (2009: 9) suggest that 'It is pointless for creative writing practitioners to work within the university unless the university environment responds to them and they respond to it'. Given the strength of such a claim, what then can we say about the relationship between creative writing and the academy? More specifically, what importance and value does creative writing bring to the academy, and how does the nature of the university environment impact the discipline?

We know that creative writing course/program enrollment in the United States, United Kingdom and Australia continues to climb. The Association of Writers and Writing Programs (AWP) 2011 *Guide to Writing Programs*, for example, points to a significant rise in US creative writing programs, and this increase is in spite of university funding cuts and an overall decline in Humanities' majors. The 79 undergraduate and graduate creative writing programs recorded in 1975 pale in comparison to the reported present figure of 813. Of this number, more than 346 are at the graduate level (37 award the PhD), and tens of thousands of students enter and graduate from the programs each year. Likewise, even though creative writing programs are comparatively new in Australia, PhD program numbers have increased from eight in 1999 to the 25 doctoral programs available in Australia and New Zealand today (AAWP, 2011). To add to this growth, what began as a 'single, experimental course' in the UK, has developed 'in the space of 40 years to 139 institutions offering HE [Higher Education] qualifications of some sort in Creative Writing'(Munden, 2011: 222). In the United Kingdom, 60 (at the time of writing) graduate creative writing programs are included on the NAWE website, with some emerging programs perhaps yet to be recorded.

The reasons students enroll in creative writing courses and degree programs differ significantly as creative writing courses/programs often draw students from a varied disciplinary base. Whether students want to write within an interactive environment, experiment with poetic or fiction forms or other genres, or explore creative literacies, the courses satisfy a broad spectrum of student interests. Creative literacy, Steve Healey concludes in Chapter 4 of this collection, 'has spurred the boom in creative writing' as 'students want access to a kind of cultural capital that's not specifically "literary" but much more amorphously "creative"'. Brian Castro[1] (University of Adelaide) insists that creative writing 'flourishes on many fronts: from publications by students to connecting with the community'. Our contributors contend that there is more to creative writing than getting published, more, Katharine Haake suggests, than 'simply professional training for writers of poetry, fiction, and other literary genres'. In Chapter 5, she questions, 'if we limit our objectives to the teaching of "good writing", once somewhat vaguely defined as writing of "publishable literary quality", we miss an important opportunity to raise larger questions about writing itself – what and how it is and what it means and how it moves through the world'. Haake offers that 'These larger questions are transferable, across disciplines and discourses'. Graeme Harper (2010: xi) connects the public experience that students reference in their creative writing coursework (e.g. that which relates to 'culture' or 'society', 'literature', 'readers' or 'writers') to the personal experience factor, and notes that the fluidity of students' ideals and ideas between individual and holistic influences 'is indicative of the fluidity of Creative Writing as a practice'. Harper (2010: xi) concludes that similarly, 'Creative Writing, as a range of results rarely stays still for long'. In Chapter 9, Indigo Perry charts the creative writing course as 'an ocean – always changing water, currents, levels, temperatures, boundaries, colours and textures'.

The university environment offers 'a natural place for writers to meet with students who wish to write' (J. Robert Lennon, Cornell[2]), and a 'quick and immediate place and community within which to work and be creative' (Virgio Suarez, FSU[3]). Although the practice-based process of creative writing practice is not unlike other academic disciplines, particularly the practices of the creative arts, J. Robert Lennon[4] suggests that creative writing does not necessarily 'lend itself well to the kind of apprenticeships other art forms enjoy'. In other words, Lennon clarifies 'a young writer is not going to have the opportunity to tour with a writing troupe, or play in a writing combo, or serve as a writing studio assistant', but the university environment does provide opportunities for students to discover, practice and connect with a writing community. It also 'provides a framework for research which works conjointly with creative activity', adds Brian Castro,[5] and he notes, 'this is the way it should be'.

What are the areas of differentiation among creative writing programs in the United States, Australia and the United Kingdom? Many undergraduate programs offer creative writing classes to what American colleagues call 'non-majors', and some programs have integrated the creative writing course in the US as a general education requirement, meaning it is available to students pursuing all disciplinary specialisms. While the MFA program in the US may range from a studio-based program to a program that requires intensive creative writing coursework as well as academic studies similar to that of a literature major, globally the PhD has been called 'the high point of investigating, understanding and pursuing creative writing' (Harper, 2005: 80).

Creative writing PhDs in the UK and Australia were not directly modeled against the US creative writing graduate degree. As such, creative writing did not share a history with composition studies as it did in the US, and 'one reason for the emergence of the PhD in Creative Writing in Britain was the incredible popularity of MA programmes' (Harper, 2005: 80). Harper (2005: 80) suggests that 'English Departments, in particular, were under pressure to produce financially viable new ideas to match the strong growth of subjects such as Business Studies, Leisure Studies, Psychology and even Media Studies during the late 1980s and early 1990s. This story of academic competition is not vastly different to that experienced in the USA'.

The majority of United Kingdom and Australian graduate students complete a creative dissertation and a substantial critical response (of which the latter contributes to disciplinary knowledge) while the creative dissertation in the US is recognized as the Master's or doctoral academic equivalency of research output. The hybridization of creative and critical considers not only the processes of creative writers in action, but also 'an original investigation undertaken in order to gain knowledge and understanding' (Candy, 2006). In other words, the 'creative work acts as a form of research' in that the creative practice – 'the training and specialized knowledge that creative practitioners have and the processes they engage in when they are [writing a creative piece]' – leads to 'specialised research insights which can then be generalised and written up as research' (Smith & Dean, 2009: 5). Smith and Dean (2009: 5) explain that '[t]he first argument [*practice-based research*] emphasises creative practice in itself, while the second [*practice-led research*] highlights the insights, conceptualisation and theorisation which can arise when [writers] reflect on and document their own creative practices'.

Secondly, university regulations and the expectations of the academy strongly steer research practices in the UK and in Australia, and the agencies behind these regulations and expectations are government funding bodies. In contrast, there is not really any primary funding impetus for the US to design practice-led research programs as part of graduate creative writing study. As a further deterrent, little pressing professional impulsion exists at the academic level for creative writing teachers to engage in the critical study of creative writing. In fact, Moxley (2010: 231) places 'the constraining force of the existing faculty reward system' in perspective when he indicates not only 'how slow the discipline is to evolve', but how his groundbreaking scholarly 1989 collection *Creative Writing in America: Theory and Pedagogy* did not count toward his tenure. Add to this limitation the didactic nature of staggering 2010–2011 student enrollment numbers with major university 'cut-backs' (moratoriums, in some cases) on faculty hires and resulting increases in undergraduate class size (to the tune, in some cases, of 60–90 students per class) and *time* for creative writing teachers becomes a valued commodity to pursue only those creative works that advance promotion portfolios. Moreover, while there is movement toward exploring creative writing practice in the US – recent scholarship suggests moving the discipline to a more practice-led model – in that teachers question *what* they teach and *how* they teach, the discipline remains more practice-based, more pedagogical than critical and theoretical in its approach.

Many of the differences that exist among creative writing programs in the US, UK and Australia relate to university and funding initiatives. What is similar across all programs (but for different reasons) is the nature of the university environment, which challenges the discipline of creative writing through its conflicting demands of creativity and criticism and sometimes through its rigid taxonomies and methodologies that relate to disciplines vastly different to creative writing. With this background in mind, some have questioned whether the postgraduate creative writing discourse meets the same research standards as other disciplines; others have asked, alternatively, whether it ever should meet those standards, given the origin of those standards. In the United States, while graduate creative writing students may be influenced by creative processes, they are not, as noted earlier, expected to submit scholarly work that complements their creative dissertations. Moreover, government funding mechanisms do not really support the kind of practice-led research in creative writing that would ultimately lead to the discovery of widespread knowledge in the field, via such investigations. Reflections may come in the form of individual writers' self-reports; also, diligent inquiries impact the authenticity and credibility of a story, novel or poem (or hybrid/multimodal genre) as these are necessary developmental processes – yet, the creative work is expected to stand on its own as evidence of a research achievement. In fact, US practitioners are asked to evidence their creative activity in their annual faculty evaluation applications. A growing number of US graduate creative writing students and teachers do engage in connected research activity, and the results of such activity may present in writing conference forums or other scholarly publications. And recently, a small number of MFA and/or PhD programs complement the creative work with a critical study as part of the degree, and such an impetus may position the discipline in a more 'mainstream' academic light in these selected universities. It is also possible that the growth of creative writing PhD programs, in particular, may influence an academic movement, embracing a new sense of the relationship between creative writing endeavor and critical examination.

In the UK and Australia, the PhD degree (or other doctoral qualification) in creative writing has increasingly been standard for a university teaching position. Creative writers are thus more often asked to conform to research agendas that demonstrate evidence of knowledge acquisition, investigation and advancement. As such, creative writing programs in the UK and Australia are challenged to compete with other disciplines for research monies, and they are increasingly engaged in defining how creative writing as a discipline can define its research territory and research practices.

Organizations that assess US doctoral programs also impact creative writing's critical standing in the academy. The National Research Council (NRC, n.d.) assessment of research doctorate programs, tracks 20 variables that it considers to be program quality measures. The results, taken seriously by academic leaders, allow prospective students to compare graduate studies programs. Data collected to assess faculty research activity includes faculty honors and awards, publications, citations and grants. NRC does not rank creative writing as a component of the English department, likely because in such research terms the discipline doesn't have critical mass. Should the NRC include creative writing as a ranked field, the discipline might consider how literary studies came up short in the 2010 rankings mostly because 'the apparatus used to calculate citations in the sciences . . . picks up only a portion of humanities journals and no humanities monographs' (Bauerlein, 2010). As such, 'Scholarship [is] pretty much the single measure of research activity in English . . . The focus ends up gauging quantity, not quality' (Bauerlein, 2010). Mark Bauerlein (2010) suggests that 'If humanities departments were wise, they would respond to the NRC report with effusive thanks and a polite request to recalibrate the rankings for their own fields'. A cautionary tale for creative writing is embedded in the discussion above: if the discipline is to have critical mass and a visible presence in the academy then it might begin now to take stock of its benchmarks of research activity – its faculty scholarship, grants, honors and awards.

Quite apparent differences among the research assessment bodies in the US, UK and Australia exist. Some of these research assessment bodies are tied to funding initiatives and consequently link with recognition of creative writing in the academy. While in the States there is no funding body that awards creative writers for participating in research activities, its National Research Council (NCR) ranks American universities and college institutions based on (among many other variables) teacher value, quality of programming, and publications. The NCR study is released approximately every 10 years although there was a 15 year gap between the 2010 release and the previous study. The Research Assessment Exercise (RAE), a national measure, has considered research performance units in the United Kingdom's Higher Education Institutions (HEIs) periodically, initiated by the Thatcher government in 1986. The last RAE in the United Kingdom was in 2008, and the next research assessment, now called the Research Excellence Framework (REF), is to take place in 2014. Results have been compiled by appointed RAE (now REF) panels, and the results of such assessments impact directly on government research funding allocations to institutions. The REF is managed for the UK by the Higher Education Funding Council for England (HEFCE). In Australia, the government initiative Excellence in Research for Australia (ERA) has also evaluated research performance in HEIs. A 2009 ERA trial included the assessment of the Creative Arts cluster, which contains the creative writing discipline, and the study continued in 2010 and was scheduled again for 2012. The ERA built on Australia's earlier Research Quality Framework (RQF), as well as relating its approach to that seen in Britain's RAE.

Also among the differences are research funding bodies and research assessment credit for journal publications. Australian and UK research councils count peer-reviewed journal publications as indicators of scholarly achievement, and do not usually count, for instance, the published equivalents of the many how-to books that have dominated the US market since the onset of New Criticism guided textbooks. Although there are significant differences among US, UK and Australia research assessment bodies, all entities seek to measure the research quality of HEIs. As such, noting how research quality in creative writing can be viewed is pressing. On a global plane, what would now prove valuable is a common language that addresses benchmarks for creative writing research as well as a strategic plan to increase the national and international visibility of creative writing's contribution to human knowledge, understanding and critical engagement with the world around us. Of equal importance in this aim is gaining the attention and understanding of university and governing bodies of the significant work that is done in undertaking and investigating creative writing and the undertaking of creative writing.

As creative writing has competed in the modern academic environment, there has often been some degree of tension between the discipline and the academy in part because of the way in which the 20th century economy shaped creative writing's public face; and, likewise, how it shaped the academy. To date, influenced by this 20th century agenda, student interest has largely been the force propelling creative writing programs in HEIs. The discipline's continued growth is also often measured by students' widespread enthusiasm and investment in the writing of their own work. Unlike other leading areas in the academy such as the physical or technological sciences, creative writing is not a major income-producing discipline, beyond that core student recruitment income. Even in the United Kingdom and Australia, where government funding is more directly tied to research, creative writing doctoral candidates have most often been less than successful in their attempts to attract Research Council funding, despite evidence that the discipline may produce more published, assessable, knowledge-based outputs than many other humanities' programs. For example, by 2010, 'Creative Writing had a higher national rating in the Australian Government's Excellence in Research (ERA) report than either literary studies or cultural studies, and produced twice as many research outputs' (Dale, 2011).

For the past decade, 'creative writing has been one of the most rapidly expanding and popular disciplines in United Kingdom higher education' (Steve May, Bath Spa[6]). Steve May, who heads the Creative Writing and Publishing Department at Bath Spa University, explains that finance officers 'like high and easy recruitment'. However, the UK government's response to the current global recession may impact the discipline's continued growth as the government is scheduled to withdraw its funding for education and 'transfer the cost of higher education to the student consumer' (Threadgold, 2011). Terry Threadgold, Pro Vice-Chancellor at Cardiff University, relates that 'From 2012–13, universities will be able to charge UK and European Union students up to £9,000 [$14,355.93 US dollars], up from the current £3,500 [$5,582.86 US dollars]'. Threadgold predicts that this fee may be too high for the humanities. Another variable is that parental income (an equivocal factor in student attendance at universities) may now direct a student's focus of study. With funding moving to government priority areas (science, technology, engineering, mathematics), parents may direct their college-bound children 'to study "hard", "old fashioned" subjects to give them a better chance in the contracting job market'

(Steve May, Bath Spa[7]). Combine this factor with the awareness that funding for the Arts and Humanities Research Council has been reduced, and the concern remains over how the creative writing discipline will sustain its current posterity in the United Kingdom.

Based on the findings of the Bradley Review of Australian Higher Education, the Australian government will increase funding to universities. Part of that financial support is related to a 'demand-driven' funding system that allows HEIs to enroll and provide students with an undergraduate degree. The Australian Government manages higher education funding, defines the quality of higher education and its costs, assesses the benefits of higher education to the public and knowledge community, [and] decides 'what funding model provides the best incentive to universities to deliver on the Australian Government's commitment to equity, skills, growth and quality' (Higher Education 2020 Newsletter, 2010: 8). John Dale admits that getting creative writing accepted and integrated into the university 'to the same degree of acceptance that it receives in colleges and universities across the US' was a challenge, and Brian Castro[8] (University of Adelaide) does not think that 'a lot of the old hierarchy quite understands it'. Castro[9] contends that while [the discipline] attracts and brings in money, it is largely invisible in the university, which he laments is 'now a corporation'.

In today's deflated economy, many American universities hope for a budget with no new reductions in state funding for higher education. 'Flat is the new up', is the way Rebecca Wyke, vice chancellor of finance and administration for the University of Maine system sees it. With '[r]evenue not expected to return to 2008 fiscal-year levels until 2014', Wyke predicts that 'the state will be struggling to maintain all of its services, and pent-up demand for funding will be very competitive over the next few years', and to this she adds, 'We're happy to be where we are right now' (in Biemiller, 2011). The University of Maine is representative of the kind of financial constraints many state university and college leaders face when it comes to negotiating tuition, instruction and other operational issues in these challenging economic times.

While reshaping the university infrastructure, shaving physical plant costs and exercising fundraising efforts are measures practiced by administrators to best operate in these lean years, raising tuition costs is one effort that has significant rippling effects throughout the academy. Consider that today's creative writing college degree 'is up some 3,400 percent since 1972', but 'household incomes haven't increased by anything close to that number' (Jaffe, 2011). Present and forecasted unemployment rates as well as credit card and housing bubbles make investing in degree programs more challenging. The 2007 recession is still upon us, and both students and administrators feel the crunch. From the university's perspective, the academic and financial future of the university is in science and technical engineering and the training programs that will lead to jobs (Thaxton[10]). The small creative writing class size makes the discipline an expensive capital venture despite the increased student interest in the program track.

While the job market is intensely competitive, the thready pulse of creative writing as an income-producing entity within the academy should give us pause to respond to university administrators in dynamic and realistic ways. What then, does this 'never-enough evolution' of sustainability (Thaxton[11]) mean for creative writing practice in the academy, a practice that is poorly funded and now includes, in many universities and colleges, student-teacher inflation ratios, a mixed-mode curriculum and larger class size? Is there a way to make the discipline more manageable for university administrators? Terry Thaxton,[12] panelist at the 2011 AWP Conference, insists that 'We need to talk about [creative writing] before we lose it'. Nigel McLoughlin predicts in this collection that 'It is certain that there will also be further economic pressures to find new ways of teaching which respond to funding cuts and efficiency drives but also maintain the quality of teaching and learning experience'. Given this forecast and the realistic understanding that we cannot continue (for the most part) to teach within the same framework as we have in the past, what is the best way to talk about creative writing practice in the academy today? Is the field, as Indigo Perry suggests, 'ripe for change'? If so, what will be the drivers for such change? How might we consider the shape and space of creative writing in the academy, the 'possibilities for spaces, environments, habitats for the teaching and learning' (Perry) – habitats as 'the layered engagement with space and time' (Harper), the 'unfettered spaces' (Donnelly), the 'spaciousness around thinking about teacher/student, professional/amateur and producer/consumer binaries', 'around genre and form' (Perry), around 'a both/and formulation' and binary assumptions which are seen as 'multiple and fluid' (Haake). As any field of knowledge surely benefits from being explored within a university, the purpose, aim and focus of this collection are to investigate the critical areas of creative writing in Higher Education institutions from a variety of approaches, and a number of places in the world. *Key Issues in Creative Writing* introduces a range of issues that inform the practice and understanding of creative writing. It examines creative writing as a subject in universities and colleges and discusses the ways in which the subject uses and explores a range of creative and critical knowledge. The collection outlines issues (areas of investigation) that arise because of the nature of creative writing, and suggests ways in which those issues might form the basis of a disciplinary understanding that impacts the ways in which courses, or programs of study, are developed and become successful in today's academic environment.

The first part of the collection locates creative writing within and throughout the academy and explores variable key issues related to creative writing habitats, genre, hybridity, research and knowledge. The latter section considers variable university teaching perspectives and studies related to successful creative writing course and program design. *Key Issues in Creative Writing* is an inquiry-based study and, as such, issue-based questions drive this collection forward.

Key Issues in Creative Writing

Part 1

(1) How might we move the discipline forward within the modern economy and critical academy? In what ways can we add agency and power to its position in HEIs and respond as champions for the discipline, as proactive rather than reactive agents of change? Terry Threadgold (2011) urges that 'the future success of higher education institutions depends on universities learning to re-imagine themselves regularly'. In 'Reshaping Creative Writing: Power and Agency in the Academy', Dianne Donnelly interrogates what this 're-imagining' might mean for creative writing in the academy, noting as she does that 'the future success of creative writing depends on our agency – on the ways in which we go forward, on the ways in which we intentionally design our coursework and programs and the ways in which we stay attuned to our students' needs, to the modern economic critical academy and to our community coalitions'.

(2) How important is the understanding of creative writing's history to its practice and development? Mimi Thebo explores creative writing's history and its relationship with the academy, asking as she does, 'How did we get t/here?' 'Do we belong t/here?' 'Do we know what we are doing t/here?' She characterizes creative writing in terms of 'otherness' and 'wildness', and laments its lack of 'aboutness'. In 'Hey, Babe, Take a Walk on the Wild Side – Creative Writing in Universities', Thebo explains the dualities of metacognitive language and advances the intellectual and ethical development of students' stages of development or 'graduateness'.

(3) What is a creative writer's 'creative writing habitat'? And what are the nature, forms and applications we associate with the habitats created, adopted or adapted by writers for their creative writing? Graeme

Harper explores how a creative writing habitat comes about and the influences (in terms of time and in terms of space) it has on the success and failure of creative writing projects. By implication, as well as by direct address, he explores: what might be the sorts of things we might teach and learn about creative writing habitats?

(4) What does creative literacy mean for creative writers and the academic discipline? Steve Healey suggests that 'many creative writing students are not particularly attached to traditional literary genres but seek access to a more general creative literacy'. The 'practical implication' is that 'creative writing can and does lead students to a much wider range of careers and professional paths than is often acknowledged'. In 'Beyond the Literary: Why Creative Literacy Matters', Healey sees creative writing as a way to distribute creative literacy throughout the academy.

(5) How do we define genre in today's creative writing discipline? Katharine Haake explains in 'To Fill with Milk: or, The Thing and Itself', the 'transgressable' nature of genre, as that which is 'stable enough to hold together as its function and fluid enough to allow for its own transformation'. She teaches her students to 'think systematically about what they are doing when they're writing and the kinds of choices they are making', encouraging as she does, a 'both/and practice', where writing is located 'in relation to larger and historical trajectories', where writing is fostered as a 'conversation', as a 'positive value', as 'interstitialty'.

(6) What are the key issues in creative writing *as* research and in creative writing research? In what ways does critical understanding play a role in creative writing? Graeme Harper explores the relationship between private and public knowledge in creative writing and the ways in which we might negotiate and develop this relationship. He queries: how do we assess graduate work in creative writing where many outputs are possible, but where assessment of critical understanding is often incorporated?

(7) In what ways is creative writing a knowledge-based discipline? Does creative writing knowledge have further opportunities to inform our views and ideas about the world? Dianne Donnelly explores creative writing as 'a field of intellectual inquiry' and as 'a practice-led academic discipline committed to the advancement and expansion of knowledge in its field'. In 'Creative Writing Knowledge', Donnelly frames the epistemological shape of creative writing, compares it to other domains, and builds on the knowledge discoveries of its creative writing body.

Part 2

(8)   What teaching practices exist that consider the actions and under-
       standing of creative writing in the academy? In addition to teaching a
       diversity of craft elements and strategies writers can use across all
       genres, Stephanie Vanderslice prepares her students for the world *they*
       live in by teaching core 'habits of the mind'. In 'Teaching Toward
       the Future', Vanderslice considers for her 'writers in the digital land-
       scape', common objectives related to 'digital competencies', 'industry
       awareness and initiative' and 'resilience'.

(9)   In what ways do the critical processes of research, study and theory
       impact creative writing pedagogies? Like Vanderslice, Indigo Perry
       situates her chapter with perspectives on the landscape in which *she*
       learned and notes how different the landscape is for today's creative
       writing student. The future for teaching and learning creative writing,
       Perry shares, is about space and spaciousness, the 'holding on' to the
       theory of creative writing and the 'letting go of boundaries in our
       course design, teaching and assessment'.

(10)   Can creative writing program design be better or worse and, if so, then
       in what ways? Nigel McLoughlin considers this question in his case
       study of a successful program design at the University of Gloucester-
       shire. He contends in 'Building a Better Elephant Machine: A Case
       Study in Creative Writing Program Design' that 'it is no longer suffi-
       cient [or efficient] to design a programme that replicates unthinkingly
       the Iowa Workshop model, or to replicate what has been standard
       practice'. The program design emphasis at the University of Glouces-
       tershire is on 'progression for the student', a '"writerly" degree, a
       craft-focused, student-centered and critical curriculum that focus[es]
       on making writing and reading as a writer'.

       Patrick Bizzaro, in the second part of this chapter, positions Quan-
       tum Rhetoric, 'which combines training in creative writing at the
       graduate level with graduate study in a professional/technical field, as
       a way to situate creative writing in the academy'. In his essay 'The
       Future of Graduate Studies in Creative Writing: Institutionalizing
       Literary Writing', Bizzaro projects that 'creative writing might help
       future professionals better describe new discoveries' and might 'teach
       writing skills that are not currently being taught generally in the uni-
       versity, skills we currently do not know how to teach in any other
       way right now except as "creative writing"'.

Creative writing, as a range of results, rarely stays still for long. With
this in mind, how might the key issues of creative writing we interrogate in

this collection impact the future of the discipline? Patrick Bizzaro forecasts: 'the future holds a great many things', for creative writing, 'some unimaginable to us right now', and the discipline 'will be used in the university in increasingly innovative ways'. Nigel McLoughlin reminds us that 'in an era of student choice', universities will demand 'more distinctive programmes . . . that fit niche markets', and 'program design will be more informed by theories of how students learn and what research tells us about how the creative process works'. Indigo Perry sees a future that allows 'far greater intellectual engagement', more 'space and spaciousness for the dynamic energy of creativity; indeed, the dynamic energy of practice'. While *Key Issues in Creative Writing* examines the dynamic and fluid nature of creative writing and the ways in which the discipline has evolved, the collection also suggests gaps and ways of exploring and narrowing those gaps in understanding – with an eye on the discipline's future role in the academy and in the world at large.

Notes

(1)   B. Castro (personal communications, May 15, 2011)
(2)   J. Robert Lennon (personal communications, May 10, 2011)
(3)   V. Suarez (personal communications, May 10, 2011)
(4)   J. Robert Lennon (personal communications, May 10, 2011)
(5)   B. Castro (personal communications, May 15, 2011)
(6)   S. May (personal communications, May 10, 2011)
(7)   As above
(8)   B. Castro (personal communications, May 15, 2011)
(9)   As above
(10) T.A. Thaxton (AWP Conference 'The Future of Creative Writing in the Academy', Washington, DC., Feb. 4, 2011)
(11) As above
(12) As above

References

Association of Writers and Writing Programs (AWP), accessed 6 June 2011. Available at: http://guide.awpwriter.org/.

Australasian Association of Writing Programs (AAWP), accessed 17 May 2011. Available at: http://www.aawp.org.au/.

Bauerlein, M. (2010) Two problems with the new doctoral rankings. Minding the Campus: Reforming our Universities, accessed 8 August 2012. Available at: http://www.mindingthecampus.com/originals/2010/09/two_problems_with_the_new_doct.html.

Biemiller, L. (2011) 'Colleges keep an eye on reports about jobs, revenue – and crops', *The Chronicle of Higher Education*, accessed 17 January 2011. Available at: http://chronicle.com/article/Keeping-an-Eye-on-Reports/127857/?sid=at&utm_source=at&utm_medium=en.

Candy, L. (2006) 'Practice-based research: A guide', Creativity and Cognition Studios, University of Technology, accessed 13 January 2011. Available at: http://www.creativityandcognition.com.

Dale, J. (2011) 'The rise and rise of creative writing', *The Conversation*, 25 May 2011, accessed 12 January 2012. Available at: http://theconversation.edu.au/the-rise-and-rise-of-creative-writing-730.

Harper, G. (2005) The Creative Writing doctorate: Creative trial or academic error? *New Writing: The International Journal for the Practice and Theory of Creative Writing* 2 (2), 79–84.

Harper, G. (2010) *On Creative Writing*. Bristol: Multilingual Matters.

Higher Education 2020 Newsletter (2010) Department of Education (Dec.) 11, accessed 8 December 2010. Available at: http://www.deewr.gov.au/HigherEducation/Publications/.../NewsletterIssue11.rtf.

Jaffe, S. (2011) 'The next bubble is about to burst: College grads face dwindling jobs and mounting loans', *AlterNet* (June), accessed 16 December 2010. Available at: http://www.alternet.org/story/151149/the_next_bubble_is_about_to_burst%3A_college_grads_face_dwindling_jobs_and_mounting_loans/.

Moxley, J. (2010) Afterword: Disciplinarity and the future of creative writing studies. In D. Donnelly (ed.) *Does the Writing Workshop Still Work?* (pp. 230–238). Bristol: Multilingual Matters.

Munden, P. (2011) Sharing the art, craft and imagination: The National Association of Writers in Education. *New Writing: The International Journal for the Practice and Theory of Creative Writing Special Issue*, 215–237.

National Bureau of Economic Research (2011), 5 August 2011, accessed 14 July 2011. Available at: http://www.nber.org/.

National Institute of Health, accessed 14 July 2011. Available at: http://ohsr.od.nih.gov/info/sheet3.html.

National Research Council, accessed 18 July 2011. Available at: http://www.nationalacademies.org/nrc/.

Smith, H. and Dean, R.T. (2009) Introduction: Practice-led, research-led research – toward the interactive cyclic web. In H. Smith and R.T. Dean (eds) *Practice-Led Research, Research-Led Practice in the Creative Arts (Research Methods for the Arts and Humanities)* (pp. 1–38). Edinburgh: Edinburgh University Press.

Threadgold, T. (2011) 'The global impact of UK university funding cuts', *The Conversation*, 17 May 2011, accessed 18 December 2011. Available at: http://theconversation.edu.au/the-global-impact-of-uk-university-funding-cuts-864.

Part 1

1 Reshaping Creative Writing: Power and Agency in the Academy

Dianne Donnelly

Terry Threadgold urges that 'the future success of higher education institutions depends on universities learning to re-imagine themselves regularly'. This chapter interrogates what this 're-imagining' might mean for creative writing in the academy, noting that the future success of creative writing depends on the discipline's agency – on the ways in which creative writing goes forward, on the ways in which its practitioners intentionally design their coursework and programs and the ways in which creative writing programs stay attuned to their students' needs, to the modern economic critical academy and to their community coalitions. This chapter urges the ways in which creative writing (administrators/ teachers) can visibly impact their students and the academy through (1) hybridization and cross-pollination, (2) new teaching formations and directions, (3) more flexible and appropriate career pathways for graduate students, and (4) through the building of stronger public and academic communities to include a stronger relationship with government bodies as well as more fully-integrated international partnerships and associations.

> *Everything we do is embedded in time, and time changes not only us, but our point of view as well*
> Margaret Atwood, 2005: xiii–xiv

Looking back on some of the essays she's written, Margaret Atwood (2005: vii) reflects on whether she'd write them differently today or whether she'd write them at all. She says, 'One year's prophecy becomes the next year's certainty, and the year after that, it's history . . . We're always looking over our shoulders, wondering why we missed the clues that seem so obvious to us in retrospect'. Creative writing's story in the academy tends to mimic this reflective cycling. For years, the discipline promoted literature for its own sake in the US until its intersection with postwar program expansion and rising enrollment. Patrons of university subsidies and National Endowment for the Arts (NEA, n.d.) funding made available hiring opportunities that tripled what is available in today's job market. In the eighties, the road traveled by creative writing promoted the production of writers and teachers until the 1990s, when once again, creative writing situated at a crossroad; this new position no longer in sync with a favorable marketplace. Looking over our shoulders, we can see that as a discipline, creative writing had been part of a fractured community signaled by its long history of subordination to literary studies, its lack of academic status and sustaining lore, and its own resistance to reform. These factions *had* kept creative writing from achieving any *central* core in the academy.

Still, Allan Tate predicted back in 1964 that the discipline 'is here to stay, at least for a long time' (p. 181), and part of the catalyst that not only sustains creative writing today but also propels it forward, is its mobility and its transferrable and generative properties that intercross disciplinary boundaries. Yet, perceptions of creative writing as a significant contributor to the academy waiver even in light of the discipline's growing student enrollment and degreed programs in the US, UK and Australia and even in view of its competence as a substantiated site of knowledge. With the perspectives we've gained by considering the past and the crossroads we've encountered, we can (1) shed new light on the history that informs our pedagogies and writing practices, (2) reshape, as needed, the space of creative writing, (3) move the discipline forward within the modern economy and critical academy, and (4) respond as champions for the discipline as proactive rather than reactive agents of change. Responding as champions of our discipline means that although we may have fewer choices given the direction of the economy and the inevitable changes that impact the academy, we can also focus our attention on the opportunities that exist for creative writing to succeed in our many different academic environments and administrations.

Terry Threadgold (2011) reminds us that 'The levels of government scrutiny we are facing, along with the funding crisis, will be drivers for change'. He suggests that 'future success of higher education institutions will depend on universities learning to re-imagine themselves regularly'. This chapter suggests that we can visibly impact our students and our academy through (1) hybridization and cross-pollination, (2) new teaching formations and directions, (3) more flexible and appropriate career pathways for graduate students, and (4) through the building of stronger public and academic communities to include a stronger relationship with government bodies as well as more fully-integrated international partnerships and associations.

Hybridization and Cross-Pollination

Foucault (1980: 112)[1] sets up a dichotomy related to the conditions of *space* when he says that space can be a theater of operation for power dynamics because of competing ideologies, but it can also be a sector of freedom which is unconstrained by barriers. Power dynamics come into play in the academic environment when research monies and employability factors influence administrative priorities. Although creative writing enroll-ment numbers may prove favorable to administrators, low teacher-student ratios and other associated overheads impact operational costs. Moreover, the discipline's effective practice and academic value has been somewhat dissociated from the university and less understood by administrative leaders who focus more attention on programs that achieve critical mass.

However – as research universities begin to respond more flexibly to the changes in the economy's and society's demand for certain skills and knowl-edge, as they react to the growth in the media-related sector, and become more aware of the 'seismic shift now underway in much of the advanced world from the logical, linear, computerlike capabilities of the Information Age' to the kind of creativity associated with the 'inventive, empathic, big-picture capabilities . . . of the Conceptual Age' (Pink, 2006: 1–2) – the cross-disciplinary activities of creative writing will become even more productive and meaningful to the academy, its profession, its creative economy and critically – to its student body.

Joseph Moxley (1989: 25) reminds us that 'the general segregation of creative writing from literature and composition [or cultural studies, for that matter] corrodes the development of a literacy culture'. More specifi-cally, Moxley wonders if 'our passion for specialization within writing departments has caused us to divide and subdivide (potentially) consolidat-ing processes of discovering and shaping meaning' (p. 25).

With this in mind, Foucault's concept of unfettered space seems reason-able to apply to creative writing's cross-pollination in the academy, for as Foucault (1980: 112) relates space, knowledge and power as that which is necessarily related, he notes 'it is somewhat arbitrary to try to dissociate the effective practice of freedom by people, the practice of social relations, and the spatial distributions in which they find themselves.' Consequently, if we are to renegotiate the space of creative writing, its boundaries and its power, while considering the shifting nature of students' skills with tech-nology and various art forms, the rapidly changing university environment, and the impetus of community as the prime mover of discourse, then there exists such potential for the discipline to connect with its relations within departmental and university systems and within the global network as a way to lead to a wider field of vision. Creative writing's strong construc-tionist base, social and cultural agencies, close reading skills and growing repository of knowledge establish a common ground that transcends academic boundaries.

What are some of the crossover possibilities for creative writing? At a departmental level, Paul Dawson (2005) sees the common goal between creative writing and literary studies as one based on a vision of social agency rather than a theory of generic form or of the creative process. He collapses the writer and critic into the figure of the public intellectual and argues for a particular 'mode of literary research within the academy', one which would entail 'literary and critical writing as complementary practices' (pp. 178–9). Additionally, creative writing and cultural studies are tied to the idea of an all-round aesthetic education for our students. Such integra-tion with cultural studies leads Kevin Brophy (2000: 203) to conclude this synthesis is critical 'if creative writing students are to maintain a level of sophistication and security important to resisting rigidity in their approaches to writing'.

Consider as well the blurring of lines between creative writing and com-position studies that began with the early scholarship of Joseph Moxley (1989) and Wendy Bishop (1994), and forged ahead by Tim Mayers (2005) and most recently by Douglas Hesse (2010) and I have also addressed this intersection as well (Donnelly, 2011). Many of us who attend the Conference on College Composition and Communication (CCCC) and the Association of Writers and Writing Programs (AWP) conference are creative writers who also teach composition. As such, our teaching pedagogy is informed by both disciplines as research methods mix with observation – experiential skills with bibliographic – inquiry with pedagogical scholarship. We represent a fused model of a collective identity that naturally invites the blurring of disciplinary boundaries.

Spatial distributions such as the ones described above demonstrate how creative writing can negotiate a space of freedom and still integrate with its departmental relations. Creative writing is already at work shaping a new era through its cross-pollination efforts into other interdisciplinary areas. As a practice, the new creative writing follows what David Starkey (1998: xiv) certifies as a 'polyculturalist' approach to writing instruction, which is constructed by 'teacher theorists who, over the years, have actively cross-pollinated areas of writing that had once been isolated from each other'. Such interfaces propel creative writing into new and interesting spaces, spaces that position the discipline as a pedagogically and programmatically sound entity fully empowered in its own identity and scholarship. Today, writing is less bound by genre and instead has been liberated by recent efforts to adapt the course in creative writing to the interests of our students who come into our classroom increasingly savvy about creativity as a product of experience in the cyber community. In an effort to broaden the expanse of writing, teachers partner with those in such fields as creative arts, media, film and technology studies. As such, creative writing teachers are changing the shape of the workshop model and hybridizing the classroom by introducing more outlets for expression, more venues for creativity and more activity and demonstration. The kinds of writing that emerge as a result often challenge mainstream genres.

We witness creative writing's mobility as teachers embrace and incorporate more technological literacy skills (e.g. literary hypertext, digital narratives, podcasts) into their design. We see creativity and technology merge in ways that transcend the digital cultures of universities and consider – for our students as creative artists now more than a decade into the 21st century – new audiences as well as relative skills and practical opportunities in writing in digital environments. As students engage in digital media, they are building new literacies that are more complex than conventional literacies.

Creative writing also uses space theory in interesting ways (i.e. hypertext, photos, maps, vlogs, wikis, music) that interfaces with textual dimensions, digital tangibles and online platforms. While digitalization invites readers in at a new level, it also invites students to bring together constructions from other disciplines, welcomes disciplines to partner in unexpected ways, and positions writers to consider how the visual arts might enhance the hybridity of stories and essays through manipulations and juxtapositions of photos/videos and text. When it comes to visual methodologies, Gillian Rose (2005: 68) asks, 'Why split things apart when they are almost always found in spatial proximity?' We might apply this rationale to creative writing's hybridization and cross-pollination throughout university systems by asking, why compartmentalize creative writing when the discipline is almost always found in spatial proximity – programmatically – to our university relations? As creative writing crosses boundaries within the university system, we see more potential for new disciplinary partnerships, new relations and new ways of redefining literature. Chad Davidson and Gregory Fraser (2009: 76–77) concur that 'practicing writers embrace rather than ignore other fields of study. And a college campus provides an excellent place to facilitate connections and strengthen the imagination'. Brian Castro, [2] co-director of the J.M. Coetzee Center for Creative Practice at the University of Adelaide, agrees that 'hybridity and cross-discipline collaborations are key words'. He asks 'why not write ethnography creatively, or research narrative through film and images, providing the research is vigorous?' We know that there are traditional methods associated with field methodology, yet ethnographers can be scholars and literary writers adept at weaving narratives in creative and scientific ways. We also know that the intersection of creative writing and film studies is useful to illustrate dialogue, the use of metaphor and the construction of scenes and other organizational principles.

As teachers, we respond to the shifting nature of students' reading and writing by crossing the interstices between disciplines. More universities now offer courses that transition students to write in the new digital age, and some universities now require at least one digital narrative as part of a creative writing course portfolio. Cross-pollination between creative writing and other university relations exposes our students to more performative arts in an effort to broaden their expanse of writing. Students write dialogue that is acted by drama students, action that is produced on stage, and/or poems expressed in music, sculpture, dance. Teachers combine creative writing with 'dance studio sessions or visual arts life drawing classes' (Indigo Perry, Deakin University[3]). Other teachers address the teaching of fiction as a method for creating games. James Paul Gee (2003: 207–212), author of *What Video Games Have to Teach Us About Learning and Literacy*, suggests that students of the gaming generation become insiders, teachers and producers when they create environments, interactive stories, characters and animation. The self-knowledge principles inherent in such a learning environment allow students to 'take risks in a space where real-world consequences are lowered', to master 'semiotic domains', to appreciate 'interrelations within and across multiple sign systems', to 'understand texts as a family ("genre") of related texts', and to develop active and critical thinking skills.

Mehrdad Massoudi (2003) asks if scientific writing can be creative. Neuroscience journals call for creative writing stories related to the field. Studies indicate that physicians and nurses who write descriptive narratives (in addition to clinical notes) are more compassionate, observant and engaged with their patients. At Cornell, writers are paired with scientists, musicians, dancers and visual arts (J. Robert Lennon[4]). There are opportunities for creative writing to intersect with business and communications faculty, to invite corporate recruiters to class, to encourage internships that would support such creativity in the business world. Karen Bender[5] (University of North Carolina Wilmington – UNCW) appreciates that 'more interdisciplinary work – with English, theater, film, history departments – would enhance all university learning experiences'. These paradigm shifts give us the courage to envision the teaching of creative writing skills beyond the creative writing classroom, beyond the 'either-or logic – where creative writers cordon themselves off from their peers in other disciplines'. Rather, creative writers 'increasingly adopt a "both-and" mentality that encourages border crossing and cultural exchanges' (Davidson & Fraser, 2009: 78).

Consider also other academic community partnerships that might exist with language studies in an effort to 'expand possibilities for *reading* across cultures' (Camens & Wilson, 2011: 1) and to open opportunities for literary translations. Castro (2011: 5) proposes that 'all Creative Writing programs should look at some form of literary "translation" as a possible adjunct to their courses', and notes that 'working creatively across languages is an incredible boon for all creators'.[6] For example, Queens College, Flushing, New York offers a tract in creative writing and one in literary translation. Also serving as a model for literacy translation/writing workshops is the partnership between the British Centre for Literary Translation and the School of Literature and Creative Writing at the University of East Anglia. Such a joint venture gives students an opportunity to 'workshop writing-in-progress with students in Spain learning the art of literary translation' (Camens & Wilson, 2011: 2). Isagani Cruz (2011: 11), chair of the Asia-Pacific Writing Partnership, supports a multilingual literary theory that emphasizes the intersection of creative writing and language studies in his appreciation that 'students with a command, no matter how slight or uneven, of more than one language have a new and relatively unexplored tool on hand for producing works of art'. Such examples of cross-talk and cross-disciplinary practices do position creative writing in new tenable and flexible ways. For instance, as the building of creative borderlands within the university establish 'new hybrid learning styles that draw on the strength of varying discourses' (Davidson & Fraser, 2011[7]), these hybrid learning styles lead to 'hybrid fields', which soon 'begin to "talk back" to standard modes of inquiry, in ways that are as exciting as they are daunting' (McWilliam *et al.*, 2007: 9).

If we are to become a place where students can generate ideas, try out these new ideas, and continue a quest for human expression and knowledge acquisition, if we consider that writing spaces influence what we write and how we interact with others, then we should collaborate with all our relations and open spaces for learning across interfaces.

New Teaching Formations and Directions

While hybridization and cross-pollination progresses creative writing across interdisciplinary planes, the management of creative writing within the modern academy challenges the discipline to consider new teaching formations and directions. Lisa Spaar[8] (University of Virginia) confers that 'what happens to creative writing in the academy will, of course, be affected by larger issues facing institutions of higher learning: budget cuts, a move toward adjunct teaching, and the need to make fewer faculty teach more students'. She expresses my wholehearted sentiment in her optimism that 'even in the direst scenario, creative writing will find ways to flourish and evolve'. It is important to note that institutions differ in many facets, and so discussions related to program design and operating costs are always contextual. What is a directive in one program is sometimes not an issue in another. However, proactive assessments of *how* we teach creative writing and *what* we teach can help us balance the needs of students *and* administrators, as much as this is possible. As the academic and financial future of the university is still felt to be with STEM programs – science, technology, engineering and mathematics (though the disciplines included in the acronym STEM vary, depending on particular universities and international differences) – funds to sustain creative writing programs which do not lead to jobs (to the degree that STEM programs might), or generate critical research grants, are more at risk. Although creative writing does yield considerable student interest and generates community favor as well, the discipline, generally, does not add to the university's profitability. Operation costs to maintain the small class size and teacher-student ratio inflation affect the academy's bottom line. Outside of the 10 or so top-ranked programs which may receive major endowments, most creative writing programs receive little funding, and administrators attach available monies to the maintenance of facilities and to the training of students in income-producing programs. Some administrators have sought ways to reduce their overhead by increasing the creative writing cap and by asking practitioners to find more cost-effective ways to operate and teach the creative writing course. In these more dire scenarios, Terry Thaxton[9] (University of Central Florida) tells us that we 'have to think about what we can do usefully'. When the directive is to increase class size and reduce operating costs, what options could best offer a variety of experiences for undergraduates? What follows is not a prescriptive solution, but rather an explorative look at strategic teaching formations and directions that consider alternative program tracks, independent writing centers and fully-integrated general education programs.

In the introduction to *Does the Writing Workshop Still Work?* (Donnelly, 2010: 18–19), I propose two program trajectories at the undergraduate level that may serve as alternatives to the open-admission, small-class-sized programs in many universities. The first sequence 'functions as a series of courses under the general education track' available to any student interested in 'the advancement of [his/her] writing (and reading) for its own sake (creative writing's early pedagogical goal)'. In this track, there is no creative writing major, no specific focus on career trajectories or life planning, and no objective for students to publish. With universities that include post-graduate teacher training programs in creative writing or include creative writing pedagogy coursework, second-year graduate students might offset faculty course loads and coordinate undergraduate course breakout sessions 'to advance writing and discussions relevant to lecture topics' (Donnelly, 2010: 22).

The second baccalaureate track considers the more advanced creative writer, 'one whose placement in the program is dependent on a sample of student work' (Donnelly, 2010: 19). This more specialized program would require smaller class sizes; however, students might not commit to this program major until after they have completed the introductory classes noted above as pre-requisites for admission into the creative writing program. Some universities also employ non-tenure-track faculty who receive course releases to facilitate the creative writing thesis projects.

Rethinking and restructuring the creative writing learning experience might also include online coursework or mixed mode/blended learning formats as an option. This differentiated instruction may require a combination of traditional classroom sessions, online work, independent small group workshops, attendance at special reading series or visiting writer Q & As or webinars. The benefit of such a mixed mode curriculum is in the variety of learning experiences available to undergraduates that often simulate the negotiated writing spaces outside of the academy, and the costs associated with traditional teaching formats are offset with this model. The challenge, of course, is in the careful design of the program and the coordination of what will inevitably be a larger class roster.

Other program options – MFA and PhD programs in the US, MA and PhD programs in the UK and AU, and DCA (AU) and MPhil (UK) – may be less conducive to large class sizes and mixed mode curriculums. However, program design that considers student motivation along with more flexible and appropriate career paths that extend beyond university teaching would not only respond to any question as to what constitutes our responsibilities to our students, but might also nudge profitability in creative writing's favor.

While alternative program tracks may work in some academic settings, independent writing centers that negotiate bureaucratic and operational issues such as funding, staffing, curriculum, and questions of how such an independent writing program would gain acceptance within the existing structures of universities, assume a unique configuration of space. Independent writing centers place creative writing at the administrative table, establishing a much needed voice for the discipline in academia. While many institutions cannot position creative writing as a separate entity located within its own edifice, the discipline, because of its transferrable and generative properties, may be fully integrated at the core of the university. The University of Georgia[11] is one such program that has implemented the cross-fertilization and cross-cultural benefits of creative writing as a generalized [undergraduate] course.

Convincing the administration that such integration has value means demonstrating the ways in which the process of creative writing and its focus on language bears import and resemblance to other fundamental education units. In fact, creative writing courses – particularly when they include multimodal literacies and disciplinary collaboration – provide value-added relevance as a core requirement of the college curriculum. More than two decades ago, Wendy Bishop suggested implementing the creative writing course as a general education requirement, and renewed interest in creative writing as a foundational course appears on the rise as evidenced by a 2011 AWP conference session where panelists energized the claim that creative writing can enhance the outcomes embedded in the university's core curriculum. One of the challenging aspects to transitioning the discipline to a foundational course may involve paradigm shifts when the transference requires a physical location change. The creative writing unit at the University of Georgia is now housed in the Fine Arts Department. Chad Davidson and Gregory Fraser[12] advise those thinking about such a fully-integrated program to expect some 'colonizing anxiety' that may result from such a move.

Program design is a critical factor in determining a cost-effective, efficient and successful creative writing program. Assuming a proactive position within the university system means creative writing situates and demonstrates its critical contribution. Such positive action also means the discipline carefully considers its expected outcomes, student population, versatility, flexibility and larger purpose within the scope of the academy. Scaling down is not always the knee-jerk answer to economic challenges and assuming a head-in-the-sand posture certainly won't put the discipline at the administrative table. Reshaping creative writing, rather, is an attentive, championing effort, one which adds for the discipline, power and agency in the academy.

More Flexible and Appropriate Career Pathways for Graduate Students

In 2009, more than 2000 MFA and PhD graduate students in the United States competed for the approximately 100 tenure-track faculty jobs in creative writing (*AWP Job List*, 2009). Currently, there are at least 3000 MFA and PhD graduate students contending for the approximately 78 tenure-track positions in the 2009–2010 *AWP Job List*. Since the 2009 statistics, there has been a 20% drop in creative writing tenure-track positions and a 50% increase in the number of graduates possibly vying for these jobs. The numbers suggest that the discipline might consider ways in which its program design can be more practically applicable to the university and to its students' future livelihood. Of course, any discussion related to program change might consider several factors: first, a motivating goal for creative writers to attend a graduate program as a pursuit of self-knowledge is legitimate. Peter Conn (2010) and others believe we enroll 'too many PhD students', 'spend far too long in guiding them to their degrees', and then appropriate them to a 'dysfunctional job market'. In response, Graeme Harper (2010) suggests there is value in the humanities and liberal arts degree in the 'growth, creativity, and the widest possible intentions and aims of human exploration'. Harper remarks that 'Employers need these things; but so does Humanity generally', and he cautions that we not 'sell ourselves and our students short' in 'fixed, time-conscious ways'.

There is no argument in contesting such aims of human exploration and in responding to what the marketplace yields. While students who hope to teach creative writing in higher education universities should appreciate the fierce competition of qualified candidates in this field, the university ought to accept some obligation in demystifying this particular outcome as one which motivates students to invest in the graduate creative writing program in the first place. Scott Smallwood (2001) reports that departments perpetuate this dilemma when they claim, 'Some of our more illustrious alumni are at Wisconsin, Harvard, Yale and Princeton', rather than attesting to a broader base of achievements by sharing, 'of our last 30 graduates, here are the 30 things they are doing'. Maggie Butt (2001: 2) responds to the 'graduateness' of our students, noting that 'They have developed their ability to write well, to express themselves with clarity and vividness in a range of genres; a skill which can be applied to writing a good business report, as much as to writing fiction, and satisfaction which comes with any creative activity'. What do students do with a creative writing degree? Butt suggests:

> A small minority choose the writer' life, perhaps going on to post-graduate study, aiming to become recognized as playwrights, novelists or poets, and usually supplementing their income with some other 'day job'. Some of our students have gone directly into work as professional writers, journalists, advertising copywriters, script-writers, dramatists.

Others have chosen to use the insights and skills they've gained as teachers, PR people, art therapists, web-site designers, book editors, sub-editors, TV researchers, literary agents, librarians . . . parents. (p. 2)

Finally, in no way do I suggest that creative writing programs become employment brokers for their students as I agree with Pro Vice Chancellor at Cardiff University Terry Threadgold's (2011) caution that universities not be 'reduced to becoming factories for business and industry'. Rather, I offer, instead, the possibility of engaging in a realistic discourse in student outcomes. As universities differ as to the kinds of coursework and teaching provided, I contend that students should explore the programming that best meets their academic and postgraduate plans, but I add that creative writing practitioners and administrators might also look to what else is possible for our students in the creative writing classroom and in creative writing integration across the university.

Such proactive agency means taking the pulse of the marketplace and designing courses and programs that prepare our students for the many different areas of creative practice that best reflect the burgeoning opportunities that exist for creative writers in film, journalism, television, design drama, new media and the digital content industries that incorporate digital communication, computer games, digital video and film, postproduction (editing, computer-generated imagery, sound effects, etc.), animation and more. Daniel Pink (2006: 1) tells us that 'the future belongs to a very different kind of person with a very different kind of mind – creators and empathizers, inventors, designers, and meaning makers'. Creativity, 'the buzzword of the business world' (Healey, 2009) has real market value if we consider that Richard Florida (2003) and others 'estimate nearly one-third of the future workforce will be identified within the "Creative Workforce" because the nature of their work is turning latent symbolic value of their work into economic and social assets' (McWilliam et al., 2007: 2). Sir Ken Robinson calls creativity a 'strategic issue' and notes that 'in times of economic crisis creativity is an urgent imperative' (in Fera, 2011). Moreover, creativity has been identified 'as the single most important leadership competency' by more than 1500 CEOs worldwide as per the 2010 report 'Capitalizing on complexity' (IBM, 2010: 10) compiled by the IBM President and CEO.

In Australia, government policies connect economic and social access to the creative enterprise as a way to resituate knowledge, and this alignment has reorganized disciplinary boundaries in some higher education institutions (see Queensland University of Technology, Griffith University, the J.M. Coetzee Center for Creative Practice, Deakin University, RMIT University). The creative economy in Australia is 'estimated to contribute

$31.1 billion towards the nation's GDP [Gross Domestic Product] (2007/08) which is higher than the contributions by other Australian industries such as agriculture, forestry and fishing' (Asia-Pacific Cities Summit, 2011). The Australia Government's Council for the Arts directs that Australia should 'seek new and liberating ways to bring together the arts, popular culture and the creative industries' (Australian Council for the Arts, 2011). Creative industries are gaining momentum especially since the government affirms the economic contributions of the industry, and as such, it looks to HEIs to develop graduates who can participate in this field and boost the economy. The Arts and Creative Industries report, commissioned by the Australia Council as part of a long-running and productive relationship between the council and the ARC Centre of Excellence on Creative Industries and Innovation at the Queensland University of Technology, considers the way in which the 'policy relationship between these often polarised sectors of arts and creative industries might be re-thought and approached more productively' (O'Connor, 2011). In the end, the report suggests that national policy should reflect no division 'between publicly-funded arts, popular culture and the blossoming businesses of the creative sector' (O'Connor, 2011), and HEIs play a pivotal role in the integration of these areas.

British Prime Minister David Cameron's May 2010 speech (Cameron, 2010) on ways to transform the economy highlights creative industries as a growing knowledge-based business. Furthermore, the Department for Culture, Media and Sport (DCMS, 2010) report notes that 'creative industries contributed 5.6% of the UK's Gross Value Added in 2008', '41% of all goods and services exported' were generated by creative industries, and 'approximately 182,100 businesses in the creative industries [were listed] on the Inter-Departmental Business Register (IDBR) in 2010'.

The United States government may influence funding in state higher education research institutions, but it does not necessarily emphasize the importance of creative industries as a growing knowledge-based business or link the potential for creative capital to higher education institutions to the same degree as governing bodies in Australia and the United Kingdom do. This year, the White House began a 'Startup America' initiative that focuses on investing and creativity as a way to facilitate new businesses. Also, research commissioned by President Obama recommends that creative activities merit 'an unambiguous place in the curriculum' (Peirce, 2011), yet support is still undeniably directed to the fields of science, technology, engineering, mathematics or medicine (again – depending on global definitions of STEM).

One can find on the Americans for the Arts website (Americans for the Arts, n.d.) Dun & Bradstreet data that reflects creative industry growth per congressional districts, but there is nominal governmental imperative to grow such an industry. What we do know relates to the consumer behaviors of the American public and the business-savvy development of knowledge technologies. As a nation, 'Americans spend more money on entertainment and recreation than they do on automobiles, health care, apparel and shoes, or housing and utilities' (Rifkin, 2000: 161), and as such, entertainment has replaced 'defense' as 'the driving force for new technology' (Rifkin, 2000: 161). In 2008 there were nearly '361,900 wage and salary jobs in the motion picture and video industries' alone, and the multimedia and digital visual effects industry has emerged at a rapid pace since the 1980s (US Bureau of Labor Statistics, 2010–2011); nonetheless, there has been little concerted effort to align creative arts in the American academy with the potential for economic benefit and job creation. Given what seems to be convincing data, we might further reflect on what role higher education institutions and, more particularly, creative writing programs have in preparing students for this creative workforce.

With regards to other flexible and appropriate career pathways for graduate and undergraduate students, the United States Bureau of Labor Statistics reports that writers and editors held 281,300 jobs in 2008 of which 50% worked in industries related to advertising, public relations, periodicals, books and directory publishers and 50% worked in broadcasting, professional and social organizations and those creative industries that involved motion picture and video industries. Salaried editors worked not only for publishers but also for editorial positions related to web content. The bureau contends that the demand for writers and editors, 'especially those with Web or multimedia experience', grows as 'many organizations move their publication focus from a print to an online presence and as the publishing industry continues to contract'. One only need visit the latest *AWP Job List* to witness the rising number of editorial posts. Fortunately, we're headed in the right direction with recent movements by universities to offer graduate diplomas and master's and bachelor's degrees in publication and editing and to coordinate publishing and editorial internships as well.

Stronger Knowledge-Based Communities

Creative writing has typically occupied low-profile spaces in the academy. Its 'courses [have been] seen as "lesser" courses, less serious and less august, more "radical" and not benchmarked' (Castro[13]), and even its practitioners have perpetuated a century old isolationist posture in the US that led Patrick Bizzaro (2004: 296) to conclude a requisite of creative writers' 'skepticism of anything academic'. However, the discipline's value is becoming more fully recognized not only in the many integrated ways discussed earlier, but also in its potential to heighten and promote creative practice and awareness through strong community relationships. 'Creative Writing', Danielle Nettle (2009: 101–2) remarks, 'is a cultural activity', a 'cultural invention', also a bridge to cultural development, and as such, 'it will flourish if it is successful at capturing the attention and motivation of a significant number of people, and it will wither if it does not'. Creative writing prospers as it partners with community programs, as it creates and disseminates knowledge; and as it builds a knowledge culture with the public community, the academic community, the governmental granting bodies, as well as with the global community. Partnerships such as these further demonstrate creative writing's breadth of influence and impact.

Public community development

Most creative writing programs include literary community activities such as readings or lecture series that are open to the public. Here visiting writers, faculty and students often participate in community outreach events by reading their work in a public forum. Some programs engage their students in more immersive community work and enter into supportive partnering with community programs to foster a commitment to the literary arts. Annie Finch[14] (University of South Maine) foresees creative writing 'moving further out of the academy and into the community, as the changing economy mandates that writers learn to address a more general audience and the changing society mandates that more and more people benefit from the healing work of writing'. She sees these changes 'naturally leading to greater collaborations between creative writing and such academic disciplines as social work, nursing, psychology, and fine arts'. Such a forecast materializes as creative writers at Ball State University collaborate with community services and social services through their participation in an immersive learning course (Ball State University, n.d.). Students 'partner with community members to create and read a collaborative collection of works that is a venue for the voices of children at risk, the aging population, and persons with mental and physical disabilities'.

To add to this collaborative model, the interdisciplinary MA Program in Creative Writing at Eastern Michigan University engages students in a community outreach practicum and seminar by asking them 'to explore the significance of literary culture in communities beyond the university' (Eastern Michigan University, n.d.). The international obligations of the University of Nevada, Las Vegas' (UNLV) Master's International/Peace

Corps Program permits creative writers to 'become bilingual', and to 'study the creative process across traditional borders of language and culture' in an effort to integrate 'a more global and contemporary perspective on their craft', while also 'serv[ing] the current needs of the third world' (UNLV, n.d.). Stephanie Vanderslice (2011: 108) suggests that creative writing programs in the academy 'have a vested interest in such initiatives, in community partnerships that expand and enlarge literate culture'. This comment is supported in the *AWP Director's Handbook* (2011), which advocates community partnerships in its policies and information for creative writing programs. The program guide notes that an effective program 'fosters relationships with its surrounding community', by 'forming partnerships with local arts organizations, and doing outreach to other area schools, including secondary schools' (p. 72). Many programs model this practice by partnering with Writers in School, a non-profit organization that may provide, depending on the locale, residencies for creative writers in schools, hospitals, community centers, museums and other public settings. Moreover, as a 2013 initiative, the Higher Education Funding Council for England announced that 'university departments will also have to provide case studies proving the impact of their work beyond their institution' (Lipsett, 2011). To initiate such community impact, creative writers in the academy might partner with local, regional and national councils for the arts to promote creative awareness, produce innovative projects and increase the visibility and effectiveness of the discipline's contribution to the academy.

For example, on the principle that 'digital content industries can be seen as the nexus, where art, science, and technology combine', the Australian Council for the Arts (ACR) partnered with the Australian Film, Television and Radio School in 2006 to produce *The Writer's Guide to Making a Digital Living: Choosing Your Own Adventure* with an aim 'to create a freely available and widely accessible repository of knowledge and information on the theme of professional creative writing in a digital context' (Fingleton *et al.*, 2008: 6). The ACR also provides grants for new work in digital and new media writing this year. The British Council UK Writer-in-Residence Program (British Council, n.d.) partners with the University of Iowa's International Writing Program, and the British Council for the Arts invites strategic partnerships with higher education institutions, and the National Endowment for the Arts (NEA) funds new media performance projects at higher education institutions.

Recently, in a February 2012 *Inside Higher Education* article[15], John Warner hypothesizes what might happen if the critical mass of the 2012 AWP attendees spent their time 'growing the pie' by increasing the readership of the city of Chicago through the offer of free books raffled on Daley

Plaza or through the placement of 'a creative writer in *every single classroom* in the city for half a day'. Warner imagines a 'supernova of art, exploding out of the [AWP] conference center in order to destroy hearts and minds in the best of ways'. Vanderslice[16] notes that such an outward energy-bound effort may have, in fact, materialized if we are to consider as evidence, the several 2012 AWP sessions that 'centered on teaching creative writing in prisons', or those that 'talked about teaching creative writing to bilingual students', or the panels that 'looked at the best ways to engage youth, at-risk and underserved populations' or 'advocated social justice and service learning' or 'examined the best ways to help veterans transition from the military to the academic world of colleges and universities'. Vanderslice wonders what might happen if every audience member at these panels converted their 'enthusiasm back to their communities in the form of sustained programs that last more than a half a day', if the 'aptly described "supernova of art" that Warner hopes for has already exploded out of the 2012 conference'. Moreover, where creative writing programs can partner with community-based organizations, they should do so for many value-added reasons to include among them, the integration of service and knowledge and the promotion of creative writing's visibility in the academy.

Academic community development

Lisa Spaar[17], who has directed the creative writing program at the University of Virginia these past 11 years, appreciates that the early organization of creative writing in the academy 'was met with varying degrees of suspicion, bemusement, even condescension by some academic and scholarly constituents of the academy'. In places 'where tension was especially divisive and intense, creative writing programs often separated themselves from academic silos, but other institutions embraced creative writing'. At universities like the University of Virginia where undergraduate and graduate programs are accepted 'by the Department and at the decanal and university-wide levels as a kind of jewel-in-the-crown of Arts & Sciences', the discipline has more opportunities to engage in productive conversations regarding program design, development and integration.

Bender[18] (UNCW) offers that 'creating [an] infrastructure is important to show students that literary writing is culturally significant'. She adds that 'creative writing needs to be taken seriously by academic organizations, not just to nurture young writers, but to help students learn about themselves and the world in a creative context'. I would add that rather than projecting a defensive (or isolationist) posture as it relates to the effectiveness and functionality of creative writing in the critical academy, practitioners might empower a more deliberate and receptive stance as they consider the ways in which the discipline can best meet the needs of the university and its student population. As such, the liaison between the discipline and the academy should be a mutually reciprocal one in that each cog in the wheel has an invested interest in moving forward. In centers where (1) administrators respect and value the creative writing programs, (2) where creative writing can negotiate program design with administrators in the contemporary academy, and (3) where creative writing crosses boundaries and touches students' lives in multiple disciplines – mutually beneficial partnerships connect student and program outcomes to university initiatives. To add a much needed voice for the discipline in the academy, creative writing could also benefit from more representation at higher administrative levels.

As recipients of awards, fellowships, foundations and grants; creative writing teachers can demonstrate the importance and value of the discipline in the academy and increase its visibility, validity and influence in the field. Some awards require nominations; some require residency in a given country, and application deadlines vary, of course. The Alliance of Artists Communities (n.d.), a national and international association, sponsors residencies for creative artists who wish to pursue their work. The organization also publishes a comprehensive directory of community residencies. Coveted artist communities include Yaddo, MacDowell, Ragdale, Banff and others. The National Endowment for the Arts and the Guggenheim Fellowships are influential grants, the USA Government Grants (USG) provide creative writing research grants at times, and Fulbrights and residencies at international colonies such as the Rockefeller Foundation and Bogliasco Foundation in Italy are the top international grants.[19] There are a host of other awards, foundations, grants and fellowships for creative writers to consider.

Governmental granting bodies

University regulations and the expectations of the academy steer research practices in the United Kingdom and in Australia, and the agencies behind these regulations and expectations are government funding bodies. Castro[20] believes *less* that the academy resists the expansion of creative writing and *more* that 'governmental granting bodies and media representatives' do not yet appreciate 'the academic and economic value of creative writing'. Although the critical exegesis complements the creative component of the United Kingdom and Australian creative writing doctoral degrees, the research taxonomies and accepted methodologies for gathering such research are not yet universal. There has been much effort to make clear the requirements for the postgraduate creative writing exegesis; however, there is still no consensus as to what comprises the critical component of the award. Under the terms of the Research Assessment Exercise (RAE), 'research' refers to that which is based on 'the invention and ideas, images, performance and artifacts including design, where these lead to new or substantially improved insights' (RAE, 2008: 5). It should be noted that the RAE will be replaced by the REF – Research Excellence Framework – by 2014, and it will use assessment data (2015–2016) to advise its research funding, and we will stay abreast of any revisions to research definitions and requirements. Similarly, for the purposes of the Excellence in Research Assessment (ERA), the Australian Research Council Assessment defines 'research' as 'the creation of new knowledge and/or the use of existing knowledge in a new and creative way so as to generate new concepts, methodologies and understandings. This could include synthesis and analysis of previous research to the extent that it is new and creative' (ARC, 2008: 1). As of yet, there is no vocabulary in the ERA or RAE criteria that supports the writing of a novel, screenplay or volume of poetry as research activities. Rather, government imperatives challenge creative writers in the academy to substantiate how their work represents a body of research and contributes new knowledge in the field. The governing research guidelines do not generally discern research methodology differences between disciplines, and though creative writing is a practice-based discipline, councils often ask creative writing researchers to conform to the scientific methods that demonstrate evidence. As such, creative writing programs in some areas are challenged to compete with other disciplines for research monies. Further impeding efforts to establish benchmarks for research practices are the dichotomies associated with creativity and research. Steve May[21] posits that there are 'those that complain that rules and regulations impinge on creativity', and others who criticize that such complainers are often 'those who find it hardest to self motivate and finish creative work'.

Castro[22] suggests, in part, that one way to get the recognition of government bodies is 'to make [creative writing] more visible, to encourage excellence through rigour, to "brand" [the discipline] not only through publication but to make creativity central in all vocations and professions as an inevitable *writing* exercise'. Beyond the 'future of the book', he notes, 'are social relations, communication and transmissions of culture, inspiration and invention. These cannot be explained in any historical way unless they are written'. And they cannot be explained unless we appreciate that there are three intersecting components to building a stronger community between creative writing and governmental research councils. One relates to creative writers being 'more aware of their status as researchers' (May[23]), more aware that in order to create new understandings and new knowledge and to 'understand their place in the culture ... [creative writers] must understand – as scientists must – what else is being done in the field' (Kroll, 2004). Add to this cognizance the 'knowledge acquisition activity' with the 'on-site opportunities' that the university offers for creative writing researchers to 'uncover [the] new theory and knowledge' that 'runs parallel to practice' (Scrivener, 2000). In particular, Hazel Smith and Roger Dean (2009: 1) suggest 'As soon as higher education becomes more accepting of creative work and its existing and potential relationship to research, we also see changes in the formation of university departments, in the ways conferences are conducted, and in styles of academic writing and modes of evaluations'. The third factor in constructing a stronger community with the governmental research councils is gaining the attention of the governing bodies to the distinct methodologies that set creative writing apart from other research disciplines. 'Research', Castro suggests 'is without question, a creative exercise'.

Global community

In a special issue of *New Writing: The International Journal for the Practice and Theory of Creative Writing* (*New Writing*, n.d.), called 'Making connections: Creative writing in the 21st century', Graeme Harper (2011: 204) proposes that '... if we are in an era in which connected human experience is far more the norm, human interaction beyond our geographies and across our timezones, then we are also in an era in which opportunities arise to share our creative activities as they happen, to exchange knowledge, to develop our understandings and our collaborations, to work together'.

Given that creative writing is a well established discipline among universities in the United States, United Kingdom, Australia, New Zealand, the Philippines, Hong Kong, Fiji, Africa, Ireland, Scotland and Canada, with a presence in many other countries, we see potential for such opportunities to share, exchange, collaborate. Tim Mayers notes this distinction of creative writing's international focus as one that is not assumed by others in the humanities department. In the scope of this critical global mass, it seems reasonable to ask how might we advance a more global understanding of how creative writing can strengthen its academic presence as well as contribute new knowledge to the field.

A sum of data that supports creative writing research as knowledge exists in UK and Australian creative writing programs as graduate students contribute to their universities' research practices, shaping the study of creative writing, as they do, as a research discipline. As such, research in creative writing becomes an increasingly important aspect of the universities' productivity and an important aspect to the development of creative writing research as a method of knowledge acquisition and production. Harper (2007) concludes that 'Because creative writing is a site of knowledge, we can investigate the nature and dimensions of this site of knowledge, and if we choose, create models, or theories, about this knowledge and the components of this knowledge'.

In the US, the relation of creative writing to knowledge is through the field's growing body of pedagogy. While we know that creative writing research methodology exists, we have not fully begun to explore our methods in any significant context. Through a collective international voice, however, UK, Australian and US practitioners can discover under what conditions meaning is to be treated as knowledge or the acquisition of knowledge so that the significance of what creative writing as a global field has to offer moves beyond any international program degree differences to a communal space in which a common 'global' language might exist from which to talk about creative writing as a knowledge-based discipline. In order to know how creative writing research can be effectively benchmarked and measured, we must open new global and international gateways to facilitate a better understanding of creative writing's particular modes of research.

As a global measure, Castro (2011: 6–7) encourages us to 'not underestimate the osmosis effect' of internationalizing creative writing. Importantly, he notes, 'Visiting writers, particularly international writers, teach apprentices how to be writers-in-the-world'. This summation is of particular interest since the United States, United Kingdom and Australian universities are international organizations with a growing number of international faculty and students. As a result, global markets provide broader learning opportunities for writers and a means for crossing cultural paths. Creative writing organizations such as the Association of Writers and Writing Programs (AWP), the Australasian Association of Writing Programs (AAWP), and the National Association of Writers in Education (NAWE); all promote creative writing pedagogy and education and facilitate a global culture and exchange through their international conferences, scholarship and higher education networks. A number of print and online publications that serve a national community and link to similar organizations overseas include AAWP's online journal *TEXT*, AWP's *The Writers' Chronicle*, NAWE's *Writing in Education*, and *New Writing: The International Journal for the Practice and Theory of Creative Writing*. In addition, Great Writing: The International Creative Writing Conference builds 'on the growing worldwide interest in Creative Writing research' (Great Writing), and the International Center for Creative

Writing Research (ICCWR) offers a new international forum that addresses creative writing in the academy. Led by Director and Chair Graeme Harper, this includes the international Creative Writing Society (CWS) and is 'a place to discuss practice-led and critical research in Creative Writing, and a channel for discussions about the teaching of Creative Writing in universities and colleges' (ICCWR). The ICCWR works through international collaboration and mutual exchange. For example, its June 2011 inaugural video-linked workshop featuring the 2009 T.S. Eliot Prize winner Professor Philip Gross, streamed live from London at the 14th Annual Great Writing International Creative Writing Conference. And in 2012, an international dialogue related to graduate studies will take place between Kate Coles (US), Nigel McLoughlin (UK) and Jeri Kroll (AU). Moreover, as part of this worldwide effort, teachers and students from the US, Korea and Australia teleconferenced in November, 2011, about creative writing in the academy and planned for a larger global translation project in the near future. In 2010, an international virtual collaborative exchange titled 'Unmade!' brought together teachers, writers and other creative artists from Montevallo, Alabama, USA; Normanville, Australia; Seoul, Korea; and Wales, UK. In April 2012, an international connection was established among creative writing teachers, artists, writers, and scholars in the US, Korea, and Australia on the subject of the critical understanding of creative practice.

We see more evidence of large-scale interest represented at a 2012 AWP international panel (US, Hong Kong and the Philippines) where panelists entered a discourse on the internationalization of MFA programs. Furthermore, a global exchange takes place in the special issue of *New Writing: The International Journal for the Practice and Theory of Creative Writing*, titled 'Making connections: Creative writing in the 21st century', which featured contributors from AWP, NAWE, AAWP as well as contributors from New Zealand, the Asia-Pacific Writing Partnership (APWP) and the European Association of Creative Writing Programs (EACWP).

Other programs that encourage the internationalization of creative writing and elicit local and global recognition include study abroad programs, international writing programs, transatlantic writing collaborations and cultural exchange programs. Moreover, creative writing teachers up for promotion (e.g. associate professor, professor, distinguished professor) at US research facilities are generally expected to demonstrate some standing beyond US borders. Rita Ciresi,[24] Director of Creative Writing at the University of South Florida, reports university guidelines that suggest academic writers can achieve this status by (1) having their work translated into other languages, (2) having presented or given readings at international conferences or writers' workshops, (3) publishing bilingual editions, (4) translating other writers' work into other languages, (5) writing book reviews, articles or creative work for international literary magazines, newspapers or periodicals, (6) writing about their own ethnicity, race or religion and attempting to place their work in international magazines that would be interested in such work, or (7) attending international writers' colonies or getting Fulbright or other international grants.

Conclusions

To 'reshape' creative writing, means taking a hard look at the relationship between creative writing practice and the academy. We know creative writing brings value to the academy; its courses and degreed programs satisfy a broad spectrum of student interests, and the discipline draws students from a wide-ranging disciplinary base. We also know that the university environment provides opportunities for students to discover, practice and connect with a writing community as well as offering 'a framework for research which works conjointly with creative activity'.[25]

Yet, we must be mindful of the ways in which the modern economy shapes creative writing in the academy and the ways in which the discipline might re-imagine itself by extending its value, importance and visibility in the university and community. Lisa Spaar[26] reminds us that 'Wonderful, daring, intrepid work is being done inside the academy, and continually refreshing the ways in which this happens should be the privilege and responsibility of everyone associated with the creative writing/academy alliance'. The future success of creative writing depends on our agency – on the ways in which we go forward, on the ways in which we intentionally design our coursework and programs and the ways in which we stay attuned to our students' needs, to the modern economic and critical academy and to our community coalitions.

Notes

(1) I discuss creative writing's hybridization in more detail in *Establishing Creative Writing Studies as an Academic Discipline*, Bristol: Multilingual Matters, 2011.
(2) B. Castro (personal communications, May 15, 2011).
(3) G. Perry (now known as Indigo Perry, survey response, February 2010).
(4) J. Robert Lennon (personal communications, May 10, 2011).
(5) K. Bender (personal communications, May 15, 2011).
(6) B. Castro (personal communications, May 15, 2011).
(7) C. Davidson and G. Fraser (AWP Conference 'Getting to the Core: Creative Writing as a Core Requirement in College Curricula', Washington, DC., May 5, 2011) .
(8) L. Spaar (personal communications, May 24, 2011).
(9) T.A. Thaxton (AWP Conference 'The Future of Creative Writing in the Academy', Washington, DC., February 4, 2011).

(10) P. Gerard (AWP Conference 'The Future of Creative Writing in the Academy', and personal interview, Washington, DC. February 4, 2011).

(11) C. Davidson and G. Fraser (AWP Conference 'Getting to the Core: Creative Writing as a Core Requirement in College Curricula', Washington, DC., May 5, 2011) .

(12) As above.

(13) B. Castro (personal communications, May 15, 2011).

(14) A. Finch (personal communications, May 10, 2011).

(15) J. Warner (2012) In which I complain about the AWP conference. *Insider Higher Education* (February 24). Available at: http://www.insidehighered.com/blogs/education-oronte-churm/which-i-complain-about-awp-conference.

(16) S. Vanderslice (2012) The view from AWP Chicago: The Writer-Con, 2012. Available at: http://www.huffingtonpost.com/stephanie-vanderslice/awp-chicago-writer-con-2012_b_1318068.html .

(17) L. Spaar (personal communications, May 24, 2011).

(18) K. Bender (personal communications, May 15, 2011).

(19) My gratitude to Rita Ciresi, Director of the Creative Writing Program at the University of South Florida, for her assistance in identifying creative writing teacher awards, fellowships, grants and residency opportunities (personal communications, June 20 and June 22, 2011).

(20) B. Castro (personal communications, May 15, 2011).

(21) S. May (personal communications, May 10 and July 11, 2011).

(22) B. Castro (personal communications, May 15, 2011).

(23) S. May (personal communications, May 10 and July 11, 2011).

(24) R. Ciresi (personal communications, June 20 and June 22, 2011).

(25) B. Castro (personal communications, May 15, 2011).

(26) L. Spaar (personal communications, May 24, 2011).

References

Alliance of Artists Communities (n.d.), accessed 7 July 2011. Available at: http://www.artistcommunities.org/.

Americans for the Arts (n.d.), accessed 8 May 2011. Available at: http://www.artsusa.org/>Path: creative industries.

Asia-Pacific Cities Summit (2011) The Business of Cities (6–8 July), accessed 10 September 2011. Available at: http://www.apcsummit.org/files/pdf/2011-APCS-industry-factsheet_creative-industries.pdf.

Association of Writers and Writing Programs (AWP) (n.d.), accessed 6 June 2011. Available at: http://guide.awpwriter.org/.

Atwood, M. (2005) *Writing with Intent*. New York: Carroll & Graf.

Australasian Association of Writing Programs (AAWP) (n.d.), accessed 17 May 2011. Available at: http://www.aawp.org.au/.

Australian Research Council (ARC) (n.d.) ERA Program Descriptors, 19 December 2008. Available at: http://www.arc.gov.au/pdf/ERA_Indicator_Descriptors.pdf.

AWP Director's Handbook (2011) Available at: http://guide.awpwriter.org/hallmarks/DirectorsHandbook2011.pdf.

Ball State University (n.d.), accessed 15 July 2011. Available at: http://cms.bsu.edu/Academics/CollegesandDepartments/English/ActivitiesandOpportunities/ImmLearningOpps/EngDeptOpps/CreativeWritingComm.aspx.

Bishop, W. (1994) Crossing the lines: On creative composition and composing creative writing. In W. Bishop and H.A. Ostrom (eds) *Colors of a Different Horse: Rethinking Creative Writing Theory and Pedagogy* (pp. 181–197). Urbana: NCTE.

Bizzaro, P. (2004) Research and reflections: The special case of creative writing. *College English* 66: 3 (Jan.), 294–309.

British Council (n.d.) United Kingdom Writer-in-Residence Program, accessed 6 July 2011. Available at: http://www.britishcouncil.org/usa-arts-literature-uk-writer-in-residence-program.htm.

Brophy, K. (2000) Taming the contemporary. *TEXT* 4: 1 (April). Available at: http://www.textjournal.com.au/april00/brophy.htm.

Butt, M. (2001) Position Paper, Sheffield Hallam University/English Subject Centre, quoted in *New Writing* 8 (3).

Camens, J. and Wilson, D. (2011) Introduction: Creative writing in the Asia-Pacific region. In J. Camens and D. Wilson (eds) *TEXT* Special issue, Creative Writing in the Asia-Pacific Region, (April) 1–5. Available at: http://www.textjournal.com.au/speciss/issue10/Camens&Wilson.pdf.

Cameron, D. (2010) Transforming the British economy: Coalition strategy for economic growth, 28 May. Available at: http://www.number10.gov.uk/news/transforming-the-british-economy-coalition-strategy-for-economic-growth/.

Castro, B. (2011) Teaching creative writing in Asia: Four points and five provocations. In J. Camens and D. Wilson (eds) *TEXT* Special issue, Creative Writing in the Asia-Pacific Region, (April) 1–8. Available at: http://www.textjournal.com.au/speciss/issue10/Castro.pdf.

Conn, P. (2010) 'We need to acknowledge the realities of employment in the humanities'. *The Chronicle of Higher Education*. Available at: http://chronicle.com/article/We-Need-to-Acknowledge-the/64885/.

Cruz, I.R. (2011) Writing with two languages. In J. Camens and D. Wilson (eds) *TEXT* Special issue, Creative Writing in the Asia-Pacific Region (April) 1–13. Available at: http://www.textjournal.com.au/speciss/issue10/Cruz.pdf.

Davidson, C. and Fraser, G. (2009) The expanding role of creative writing in today's college curriculum. *The Writer's Chronicle* 42.3, 67–89.

Dawson, P. (2005) *Creative Writing and the New Humanities*. Oxford: Routledge.

Department for Culture, Media and Sport (2010), accessed 31 July 2011. Available at: http://www.culture.gov.uk/what_we_do/creative_industries/default.aspx.

Donnelly, D. (2010) If it ain't broke don't fix it, or change is inevitable except from a vending machine. In D. Donnelly (ed.) *Does the Writing Workshop Still Work?* Bristol: Multilingual Matters.

Donnelly, D. (2011) Creative writing and composition: Rewriting the lines. In P. Bizzaro, A. Culhane and D. Cook (eds) *Composing Ourselves as Writer-Teacher-Writers: Starting with Wendy Bishop* (pp. 105–115). New York: Hampton Press, Inc.

Eastern Michigan University (n.d.), accessed 16 July 2011. Available at: http://www.emich.edu/english/creative-writing/graduate.php.

Fera, R.A. (2011) Ken Robinson on the principles of creative leadership. *Fast Company*. Available at: http://www.fastcompany.com/1764044/ken-robinson-on-the-principles-of-creative-leadership.

Fingleton, T., Dena, C. and Wilson, J. (2008) *The Writer's Guide to Making a Digital Living: Choose your own Adventure*. Australia Council for the Arts. Available at: http://www.australiacouncil.gov.au/__data/assets/pdf_file/0003/42654/The_writers__guide.pdf.

Florida, R. (2003) *The Rise of the Creative Class: And how it's Transforming Work, Leisure, Community and Everyday Life*. Annandale, NSW: Pluto Press.

Foucault, M. (1980) Truth and power. In C. Gordon (ed.) *Power Knowledge: Selected Interviews and Other Writings 1972–1977* (pp. 109–133). New York: Pantheon.

Gee, J.P. (2003) *What Video Games Have to Teach Us About Learning and Literacy*. New York: Palgrave.

Great Writing: The International Creative Writing Conference (UK) (n.d.). Available at: http://www.greatwriting.org.uk/.

Harper, G. (2007) Creative writing research today. *Writing in Education* 43, NAWE. Available at: http://www.nawe.co.uk/DB/wie-editions/articles/creative-writing-research-today.html.

Harper, G. (2010) Comment on 'We need to acknowledge the realities of employment in the Humanities'. *The Chronicle of Higher Education*, comment posted on 4/4/10. Available at: http://chronicle.com/article/We-Need-to-Acknowledge-the/64885/.

Harper, G. (2011) Editorial. Making connections: Creative writing in the 21st century. *New Writing: The International Journal for the Practice and Theory of Creative Writing* 8 (3), 203–205.

Healey, S. (2009) The rise of creative writing and the new value of creativity. *The Writers Chronicle* 41 (4), 30–39.

Hesse, D. (2010) The place of creative writing in composition studies. *College Composition and Communication* 62: 1 (Sept), 31–52.

IBM (2010) Capitalizing on complexity: Insights from the global chief executive officer study. Available at: http://www-05.ibm.com/services/se/ceo/ceostudy2010/pdf/GBE03297USEN.pdf

International Center for Creative Writing Research (n.d.). Available at: http://www.graemeharper.com/sites/international_centre/index.html.

Kroll, J. (2004) The exegesis and the gentle reader/writer. *TEXT Special Issue 3*. Available at: http://www.textjournal.com.au/speciss/issue3/kroll.htm.

Lipsett, A. (2011) 'Universities braced for heavier research burden', *The Guardian*, 28 February, accessed 13 March 2011. Available at: http://www.guardian.co.uk/education/2011/mar/01/research-excellence-framework-academics.

Massoudi, M. (2003) Can scientific writing be creative? *Journal of Science Education & Technology* 12.2 (June), 115–128.

Mayers, T. (2005) *(Re)Writing Craft*. Pittsburgh: University of Pittsburgh Press.

McWilliam, E., Hearn, G. and Haseman, B. (2007) Building trans-disciplinary borderlands for creative futures: What barriers and opportunities? Unpublished paper presented at the Creativity or Conformity? Building Cultures of Creativity in Higher Education Conference, Cardiff, Wales, UK.

Moxley, J. (1989) Tearing down the walls: Engaging the imagination. In J. Moxley (ed.) *Creative Writing in America: Theory and Pedagogy* (pp. 25–45). Urbana: NCTE.

National Association of Writers in Education (n.d.), accessed 5 June 2011. Available at: http://www.nawe.co.uk/.

National Endowment for the Arts (n.d.), accessed 3 July 2011. Available at: http://www.nea.gov/Grants/apply/Media.html.

Nettle, D. (2009) The evolution of creative writing. In S.B. Kaufman (ed.) *The Psychology of Creative Writing* (pp. 101–116). New York: Cambridge University Press.

New Writing: The International Journal for the Practice and Theory of Creative Writing (n.d.). Available at: http://www.tandfonline.com/loi/rmnw20.

O'Connor, J. with Cunningham, S. and Jaaniste, L. (2011) *Arts and Creative Industries: An Historical Overview; and an Australian Conversation*. (February 2011). Australia Council for the Arts. Available at: http://www.australiacouncil.gov.au/__data/assets/pdf_ file/0007/98431/Arts_and_creative_industries_FINAL_Feb_2011.pdf.

Pink, D. (2006) *A Whole New Mind: Why Right-Brainers Will Rule the Future*. New York City: Riverhead Trade.

Peirce, M. (2011) 'Obama research calls for creativity to be put at heart of curriculum', *TES*, 24 June, accessed 12 January 2011. Available at: http://www.tes.co.uk/article. aspx?storycode=6090301.

Research Assessment Exercise 2008: The outcome. Available at: http://www.rae.ac.uk/ results/outstore/RAEOutcomeAE.pdf.

Rifkin, J. (2000) *The Age of Access: The New Culture of Hypercapitalism, Where all of Life is a Paid-For Experience*. New York: Tarcher.

Rose, G. (2005) Visual methodologies. In G. Griffin (ed.) *Research Methods for English Studies* (pp. 67–89). Edinburgh: Edinburgh University Press Ltd.

Scrivener, S. (2000) Reflection in and on action and practice in creative-production doctoral projects in art and design, *Working Papers in Art and Design* 1. Available at: http://sitem.herts.ac.uk/artdes_research/papers/wpades/vol1/scrivener1.html.

Smallwood, S. (2001) 'Survey points to mismatch between Ph.D. students, their programs, and their potential employers'. *The Chronicle of Higher Education*. Available at: http://chronicle.com/article/Survey-Points-to-Mismatch/108651/.

Smith, H. and Dean, R.T. (2009) Introduction: Practice-led, research-led research – toward the interactive cyclic web. In H. Smith and R.T. Dean (eds) *Practice-Led Research, Research-Led Practice in the Creative Arts* (Research Methods for Arts and Humanities) (pp. 1–38). Edinburgh: Edinburgh University Press.

Starkey, D. (1998) (ed.) *Teaching Writing Creatively*. Portsmouth, NH: Boynton/Cook.

Tate, A. (1964) What is creative writing? *Wisconsin Studies in Contemporary Literature* 5: 3, 181–184.

Threadgold, T. (2011) The global impact of UK university funding cuts. *The Conversation*, 17 May 2011, accessed 18 December 2011. Available at: http://theconversation.edu. au/the-global-impact-of-uk-university-funding-cuts-864.

United States Bureau of Labor Statistics (2010–2011), accessed 31 May 2011. Available at: http://www.bls.gov/oes/current/oes271014.htm.

University of Nevada, Las Vegas (UNLV) (n.d.) Master's International/Peace Corps Program, accessed 6 July 2011. Available at: http://english.unlv.edu/mfa/peace-corps.

Vanderslice, S. (2011) *Rethinking Creative Writing in Higher Education: Programs and Practices that Work* (e-book). The Professional and Higher Partnership Ltd.

2 Hey Babe, Take a Walk on the Wild Side – Creative Writing in Universities

Mimi Thebo

Creative writing is a popular and profitable academic discipline, but its place in the academy is contentious. Its evolution as a (generally un-assessed and extra-curricular) part of English Studies and its current estrangement from critical thought in English Literature have resulted in a discipline culture that is 'wild' and 'other' and that sits uneasily in humanities. Creative writing has also inherited cultural expectations from community writing classes, which include notions of therapy, empowerment, personal development and vocational study. These expectations can cloud the intentions and outcomes of discipline engagement for faculty, students and the outside world. Using William Perry's stages of development and the UK National Association of Writers in Education benchmark statement, an excellent case can be made for how creative writing provides its students with 'graduateness'. However, discipline reasoning methods, definitions of research and the deep embedding of creative writing faculty into the academy are on-going projects.

How Did We Get T/here?

A group of young men are clustered around a teacher on the top step of a temple's portico. No, they're in a fusty seminar room, and a don nods over his pipe, listening and occasionally interrupting. Or maybe shingle-haired young women, too, with thick stockings, are sitting with them, chewing the ends of their pencils as the leaves of a New England autumn fall outside the picture windows and the professor reads from mimeographed pages.

Heads are bent over scrolls; over small, square brown books; over thick, authoritative anthologies. The mysteries of poetry are laid as bare as if the verse is on the anatomist's table.

Then the sun dips, the pipe is knocked in the grate, or a bell rings. The students begin to rise and chatter; amongst themselves, to the tutor. One shyly ducks his head and says, 'Please, Sir, I've written one of my own . . . could you . . .?' And the hand delves into the tunic/gown/breast pocket.

Since antiquity, students of poetics have sometimes shown their own creative writing (Marshall, 1976). As an academic discipline, creative writing did not invent the idea of a knowledgeable, well-read tutor helping young writers to develop. But it did get rid of the 'please'.

Students of creative writing are entitled to have their own creative work considered seriously by their tutors and classmates. This entitlement is the key-defining characteristic of creative writing instruction. The sense of entitlement is intimately connected to the development of the subject. The rise of creative writing as an academic subject is intrinsically entwined with concepts of empowerment, inclusivity and individuality in the 21st century, and these concepts, within the academy, translate into a discipline culture some may suggest is rebellious, open and iconoclastic. Creative writing has been, as David Morley (2007: 20) puts it, wild.

Although many people, including Winifred Bryan Horner (in Gaillet & Horner, 2010), have suggested that with its study of rhetoric, composition lies at the heart of English studies, along with poetics, as an element of classical education, creative expression does not have the same centrality. Composition and creative writing do, however, share the same heritage. At the beginning of the 20th century, faculty in English Literature departments on both sides of the Atlantic were engaged in teaching writing skills, but they were also providing content for students to write *about*. It is this 'about-ness' that will form the chief difference in creative writing's place in the academy.

A young man leans forward on his chair, while his tutor leans back, reading and tapping his yellowing teeth with the end of a pen.

'Ah,' the tutor finally says. 'This. This here.' Now the tutor leans forward as well. The heads almost touch over the essay. 'Not a bad thought, but poorly expressed.'

The student emits a small sound of despair.

'How would you say it? If you were talking to me?'

The student begins to perspire. 'I'd . . . erm . . . say that I thought-'

'No,' the tutor interjects. 'Never think. Never "think" or "feel" or "wonder". Either do the work and know you're right or leave it out.'

The student looks horrified, but his face also shows a faint glimmer of under-standing. He takes a moment to think. 'I'd say that the word "beauty" doesn't mean prettiness.'

The tutor smiles and leans back again. 'Good,' he says.

The student exhales and leans back himself.
'So,' the tutor asks. 'How are you going to define "beauty"¿'

The pedagogical techniques developed in composition include many of the key teaching tools of creative writing. These include looking at drafts of writing completed or attempted by students in their own time as formative assessment. This was done both one-to-one, as above, and in seminar groups.

And as above, discussion of the student's writing often leads to discussion of the student's thoughts; aesthetics and ethics as well as the understanding of a literary text (or other 'aboutness'). Creative writing has not only inherited this wide-ranging and somewhat investigatory examination of student work, but has extended it into the workshop.

In America, for practical concerns, composition was separated from the broader curriculum of English Studies. The vast numbers of students from across the disciplines passing through English 101 were not primarily interested in literature, but in the ability to express themselves with clarity on paper. These students were also the source of a major funding stream for English departments. The curriculum of English 101 gradually lost any character it might have had as an introduction to critical study and became a training ground for writing skills, later becoming allied to cross-curriculum writing centers. This movement provided a precedent for the removal of 'aboutness' in English Studies.

It did not require a huge conceptual leap to go from a stand-alone class in which writing skills were taught for essays to a stand-alone class in which writing skills were taught for creative expression. As early as the 1880s, stand-alone creative classes were emerging, and by the 1920s and early 1930s creative elements were becoming accepted for some English Studies courses across America (Myers, 1996).

But the development of creative writing as a discipline does not take place entirely within the academy. At the turn of the century, 'writing clubs' and how-to books proliferated, with the incentive of attempting publication in one of America's many short-story magazines. Such instruction imparted techniques of storytelling in the 'get ahead and win' discourse of the plain man's triumph, which was the narrative of the day. This same relentlessly positivist discourse that made magazine writers like O. Henry (Literature Collection) popular was the type of discourse that adult education 'clubs' and 'courses' used.

Twenty people sit in a brightly lit classroom; street lamps give a faint glow to the large dark windows. It is a strange collection of people – some young, some older; some prosperous in tweeds, some in cheap, shiny fabric. A middle-aged man with horn-rimmed glasses stands, clears his throat, and begins to read. The instructor, an energetic young man, nods, first in time with the reader's cadence, but then more and more quickly, until he can't bear it anymore and jumps to his feet, interrupting.

'No, no, no. You've got to get them, see?' He runs his hands through his hair. 'We've got to have the set-up on the first page. You've got your dame, you've got your fella, you've got the runaway train. It's good stuff. But you gotta get it on the first page.'

The middle-aged man sits down. The instructor continues lecturing on pace and structure, issuing very precise guidelines for writing commercial short fiction. The class takes it all in, some smirking with superiority, some scribbling down every word.

Finally, he goes to the middle aged man and claps him fondly on the shoulder. 'But don't give up. Keep on writing and one of 'em will hit the bell, you wait and see.'

In this environment, publication, not literary quality, was the measure of success. By 1934, Dorothea Brande was able to complain, in *Becoming a Writer,* of the plethora of instructional advice on technical aspects of creative writing (p. 20).

Although the Iowa Writers' Workshop (which continues, in part, to form the model for postgraduate pedagogy in creative writing) was founded in 1936 to nurture talents in literary fiction, instruction retained concepts of 'publishability' inherited from the get-rich-quick community writing course as well as the seminar teaching methods of composition (Myers, 1996: 43). Quite quickly, it established links with publishers and began to discuss success in terms of student publications.

Eight students and a tutor sit around a table. All but one of them examine extensively marked up pages. The odd one out shuffles in her seat, waiting.

'Well,' the tutor says. 'What do we think?'

An eager young man leans forward. 'I enjoyed it. It made me laugh.'

The tutor nods. 'Where did it make you laugh?' he asks.

The young man leafs through the pages. 'Page six,' he says. 'Second full para. Where Ray slips on the skate and Mary sees.'

'I laughed there, too,' says an attractive blonde woman near the end of the table.

'Me, too,' adds a colourless young woman with aggressively black reading glasses. 'I thought it showed good characterisation.'

The tutor says, 'I see.'

The young man says, 'That's it. Characterisation. That's why it was funny, because we know them so well.'

The odd one out, whose work is being discussed, glances up at the tutor for confirmation.

'Hmmm,' he says. 'What else do we think?'

Commercial success in the humanities brought a whiff of trade into the ivory tower. Creative writing, as a newcomer to English Studies, was already suspect because of its lack of 'aboutness'. Now, it seemed flashy and publicity-seeking, as well as besmirched by industrial connections.

In Britain the development of the subject was also developed largely outside of the academy as localised activity, publicly funded and/or linked to what Rebecca O'Rourke (2005: 56) calls 'enthusiasts and social movements'. Certainly, the explicitly socialist aims of the Workers' Educational Association early made inclusivity a motivation for creative writing learning in Britain, and small presses associated with various writing groups began publishing the work of the writers with the stated aim of adding other voices (particularly the voices of the working class) to counter mainstream literary publishing (Hilliard, 2005).

'Frank,' the new tutor announces, in fluting soprano tones, 'has written a poem about a betting shop.'

Frank, who was readying himself to read, objects. 'It's not about a bookies,' he says. 'It's about an old man outside the bookies.'

'Very well, Frank,' she says. 'Go ahead and read, please.'

The class leans over their desks. Frank's voice is quiet, measured. The poem is lean, but rich in imagery and detail.

When he finishes, there are small noises of satisfaction from the rest of the class. Frank folds his poem and replaces it in his back pocket.

'And what would you call that, Frank? Is it free verse . . . or stream of consciousness . . . or . . . ?'

'It's a poem,' Frank says. It's the end of the discussion.

At the very genesis of the subject, then, creative writing was allied to concepts of being other; it was outside the main curriculum of English Literature and also outside of mainstream publishing (important developments of writing education often took place far from the publishing centers of New York and London). Student writing lacked 'aboutness' and its pedagogical techniques were borrowed as much from informal community instruction as inherited from English studies.

From its very beginnings, then, creative writing was 'wild'.

Before we begin to examine the place of creative writing within the university, however, we need to muddy the waters with yet another idea of creative writing instruction – creative writing for therapy and personal development. In the 1960s and 70s, encounter groups and consciousness-raising groups used creative writing for 'self-actualisation'.[1] This brought to a wide population the concept that writing creatively was, as a practice, beneficial to mental health and personal growth.

Some dozen women sit on large cushions in a loose circle on a carpeted floor. Two hold babies; one is asleep, one is nursing – and there are sounds of children playing nearby. They lean in towards each other in twos and threes, reading a photocopied sheet.

'I can really get where you're coming from, Dana,' one finally says. 'It's true. We deal with everyone's shit.'

There's a brief moment of silence.

'Yeah,' another woman says. 'The baby, the toddler, the dog and the husband's underwear. They're all really powerful images.'

'But I'm not just talking about real shit,' Dana looks anxious. 'I'm talking about life's shit, you know? Does that come across?'

They lean forward again.

'Oh, for sure,' the first woman says. 'For sure that comes across.'

There is a general murmur of agreement.

Creative Writing for Therapeutic Practice or Creative Writing for Personal Development is now an academic subject of its own,[2] but the concept that 'creative writing is therapeutic' has been common in adult learning since this time. In addition, some learning writers come to the subject through writing in therapeutic environments.

There is anecdotal evidence from university counsellors that creative writing attracts more students with mental illnesses than other subjects, and some research seems to support this perception.[3] Certainly, studies have shown a correlation between creative writing students and mental illness (Andreasen, 1987). This too has implications for creative writing in the university. Today, even if a creative writing class does not promise, or intend, to be therapeutic in any way, students may feel certain that it is or should be (Leahy, 2005). Recent research in my own institution has shown that students choose creative writing as a subject, by quite a large percentage, because they feel it will help their self-development.[4]

Also key to issues of creative writing in the academy is the change in the critical climate. Once Barthes (1967) and Foucault (1977) reported the dead or absent author, criticism's main interest switched to the reader. Meaning of writing was now made manifest by using socio-linguistic concepts to interrogate the text.

The critical climate of English Literature had, until now, been useful to creative writers. Concepts such as the intentional fallacy (Wimsatt & Beardsley, 1954) were useful in the creative writing classroom, where divorcing the text from the author's intentions and concentrating on what could be gleaned from the page provided a rigorous and enlightening experience for the author. Deconstruction and the theory that followed it seemed, for many people involved with the creative writing curriculum, to be an abdication of critical responsibilities for textual development. Once criticism felt that it was no longer responsible for or interested in how the author has achieved his or her intentions, the authors felt similarly uninterested in criticism. As Wandor (2008: 84) puts it, 'Just as the existence of the author and the autonomy of the text are being denied . . . the notion of the text as a productive practice begins to enter the academy in the form of CW (Creative Writing)'.

The resulting philosophical fissure resulted in an uncomfortable relationship between two of the three-way split of English Studies. More creative writing departments succeeded from English Studies altogether (Media Studies seems to be seen as a more comfortable fit for many faculties in some areas such as the UK and Australia) and more stand-alone degrees were offered. Creative Writing BA and MA degree courses in America, Australia, Canada and Britain rapidly proliferated.[5]

It is a great irony that just as critics were concentrating on minority concerns (post-colonialism, feminist criticism, queer theory) creative writing programmes (which were explicitly or implicitly engaged in educating and helping a wider population of writers to achieve mainstream publication) largely disengaged from the critical tradition of English Studies. Just as issues of entitlement came to the humanities in women's studies, black history, etc., most of creative writing stepped out of the humanities' uniting discourse.

This step away has profound implications for the subject today. The concepts of other and wildness have not disappeared from creative writing, but have intensified with time.

Do We Belong T/here?

Given its other and wildness and the near total lack of interest creative writing takes in current critical discourse in the humanities, does creative writing belong in the academy? What is it doing there?

There is a strong and popular belief that writing cannot be taught – that genius comes to the academy for polish or to learn to rewrite. In Britain, articles on this topic in *The Guardian* newspaper appear regularly[6] (although, of course, they are happy to advertise courses), and the venerable Iowa Writing Workshop states twice on their webpage that writing is impossible to teach.[7]

The corollary concept is clear: students who do not bring genius to college/university are wasting their time and money by studying creative writing. This is an unusual charge for a Humanities course and contains the remnants of the 1930s 'cash in quick' motivation for writing study. Of all the humanities, creative writing tends to be most seen as vocational in nature.

We don't judge the quality of instruction in a History department on the amount of publishing historians produced as a result of study, yet creative writing departments are frequently evaluated in just this way. Moreover, the departments themselves are often complicit in this judgement, using graduate publications in advertising and marketing. These publications are, in nearly all cases, from students in postgraduate study in programmes with narrow admissions policies. We do not expect Creative Writing BA students to become professional writers any more than we expect English Literature BA students to become professional critics.

Given that most Creative Writing BA students will not become professional writers, and are not geniuses, what do they achieve from a creative writing degree? Are Creative Writing BAs proper college/university graduates?

Definitions of 'graduateness' are highly contested and largely linked to fluctuating concepts of economic value. For example, before the current economic crisis, employers were speaking a great deal about 'soft skills' – an inclusive discourse concentrating on the development of the graduate as a person. Currently, what we are hearing from employers tends to concentrate on concepts of 'good degrees from good universities', and this discourse is more about concepts of 'safe bets' and 'the best graduates'.

Instead of using graduateness as defined by employers, we can use William Perry's (1970) classic model of undergraduate intellectual and ethical development to look at creative writing's ability to develop graduateness in BA students. Does what takes place in a creative writing classroom promote ethical and intellectual development?

Perry's main concept is that students arrive at the academy early in their intellectual/ethical journey, and that the challenges they receive in their studies provoke them to change the way they relate to knowledge, authority and the world in general. I will draw upon my own practice and experience of creative writing in universities to relate Perry's stage of development to student development in creative writing, using a neat outline incorporating additional development of Perry's ideas, by William Rapaport.[8]

(1) **Dualism/Received Knowledge**: There are right/wrong answers, engraved on Golden Tablets in the sky, known to Authorities.
   (a) **Basic Duality**: All problems are solvable; therefore, the student's task is *to learn the Right Solutions.*
   (b) **Full Dualism**: Some Authorities (literature, philosophy) disagree; others (science, math) agree. Therefore, there are Right Solutions, but some teachers' views of the Tablets are obscured. Therefore, the student's task is to learn the Right Solutions and *ignore the others*!

This is the first part of Rapaport's wonderful distillation of William Perry and shows a mindset that is fully recognisable to anyone who has taught a first year workshop in creative writing. Students often believe there is a right or wrong way to write prose, poetry and script and that their task is to learn how the right way is done. Since, in workshop, they might hear other opinions from their peers than the tutor might express, they learn to ignore their peers and listen to their tutor.

Students can be comfortable in this stage of development and cling to it tenaciously, only expressing minor irritation that the tutor won't just 'show them' how to write their story/poem/script.

There is an additional problem that the concept of the Authorities can be conflated with the concept of Publishers and students may feel that the successful working writer-tutor can 'see' the Golden Tablets.

(2) **Multiplicity/Subjective Knowledge**: There are conflicting answers; therefore, students must trust their 'inner voices', not external Authority.

When students begin to doubt that the tutor has a clear view of the 'Golden Tablets' – that the tutor does not, actually, know how every story/poem/script should be written – they often go back to their own pre-college/university aesthetic, rejecting the exhortations of tutors and the examples of good writing provided.

In my own experience, I tend to see unnecessary archaic usage and proliferating gerunds at this stage of undergraduate development. The tutor can find students at this stage maddening, since nothing they say or bring into class seems to promote any progress in the student's work.

(3) **Early Multiplicity**: There are two kinds of problems:
   (a)   those whose solutions we know;
   (b)   those whose solutions we don't know yet;
   (c)   (thus, a kind of dualism). The student's task is to learn *how to find* the Right Solutions.

(4) **Late Multiplicity**: Most problems are of the second kind; therefore, everyone has a right to their own opinion; or:

   (a) some problems are unsolvable; therefore, it doesn't matter which (if any) solution is chosen. The student's task is to shoot the bull. (Most freshmen are at this position, which is a kind of relativism);

   (b) at this point, some students become alienated, and either retreat to an earlier ('safer') position ('I think I'll study math, not literature, because there are clear answers and not as much uncertainty') or else escape (drop out) ('I can't stand college; all they want is right answers' or else 'I can't stand college; no one gives you the right answers').

I find all stages of multiplicity come with apathy and attendance problems. The student believes that since everyone has their own opinion of her/his work, and that everyone's opinions are equal, there is no point to workshop and they might as well write however they'd like. The tutor's opinion is, in their view, entirely subjective and possibly unfair. Students equate the required reading with the tutor's own personal aesthetic and may resent its imposition.

Reflective writing from students at this point of their development tends to be either advertising for the creative submission ('My mescaline memoir is as good as Burroughs and all my housemates loved it') or an apologia ('You may not like my mescaline memoir, but I think it's authentic and interesting and I did everything the workshop said').

(5) **Relativism/Procedural Knowledge**: Connected knowledge: empathetic ('why do you believe X?'; 'what does this poem say to me?') vs. Separated knowledge: 'objective analysis' ('what techniques can I use to analyze this poem?').

I will interpret this as the difference between the textual discussions in Amazon reviews ('I liked this', 'I liked that', 'I thought it was boring', 'I identified with the main character') to craft-based analysis ('When the narrative voice went into the main character's point-of-view it made it easier to understand the character's motivation', or 'The way the punctuation breaks down and the paragraph goes on and on gives the feeling of breathless action').

(6) **Contextual Relativism**: All proposed solutions are supported by reasons; i.e. must be viewed *in context* and *relative to support*. Some solutions are better than others, depending on context. The student's task is to learn to *evaluate solutions*.

This is, for me, the application of the above growth in aesthetic aware-ness and craft discourse to the student's own work. The student is able to apply craft solutions to their own work ('I tried it in first person, but it was hard to understand what was going on, so then I put it in third person and it was better'), and to apply their reading of good writing to their own work ('. . . but then I remembered *The Shipping News* (Proulx, 1993) and I kept it in the third person but from my character's point of view and I liked that because . . .').

(7) **'Pre-Commitment'**: The student sees the necessity of:
    (a)   making choices;
    (b)   committing to a solution.

In creative writing pedagogy, we have a concept called 'finding one's voice'. Finding one's voice means finding a writing style which is flexible enough to be used on several writing projects and yet reflects one's own personal aesthetic. This stage of development can be seen to be about this process. The student is able to clearly identify the choices that s/he makes when writing, and understands the heritage/context of those choices ('I want to write fantasy, but on the literary end'; 'I want to write about families because I'm interested in the psychology of quiet people').

(8) **Commitment/Constructed Knowledge**: Integration of knowledge learned from others with personal experience and reflection.
    (a)   **Commitment**: The student makes a commitment.
    (b)   **Challenges to Commitment**: The student experiences implica-tions of commitment. The student explores issues of responsibility.
    (c)   **'Post-Commitment'**: The student realizes commitment is an ongoing, unfolding, evolving activity.

Here the student is ready to begin a sustained writing project in a prede-termined style. S/he will have read around his/her project, will understand the context (both historical and commercial) in which the work will take place and will have made several craft decisions before beginning. When the student begins writing, these choices will coalesce into what we might call a 'voice' – a distinctive narrative aesthetic.

However, there will be challenges that arise to this style/voice/aesthetic in the course of writing the project. The student will often need to re-evaluate her/his style in light of these challenges, which may include ethical issues of representation or authorial responsibility and limitations.

We can see the essential work of a discipline in the academy as moving as many students as possible through Perry's stages, where their 'graduate-ness' will make them truly useful members of society. The development of creative writing students intellectually and ethically may not be reflected in their marks or by the quality of their writing – Perry's work does not form assessment criteria. Some creative writing students with undoubted 'genius' get stuck at level 4a, where they view their main task is to shoot the bull, and the majority of stage 9 students are not writing compelling manuscripts. Well constructed, probably: wonderful, probably not.

If students are taking creative writing because they wish to develop personally, and creative writing is developing students, then the discipline can be read as unproblematically successful. Indeed, in Britain, the Subject Benchmark Statement from the National Association of Writers in Education has a long list of skills and attributes that students should take away from their creative writing degrees – and many of these map successfully onto Perry's late developmental stages.

But of course my representation of the student journey, however recognisable to creative writing academics, is deeply flawed, and so is my case that creative writing does the pedagogical work of an academic discipline. It contains an assumption that creative writing has 'disciplinary reasoning methods', and that words like 'workshop', 'criticism', 'voice' and 'craft' have stable and universal meaning. All of these assumptions are contentious.

Do We Know What We Are Doing T/here?

The NAWE benchmark statement says:

There are various ways in which workshops operate. In one model students might be asked to write something in a limited time within the workshop, which then might be 'shared' with the group. Or, students might be invited to bring work in, to be read or acted out, and then commented upon. In some cases they may be asked to submit work in advance so that it can be duplicated and distributed before the workshop, and people have time to look at it carefully and make written comments. Other workshops (sometimes termed seminars) might deal with exemplary writing.[9]

Descriptions of workshops typically talk about 'trust' and 'cooperation'. Student accounts range from nervousness to boredom, to enthusiasm, but tend to see the value of peer to peer learning as in this example from Gregory Light's (2002) research:[10]

I think I'm learning to differentiate between what I think I'm writing and what I've written, because ... just by hearing the responses, just realising that I thought I was saying something but it wasn't being heard and then I must have to, uh, think again about what I'm trying to say and, the way I'm saying it to get it heard more clearly. (Monica)

Stephanie Vanderslice (2000) puts it eloquently when she says that the workshop contains, 'the purposes as well as the best practices of this twentieth century phenomena, conclusions that are far too complex to begin to address and simple enough to contain in a four-word sentence: Writer, meet your Reader'.

However, Michelene Wandor looks at the workshop as 'a House of Correction'. In workshops, she says, 'Untheorised (or at best, very under-theorised) principles of "criticism" are translated into by turns brutal and patronising exchanges' which deny creative writing's 'relationship to its own histories, which are those embedded in the history of English' (Wandor, 2008).

Liz Almond says workshops 'should provide a safe environment', but that 'it takes time to develop a critical vocabulary if you're not used to responding to other people's work' (in Singleton & Luckhurst, 1996: 18, 22). To which Wandor replies waspishly, 'Yes, it's called doing an English Literature degree' (2008: 129).

Others, like Paul Dawson (2005), argue that creative writing has its own critical vocabulary, but even Dawson admits that it is 'undertheorised and idiosyncratic' (p. 90).

Certainly the vocabulary of this 'undertheorised' poetics/criticism is idiosyncratic, and despite Wandor's yearning for reconciliation with English Literature, the language is unlikely to coalesce into uniformity as a result of the forcible adoption of, say, the discourse of narratology in creative writing instruction and research.

This is only in part because such a discourse might not always be useful to creative writers (I'm not certain I could identify the 'actant models' of my latest novel or what I will learn if I do), but also because creative writing tutors are not likely to have been educated in narratology themselves, or indeed even educated in the more current and mainstream English Literature critical discourses. The revised edition of Gerald Prince's (2003) *A Dictionary of Narratology* has 103 pages of entries in eight-point font. Each entry provides a handy guide for historical reading about the concepts and origins of the terms, including many critical and philosophical texts my colleagues and I have not read.

We haven't read these texts because we have been reading other texts for our writerly research, to enable and enhance our own writing. With our commitments in the academy, we have less, not more, time to read work not in our immediate field. The time that our institutions pay for our research must be used for our own creative work because it is our area of specialty. We cannot afford, and our institutions cannot afford to give us, time to become an aspiring narratologist.

So, the problem of 'reasoning methods' remains. If 'workshop' can mean anything – from therapeutic-based methods of using recall and memory to produce writing in class, to a text-based close reading session of one student's work, to exercises using random stimulations to provoke new writing, to reading exemplary writing and discussing it together – how accurate can we be discussing it as a pedagogical model? It can be encouraging and nurturing or brutal and patronising. When I write 'workshop', which workshop am I writing and which one do you read?

Likewise, 'criticism' can mean 'critique', with its Fine Arts inheritance of peer and tutor evaluation of work in progress, or it can be 'constructive criticism', where peers offer alternative solutions to the solutions the writer chose in his/her presented draft. Paul Dawson (2005) and Tim Mayers argue that a new critical voice, a 'craft criticism' as Mayers (2005: 30) calls it, is emerging, which is concerned about literary production and may become engaged in the post-theory humanities discourse. When we say that students are developing the ability to 'look critically' at texts, which critical ability are we claiming on their behalf?

If we return to the phrase of Perry's, 'disciplinary reasoning methods', the case for creative writing's successful integration into the academy as a stand-alone discipline becomes less certain. What are creative writing's reasoning methods?

Two subject developments are helping to answer this question. One is the veritable explosion of books examining this question. Pedagogical treatises, definitions and histories of creative writing have proliferated in the last decade, and examinations of concepts of 'workshop' and 'criticism' have been published, indicating that the methods of the subject will not remain 'undertheorised' for long.

Also, the development of the Creative Writing PhD is grappling with 'reasoning methods' on the experiential end. At best, the critical/contextual components of these degrees concentrate on process – writerly research (Patrick Bizzaro gives a wonderful list of 'what we are good at' in his (2004) article for *College English*), technique and investigation into similar textual structures for guidance in the formation of the creative component. At worst, the critical/contextual components offer second-rate research in other disciplines (often Literary Criticism, Sociology and Cultural Studies) (Bourke & Neilsen, 2004). The NAWE benchmark statement on research leaves the door open for the critical/contextual element to be eliminated, by making a case that the research of creative writing might be found in the creative component itself – that a work of creative writing might be 'answering' research 'questions' (a similar strategy that is widely used in Performing Arts).

Creative writing has been slow to recognise the precedents set in the Fine and Performing Arts. In a way, it is marooned as the only practice-based subject in the humanities. Another problem in adopting performative reasoning discourse is the frequently cited 'invisible' nature of creative writing as an art form. Also, creative writing's otherness and wildness have become features of its discipline culture, further isolating it from other practice-based discourse, as well as critical discourse.

The persistence of the wild culture is, in part, due to the various career paths of the Creative writing academics themselves. Some tutors are English Literature academics who enjoy writing or who have become publishing authors. Some tutors are successful authors (by whom I also mean poets, dramatists and creative non-fiction writers), perhaps with a degree in an unrelated subject, or little academic experience at all. Some tutors have re-entered the academy after studying an MA or MFA, or perhaps even going on to do a PhD in Creative Writing. It is likely that most successful tutors will also be published authors. It is not likely that they'll all have the same conceptions of research, or feel allegiance to the same 'reasoning methods'. Although staff engaged in supporting or examining PhD candidates have been, from necessity, if not interest, engaged in various discussion groups on this very subject, consensus has not, so far, emerged.

Allegiance to 'reasoning methods' is further compromised by creative writing's relationship with industry. Promotion, pay and working conditions for creative writing academics depend less on their engagement with subject networks than on the work they do outside of the academy – in the commercial world of publishing (by which I also mean broadcasting and performance). Kelly Ritter (2007) calls this 'the emphasis of public over academic capital'. Unlike academics in, say, engineering or pharmaceutical chemistry, commercial success or esteem of creative writing academics in their associated field does not translate into institutional income; the concepts of institutional support and intellectual property are much different.

The value of creative writing academics' publishing profile to their college/university lies mainly in recruitment and the marketing of the course and institution. Although there may be a correlation between successful authors and fundraising from, say, alumni, in America, as well as some research income in Britain, the serious business of raising money for new facilities, large research projects and PhD bursaries is not generally expected of or done by creative writing staff, even though their publications may be of the highest standard and they may enjoy worldwide esteem.

As a result, the discourses of creative writing often come from the world of publishing, and the academic staff of creative writing are likely to accept these discourses because their allegiance to the academy is not as strong as their allegiance to the publishing industry. Descriptive terms from newspaper reviewing, such as 'powerful', 'dark' or 'feel-good', are brought unblushingly into the classroom without examination, as are industrial concepts, such as 'cross-over' or 'chick lit', and our notions of writing's worth often depend on industrial acceptability (i.e. 'publishable').

With these close, and often unexamined, ties to industry, its lack of 'aboutness', its lack of theorised subject discourse and its wild culture, creative writing has found it difficult to ground itself in the academy, particularly in the humanities. Creative writing academics find it difficult to successfully bid for research funding and administrative staff are unlikely to be promoted to senior management posts within the academy (despite the skills they acquire managing such disparate and fractional staff).

So, although part of this chapter title is Creative Writing in Universities, it's not certain, even after 130 years, that creative writing is wholly 'in' universities. It is an attractive, vibrant, profitable and evolving discipline, and a good case can be made for how engagement with it develops students and enhances university life. But how far into the academy creative writing has come is debatable. How far it *desires* to come in is also debatable.

If it is no longer wild, creative writing might be seen as semi-feral. It comes to the university regularly, but it doesn't yet quite call it home.

Notes

(1) Account of feminist 1970s writing circle, available at: http://www.cwluherstory. com/notes-on-a-writers-workshop.html.

(2) Lapidus website, available at: http://www.lapidus.org.uk/seminars/index.php (accessed 23 July 2011).

(3) Staying The Course Website, available at: http://www.english.heacademy.ac.uk/ archive/publications/reports/disability.pdf (accessed 23 July 2011).

(4) Artswork Learning in the Arts Survey, available at: http://media.artsworkbathspa. com/research/pages/Learning%20in%20the%20Arts/learning %20in%20the%20arts %20report-aclews.pdf (accessed 23 July 2011).

(5) There are now 284 BA programmes in America alone according to the Campus Explorer website, available at: http://www.campusexplorer.com/colleges/search/ ?location=&majorgroup=9F474C02&majorgroup2=28CF1111&major=77408FD 1&online=&rows=25&page=1 (accessed 23 July 2011).

(6)   A recent example, available at: http://www.guardian.co.uk/education/2011/may/10/creative-writing-courses.
(7)   See http://www.uiowa.edu/~iww/about.htm (accessed 23 July 2011).
(8)   See http://www.cse.buffalo.edu/~rapaport/perry.positions.html (accessed 23 July 2011).
(9)   NAWE Benchmark Statement, available at: http://www.nawe.co.uk/writing-in-education/writing-at-university/research.html (accessed 23 July 2011).
(10) For further reading in this area, see Steve May's project for the English Subject Centre, Student Responses to Creative Writing: Coherence, Progression and Purpose.

References

Andreasen, N.C. (1987) Creativity and mental illness: Prevalence rates in writers and their first-degree relatives. *American Journal of Psychiatry* 144, 1288–1292.
Barthes, R. (1967) The death of the author. *Aspen* 5+6.
Bizzaro, P. (2004) Research and reflection in English Studies: The special case of Creative Writing. *College English* (January) 66 (3), 294–309.
Bourke, N.A. and Neilsen, P.M. (2004) The problem of the exegesis in creative writing higher degrees. *TEXT: Journal of Writing and Writing Courses* (April) (3).
Brande, D. (1934) *Becoming a Writer*. New York: Harcourt, Brace & Company.
Dawson, P. (2005) *Creative Writing and the New Humanities*. Oxford: Routledge.
Foucault, M. (1977) What is an author. In M. Foucault (Trans. D. Bouchard and S. Simon) *Language, Counter-Memory, Practice* (pp. 124–127) Ithaca, NY: Cornell University Press.
Gaillet, L.L. and Horner, W.B. (2010) *The Present State of Scholarship in the History of Rhetoric: A Twenty-First Century Guide*. Columbia, Missouri: University of Missouri Press.
Hilliard, C. (2005) Modernism and the common writer. *The Historical Journal* 48 (3) (September), 769–787.
Leahy, A. (2005) (ed.) *Power and Identity in the Creative Writing Classroom: The Authority Project*. Clevedon: Multilingual Matters.
Light, G. (2002) From the personal to the public: Conceptions of Creative Writing in higher education. *Higher Education* 43 (2), 257–276.
Literature Collection (n.d.) O Henry online stories, accessed 23 July 2011. Available at: http://www.literaturecollection.com/a/o_henry/
Marshall, A.J. (1976) Library resources and creative writing at Rome. *Phoenix* 30 (3) (Autumn), 252–264.
Mayers, T. (2005) *(Re)Writing Craft*. Pittsburgh: University of Pittsburgh Press.
Morley, D. (2007) *The Cambridge Introduction To Creative Writing*. Cambridge: Cambridge University Press.
Myers, D.G. (1996) *The Elephants Teach: Creative Writing Since 1880*. Englewood Cliffs, New Jersey: Prentice Hall.
O' Rourke, R. (2005) *Creative Writing: Education, Culture and Community*. Leicester: National Institute of Adult Continuing Education.
Perry, W.G., Jr (1970) *Forms of Intellectual and Ethical Development in the College Years: A Scheme*. New York: Holt, Rinehart & Winston.
Prince, G. (2003) *A Dictionary of Narratology* (revised edition). Lincoln, Nebraska: University of Nebraska Press.

Proulx, E.A. (1993) *The Shipping News*. New York: Scribner.

Ritter, K. (2007) Ethos interrupted: Diffusing 'star' pedagogy in Creative Writing programs. *College English* 69 (3) (January), 283–292.

Singleton, J. and Luckhurst, M. (1996) In the workshop way. In J. Singleton and M. Luckhurst (eds) *The Creative Writing Handbook* (pp. 18, 22). New York: MacMillan.

Vanderslice, S. (2000) Workshopping. In G. Harper (ed.) *Teaching Creative Writing* (pp. 147–157) London: Continuum.

Wandor, M. (2008) *The Author is Not Dead, Merely Somewhere Else*. Basingstoke: Palgrave MacMillan.

Wimsatt, W.K., Jr and Beardsley, M.C. (1954) *The Verbal Icon: Studies in the Meaning of Poetry*. Lexington: University of Kentucky Press.

3 Creative Writing Habitats
Graeme Harper

Creative writing habitats are fundamental to creative writing yet we have so far failed to analyse them for the purposes of improving our knowledge of how habitats influence creative writers and creative writing. Similarly, though, creative writers have long created and recreated habitats, adopted and adapted them, we have not yet considered this set of actions from the point of view of our own creative writing, or in terms of creative writing as an occupational or recreational activity. That said, some evidence of creative writing habitats has been well examined, but not from the point of view of creative writing. Rather they have been examined primarily from the point of view of literary culture and thus these examinations, while laudable, have not provided the kinds of writerly information that research in this area could provide for creative writers. Finally, it can be argued that creative writing is itself a form of habitation. That this habitation involves place, time and memory in a distinctive way, and that this too has not yet been examined. This, therefore, is a key issue in creative writing.

Habitat Creation

Elli Muston might be more indistinct than she once was, because in her current relationship (that is, in her relationship with the novelist and occasional playwright Alan Finst) she takes a backseat on certain things – the nature and style of their home, for example – and this new approach leaves her less visible, at least to the casual observer. She has not always taken this approach.

When living for three years with Gary, her previous partner, she placed her habitation needs far higher on her spectrum of daily concerns. She actively defined what did and what did not 'work' for her and, in a manner of speaking (though she would not necessarily describe things this way), she demanded their apartment be located where she most needed it (for work and for leisure, simultaneously). When it came to the decoration and employment of the various apartment spaces she made her preferences heard by Gary and things went, more often than not, in the direction she defined.

Habitats, we recall, are not only about space but also about movement – movements within, moments through, and movements between inhabitants – and Elli's previous relationship with Gary Wu, compared as it can be to her current relationship with Alan Finst, had a dissimilar pattern of movement to that she is experiencing now. In addition, she has moved on, in her career and in her way of thinking; things are busier, yet she is (ironically, she thinks) also more relaxed. Candidly, she would rather leave the consideration of home and the movements of home life to Alan, than devote emotional or intellectual time to these things. Alan, on the other hand, seems to value those kinds of considerations, so Elli is doubly happy to step back a little – though she only recently realised that she has been habitually doing this.

In an effort to understand this dynamic situation more, were we to replace Alan and Elli here with animal characters, in the manner of a fable or an allegory – make them a pair of wolves or a mating partnership of Trumpeter Swans – we could introduce at this point quite a number of environmental factors, many of which would only partially be in Alan and Elli's control, including those aspects of habitat relating to food supply, shelter, predation, various phenomena of weather and the seasons, as well as the individual interpretative abilities of the individuals and of the pair.

Of course, human beings long ago created habitats that resist or even negate the natural world, habitats that are often highly controlled, sometimes adopted and then adapted, sustained (in terms of individual lives, if not always in terms of environmental impact) and often closely managed. Not all human beings are equally comfortable; however, all human beings are largely habitat creators, habitat manipulators. Animals can also be such, but more often than not they are habitat occupiers rather than habitat creators, and they are always far more likely to be unable to control their habitat than we humans can control ours.

Creative Writing as Habitation

The Elli Muston and Alan Finst I've described do not exist. This might disappoint anyone here who was interested in talking to them further. If someone called Elli Muston and Alan Finst do exist, those existent persons are not the fictional ones I have created here. Apologies to the real Elli and Alan should you be reading this: the characters here are obviously not you. Nor does Gary Wu exist, though the more I think (and write) about Gary the more he seems to exist, to me at least. Such is the nature of creative writing in practice, and the experience of a creative writer in engaging in it. We could, in this respect, call creative writing a form of human habitation.

As a form of human habitation creative writing involves both place and time, it involves us and it involves others (even if those others are not present, or are merely perceived versions of actual people), and it involves the taking up of somewhere and of some element of time. By this I mean, as the word habitation suggests, creative writing involves taking up residence, being present. Literary critics mostly locate this residence, this habitation, in the completed texts they encounter, even if they might not refer to this locating by these names. Creative writing critics locate this habitation firstly in the actions of creative writers and in their own actions, as creative writers, and in the evidential record of these actions, including final or completed works, drafts, notes, diaries and the range of other evidence of actions that emerges while doing creative writing.

Human habitation involves a layered engagement with space and time (current versions of place, current time, layering over previous versions, and so on) and a fluid engagement – because even if the evidential records in front of us are complete and the creative writer who produced them has passed away, creative writing criticism is strongly situational, driven almost entirely by the needs of the creative writer, so another creative writer encountering that seemingly 'fixed' evidence will renew it by their own situational needs, their own encountering of the evidence.

So it is that a layering over of space and time occurs when one creative writer produces, or encounters, evidence of their own actions or the actions of other creative writers. We can consider this in the same way as we might consider the occupying and re-occupying of any wider habitat, and the personalizing, or adapting, of a more local, personal habitat to our individual needs, desires and context.

Considering and Reconsidering Habitats

Plainly, habitats have pragmatic importance for a creative writer, as well as significant critical or theoretical significance for those considering the nature, activities and outcomes of creative writing – using the term 'creative writing' here to rightly mean the undertaking of creative writing not as a synonym for the works that emerge from this undertaking.

In the case of the fictitious novelist, Alan Finst, he has a current habitat, at very least one previous habitat, and certainly some feelings about both of these – whether he takes into account Elli's feelings is perhaps another matter! He has analysed, albeit relatively informally, the efficiency and contribution of past and current habitats in terms of his creative writing, and he has sought to maximise via creation or acts of adapting the habitat, albeit without having detailed 'data' in front of him, the positive and negative impacts of his habitats on his creative writing. As creative writing is foremost a collection of human actions, undertaken more or less fluidly, and more or less informed by the understanding and knowledge of the creative writer, Finst has created and re-created his habitats as and when he saw fit (perhaps more so as his current partner, Elli, is happy for him to determine their communal spaces and time), seemingly with a degree of extemporaneity, but often clearly informed by emotional context.

For himself, Alan has composed something along these lines, whether he has done so entirely consciously or at least partially unconsciously:

'Enter my office. There is a window to the left, curtained, but only with what are commonly called "nets". Through the netting, you can see beyond the window; but only to see shrubbery. As you enter the room, to the right there is a large bookcase, to the left there is another, both topped with piles of books. Books once slotted in bookcases are piled on books, stacked on more books, heaped on sheets of paper. There is so much paper, collapsed stacks of paper on the bookshelves and below them, on the floor, all around. It appears some book pages have caught on others as one stack fell, and they lie curled upwards over the hard covers of other books. And there is a table. Among all this – and "among" is the word, because there is no division here between pile and heap and stack and bookcase and an old round-backed chair and its sagging floral cushion – among all this there is a table even more littered and overcome with paper, books, a tennis ball, a six inch green plastic statuette of Aphrodite, a coffee tin with a silver pen sticking out of it, some silver DVDs in their unmarked cases, a pair of khaki knitted gloves, more books, more papers, pencils, a black string tie, a folded newspaper. The table is even more overcome than the floor, and on this table, in front of the round-backed chair, is a laptop computer.

'A laptop computer – it seems so totally out of place beneath the corkboard of newspaper clippings and a picture, a child's drawing of . . . well, it mostly resembles a brown bear or a roan horse I guess. But that computer screen glows on and its glow is equal, if not slightly greater, to that of the light through the shrubbery and nets and dusty window.'

Even if Alan has not set this out as plainly as this, or indeed has not reduced his analysis to a descriptive investigation, his sensory engagement in the world around him could not help but initiate or stimulate a version of this above, even if Alan's version was composed in a way that related to his personal sensory indicators and his individual dispositional parameters. That is, to what he saw, heard, felt, smelled and how he as an individual processed and responded to that sensory information. For example, a habitat might be considered by one person foremost in terms of its function, or relation to their systemic sense of interaction with space and time; by another it might be considered primarily in terms of the emotional importance of surroundings or of events, or in terms of the structural properties of these things.

Our consideration of creative writing habitats can take as many forms as the habitats themselves. After all, a habitat is hardly going to be a singular enterprise: it is made up of personal and communal physical space, as well as time sensitive movements within and through those spaces; and it also contains what can be called 'virtual spaces' (potentially, and more so now than was the case before the mid-1990s, when the domesticated digital world was only just beginning to emerge). These contemporary virtual spaces, while as the name suggests not physical in nature, can have properties of influence and attitude that impact upon, challenge or support, the creative writer – to take merely a few possible results of the existence of the virtual world.

A habitat also involves temporal cycles, events and longer term evolutionary changes (for example, a seasonal workspace or a creative writer's habitat connected to the short-term particularity of a certain publishing or performing activity). A habitat contains material objects (these might have a very wide range of forms and display an even wider range of purposes and functions, from the aesthetic to the practical, the personally nostalgic to the primarily research-orientated, from the fortuitously present to the carefully located and situated). This listing of elements could continue, and one note to make here is that habitats, and the habitation with which we are engaged, involve both macro and micro elements, larger scale actions and constituents as well as smaller scale actions and constituents.

Being People-Centred

Thus, to keep the analysis grounded in human action, the reason for introducing the fictional Alan and the fictional Elli, whose independence from each other is often as touching as the strength of their fictional relationship, was to make this discussion suitably people-centred, albeit in a fictional couple for the purposes of a theoretical exploration.

Creative writing, we know, is not analogous to the situation in which a plant germinates miraculously, after unseen winds carry its seed somewhere. Whatever we say about creative writing cannot be accurate if we begin by thinking of creative writing that way. Analogously, creative writing is not like that situation either in which a piece of ordinary wood is turned into something interesting by drifting in the sea, over time. And yet, nevertheless, metaphors of germination and metaphors of the grinding away at an object called creative writing to produce a 'final' material result have abounded in historical considerations of creative writing and continue to be common.

By this I mean that it is always incorrect to imagine creative writing without recognising it happens because people do things, people act in some way, but this recognition has not always occurred in modern times, and it still does not always occur today. Thus, Alan might not be real, but very real aspects of doing, of undertaking, of acting are focal in Alan's fictional writerly life, as well as in the real writerly life of creating him here in the first place. What evidence creative writing leaves behind is created both consciously and unconsciously by people. Therefore, to look at a poem and say 'this is creative writing' is quite obviously no more accurate than looking at the score for a symphony and saying 'listen to that wonderful orchestra' – though we cannot deny the enlivening metaphoric possibilities of doing exactly that.

This is the case too with creative writing habitats – they are being created and recreated, in motion, by people, all the time, constantly. Though some of their dynamic might be small scale – a pencil moved on a desk, a stack of papers rearranged, a different starting time for the writer's creative writing, on a particular day – other aspects of their dynamic existence might well be much larger, such as a move from one continent to another, or one home to another, or one set of personal and public relationships and another. The very largest percentage of creative writers in the world, making and remaking their habitats, will not enter anything like what we might call 'literary culture', as published or performed creative writers, though their formation of habitats will be no less significant in terms of their own creative writing and their creative writing's influence on their lives and, potentially, the lives of those around them.

Indeed, though we can look at creative writing habitats without creative writers we cannot but conclude that creative writers create them and that without the creative writer present what remains is only partial evidence of this human habitation. Similarly, we can of course look only at the habitats of creative writers who enter literary culture, but we will not then be looking at creative writing habitats; rather we will be looking at the habitats of creative writers who have entered literary culture. Stating the obvious, naturally – however, this could only be left unsaid if previous analysis of creative writing had not so often proceeded on the basis that known creative writers form the basis of all creative writing. Nothing could be further from the truth.

Moving Ahead with Creative Writing Habitat Analysis

There are many ways in which a consideration of creative writing habitats might proceed, and many forms of investigation such a consideration might take. One thing is paramount – that examining creative writing habitats should proceed on the basis that creative writers spend most of their lives in the making of something not in considering the made results of their activities.

A habitat approached from the point of view of its relationship to creative writing can consider, usefully, what was successful and what was unsuccessful about the habitat with regard to this human activity of making. 'Did the place and time with which I was engaged assist me in my creative writing, or did either or both prove a hindrance to this?' 'Did I benefit from having these materials around me, or should I have sought out other things?' 'Do I work better in the morning or at night?' 'Does noise bother me when I'm writing?' 'How much does a certain kind of writing instrument – a computer, a pencil, a mobile phone – influence the way in which I write?' 'Did I seek to adapt the habitat I adopted, or did I seek to adapt my actions to the habitat I encountered?' These are just a few habitat related questions and, at very least, getting answers to these sorts of questions would be one reason to undertake such a habitat analysis – considering that we have largely not done so to date, and considering too that what we might discover by asking such questions might well assist us in writing more successfully.

That is to say, if creative writing can itself be seen as habitation, as well as that creative writers adopt, form, adapt and/or reform habitats with some relation to their undertaking of creative writing, then it seems obvious that our dealing with habitat analysis so far in the form of investigating creative writers' homes, or creative writers' work habits (e.g. how many words they produce each day or whether they write in an office at home or in a café, on the train or in bed), has not delved deeply enough into the nature of habitat to offer useful information to creative writers about the roles and results of such habitats.

This is not to dismiss the great many works looking at the places, houses, rooms, streets, cities, occupied by creative writers, nor is it to ignore the work undertaken over many years in investigating writers' diaries, notebooks and, indeed, general outpourings on 'how' their creative writing happens. However, much of this analysis has been done only on known creative writers, mostly therefore from the point of view of literary culture, and primarily in relation to lives that might be considered as defined, foremost, more by public interest in finished works than by active interest in the actions undertaken. The issue of undertaking creative writing habitat analysis, in this sense, is indeed a pressing issue in creative writing. One which we should now address.

The Success and Failure of Creative Writing Habitats

To begin, then, if creative writers' habitats are recognized as significant, how do varieties of writerly action determine the formation and reformation of such creative writing habitats? If an individual creative writing habitat (any creative writer's habitat) is long established, what elements of it represent particular long established actions, what elements represent particular sequences of writerly activity with which the creative writer is familiar and, we would hope, with which they are pleased?

Are there points of interruption, catastrophic events even, that alter the short-term nature and operations of a creative writer's habitat? Is that habitat grounded in some way, so that longer term, more stable aspects determine its influence, positively or negatively? Are there cycles of activity that seem to form or influence cycles of success and failure for the writer – and, even, how is success and failure determined, by whom, and to what purpose? What activities might be defined as habitat adoption, habitat creation, habitat adaptation, habitat recreation or reformation?

We can relate all this to patterns of writerly composition and might consider, in doing so, if we as individual creative writers have particular, individual compositional strategies that are well represented by our habitat or, indeed, the habitats we occupy or have occupied. I've hinted earlier at some questions that could get us started on this kind of analysis, and there is some anecdotal evidence that what occurs in creative writing workshops already includes such casual exchanges – writer and workshop teacher talking about what helps them write, students exchanging stories about their successful undertakings, that kind of thing.

The more we delve the more we potentially unearth possible avenues of new knowledge, and in doing so possible contributions to the understanding of our own creative writing and that of other creative writers. For example, might there be primary and secondary habitats? Individual, group and/or shared habitats? Might we recognise these, and use them in different ways as creative writers, or be influenced by them in different ways which might or might not be orchestrated by us?

We can speculatively approach all these questions under a rubric such as this one:

(1) *Initial habitat formation*. Where do we begin to form a habitat for creative writing, why, when and in what ways? Here we can consider how much a habitat is formed anew, how much it is adopted or adapted, and in that sense already a form or recreation or reformation?

(2) *Habitation activities*. These can be considered in terms of time, so that what occurs during a day or a week or year. In addition, we can consider how many of these activities are under the creative writer's direct control, how many are partially controlled, and how many are beyond the creative writer's control.

(3) *Changes in habitat or habitats*. Brought about by what or whom, why, and to what result? How might these changes be considered in relation to specific writerly activities or, indeed, how might changes positively or negatively influence compositional practices?

(4) *Habitat awareness*. How much are we, as individual creative writers, aware of the circumstances of our writerly habitat, and its influences and contributions to our creative writing?

As our own creative writing habitat is *the place we are most likely to be found* – that being the general definition of a habitat – it surely must reflect something of the organisational qualities we individually value in our actions, and reflect habits we have formed – which may or may not be most supportive of our creative writing. It surely must also be analysable in terms of what things impact upon us but over which we have varying degrees of control. Knowing the latter could well be the clue to many things, including whether we actually get to the point of finishing something we are writing, or whether we continue as creative writers.

Knowing this must surely be useful for us as individual writers. Considering it comparatively (e.g. between creative writers, between periods in creative writing history) would be fascinating and, by starting at the point of creative writing rather than at the point of finished works or of entry into literary culture, this kind of analysis (could it be done historically, given that we have not necessarily retained information of this kind) would no doubt be revealing in terms of influence, change, decision-making and much more.

For example, what combinations of decision-making and circumstance determine the form of a long-term creative writing habitat? How many writers find their creative writing enhanced by these kinds of established habitats and how many writers have been adversely impacted upon by a habitat formed by unhelpful circumstances or by decision-making that didn't best serve their creative writing?

If all the actions of creative writers were only actions using words, or even more narrowly about creatively using words, then dismissing this kind of analysis as peripheral information would be fine. But creative writers do things that support their textual endeavours but are not in themselves actions (or results) in words – so, a writer doodling or drawing, taking photographs, recording sounds. And, of course, creative writers' actions of habitation go way beyond these kinds of things. What about a writer placing the seat in which she sits to write by the window, overlooking the beach? What about the writer choosing a particular device (pencil, laptop, smartphone) with which to write? What about the room chosen – its location in the house, its relationship with other rooms, whether it is very quiet or not, whether it is warmer in the mornings or in the afternoons, whether it has low lighting or bright lighting? And, though indeed reading often involves words (of course, reading faces does not; neither does reading the weather or reading the tides) what is the pattern of the placement and indeed moving and replacement associated with completed books and articles by other writers, poems, scripts, magazine articles? Do completed works, such as these, form the basis of a supportive organization of resources?

Thus, even though the language of discussion of creative writing must often be located in a discussion of words and texts it cannot stop there. If such a wider discussion of aspects of creative writing currently seems alien to us, this is indeed a key issue in our doing and studying of creative writing. It is an issue brought about by absences in our approach to understanding creative writing, in the past, and it is an issue if unaddressed must mean we are choosing not to explore potential avenues of new knowledge. It is difficult to see why we would choose not to discover more.

A productive way into overcoming this current limitation is to think metaphorically about the relationships and actions we need to be considering. Metaphor assists us by shifting the plane of reference and thus approaching a subject by locating it in a particular set of circumstances via avenues of resemblance or comparison. In other words, metaphor provides a technique for moving between the familiar and the unfamiliar, and for using one to enhance our understanding of the other.

Using Established Habitat Theories

Metaphorically, consider this then from *The American Naturalist*:

Strategies for habitat selection have a strong influence on individual success because abundance and accessibility of resources are discontinuous in natural environments. In addition, variations in habitat quality

> influence local aggregations and dispersal of both intraspecific and interspecific competitors . . . . That is why individual habitat selection behaviour is influenced by resource availability and density of competitors and why individual behaviour and population interactions are tightly coupled. (Křivan & Sirot, 2002: 214)

Beginning with this, I am going to ask you to take a leap of faith. My suggestion might appear a little strange, and perhaps it should at this point in our history of thinking about and exploring creative writing. Nevertheless, imagine that the first sentence of this piece by Křivan and Sirot begins 'strategies for habitat selection have a strong influence on individual writer success . . .'. Imagine that their second sentence reads: 'In addition, variations in a creative writer's habitat quality influence local aggregations and dispersal of competitors'. Imagine their third sentence says something like: 'individual creative writer habitat selection behaviour is influenced by resource availability and density of creative writers and why individual behaviour and population interactions are tightly coupled'.

While the language might appear alien in our current way of exploring creative writing, metaphorically the analysis is pointing us toward ways in which such habitat considerations might begin to be constructed. It is up to us, quite naturally, how we evolve a language of habitat discussion that best suits creative writing and those undertaking creative writing. But the key to this will undoubtedly be the recognition now that we do not currently know enough about how creative writing habitats are created, how they evolve and what their influence is on individual creative writers and on creative writers as an occupational and/or recreational group.

Investigating Creative Writing as Habitation

It was said earlier that creative writing can be considered a form of human habitation. This is far too bold a statement to leave so lightly addressed. Thus, habitation refers to the act of inhabiting. To inhabit is to be present in place and time. The reason why creative writing can be seen as a form of habitation is that creative writing naturally occurs at a place and time. There is evidence left behind of this inhabitation, but the habitation itself occurs while the creative writing is taking place or in the memory of the creative writer after it has taken place.

As a form of habitation, creative writing is not only about the present. In other words, it is possible to look at creative writing as both a current and a past form of habitation. However, in order to do so there has to be some memory of that habitation, potentially along with the records of it. That memory – as with all memory – is not simply a collection of detached observations, or observations defined by easily exchangeable evidence such as finished works or preserved manuscripts. It also includes emotional and behavioural records, physiological and psychological responses, intentions and meanings as understood by the creative writer, reasons and feelings that influenced the creative writer as the maker, the composer, the agent of the creative writing. The latter comment appears to suggest something of a detached, even mystical element – but my argument is not that such agency is controlled elsewhere but that the physical as well as psychological in the undertaking of creative writing clearly involves our individual writerly agency and, indeed, our individual free will.

So creative writing as a form of habitation in a place and time can best be investigated by the creative writer as the possessor of the fullest range of evidence, and very likely as the individual most interested in the situational relevance of that evidence. Come to understand further how this habitation occurs and it would at least seem theoretically possible that future situations encountered when undertaking some creative writing can be addressed with the knowledge gained in examining previous evidence.

This kind of analysis is not aiming to complicate a simple activity. In other words, this is not to add complexity to a human activity that might be summarised as merely 'creative writers write and if they think about their writing while doing it they will learn something of use to them later'. A statement like that, while true, hides so much. The reason why it is more productive to dig deeper is that such a statement doesn't make a strong enough claim for the ways in which creative writers can marshal their cognitive and emotional resources to help them (to help us, in fact, because I write here as a creative writer) to better understand what might be occurring in our creating and recreating of habitats and, ultimately, in our undertaking of creative writing.

'Might' be occurring, because to suggest methods of investigating our creative writing is not to suggest all answers are clearly there before us. In fact, one of the reasons to begin to actively undertake habitat analysis is that we do not yet know whether such research will reveal anything of use to us. All we can confidently state is that this kind of investigation has not yet been undertaken and that recognizing this absence would only be acceptable if we were entirely confident no new knowledge will be found in undertaking this kind of work. The key issue for creative writing, and creative writers, is that potential for new knowledge almost certainly appears far greater than the chance absolutely no new knowledge will be found.

Creative Writing Habitats and the Teaching of Creative Writing

Finally, to bring this key issue back to the teaching and learning of creative writing in universities, colleges, our schools. If we share the influence of habitats on our creative writing – which largely anecdotal evidence suggests that we do in various forms of the creative writing class – then a primary pedagogic consideration is whether habitat discussions should be more formally part of creative writing education. Creative writing is such an eclectic activity, drawing on more than word use and compositional practices. It is also one of the most individual of university subjects, for example, emphasizing the emotional and dispositional context of an undertaking as well as the results. It is one of those human activities in all levels and forms of education where questions continue along the lines of 'Can it really be taught?'

It might therefore be that part of this current key issue in creative writing is that creative writing cannot truly be taught in the way it has been taught to date and that teachers of it need to embrace a more holistic sense of what creative writing involves – including what it involves in terms of habitat formation and reformation. As creative writers it might be we recognise that already, but that modern systems of education have worked against us fully developing such a way of teaching. To take this line of thought even further it could well be that a concentration on textual evidence, on outcomes defined by finished works, and on definable material artefacts, has moved us away from creative writing not closer to it. Therefore, it would be that considering creative writing habitats, and the form of habitation that is creative writing, will bring us closer both to our own practices and to the true nature of creative writing itself.

References

Křivan, V. and Sirot, E. (2002) Habitat selection by two competing species in a two-habitat environment. *The American Naturalist*, 160 (2) (August), 214–234R.

4 Beyond the Literary: Why Creative Literacy Matters

Steve Healey

Creative writing students learn skills that they can use to produce literary works, but these skills – such as storytelling, character development, wordplay and associative thinking – are also increasingly used in a wide range of jobs and activities beyond the making of poetry, fiction and other kinds of literature. Creative literacy has become enormously valued in the creative economy, social media and digital technology; those who aspire to enter the middle and upper classes in post-industrial countries are encouraged to author many kinds of cultural texts and to access the new cultural capital associated with being a creative producer rather than just a consumer. As an academic field, creative writing has an opportunity to begin recognizing its role as a primary point of access to creative literacy, to begin shaping this role with more critical rigor and social awareness, and to help build the academic legitimacy of creative literacy throughout higher education.

Creative writing as an academic field does not exist in an isolated bubble of artistic activity, cut off from a world that hates creativity. Despite the common tendency to frame the field in these oppositional terms, creativity has in the 21st century become a pervasive social and economic value, especially in post-industrial, English-speaking countries, and this larger shift in values has spurred the boom in creative writing.

At the end of 2010, *The New York Times Magazine* released its special annual issue devoted to 'The Year in Ideas', and the lead article, 'In pursuit of the perfect brainstorm', focuses on an emerging 'quirky legion' of small companies and individual consultants who sell 'creative thinking' and 'the art of innovation' (Segal, 2010: 26) to other – mostly larger – companies. Big businesses have become so obsessed with generating new ideas for products and services, or finding creative solutions to problems, that they're willing to spend enormous amounts of money to hire these outside 'idea entrepreneurs' to think creatively for them or teach them how to become better creative thinkers.

California-based Jump Associates, for example, has worked with a number of massive corporations, including Mars, the candy producer, to help it 'define the current meaning of "indulgence"', and with Target, to help reimagine its line of 'back-to-college' products. Discussing the reasons for this creativity boom, the head of Jump, Dev Patnaik, talks about the shift in management style in the last couple of decades – while the ideal 20th century manager was good at understanding numbers and data, now, he says, 'it's about leadership, creativity, vision'. Patnaik makes an analogy to the arts, and how modern technology helped shift painting from a focus on capturing 'reality' to a focus on subjective impressions. Today's corporate creativity fever is, he says, 'the abstract-expressionist era of management' (in Segal, 2010: 27).

If it's not far-fetched to imagine businesses full of Jackson Pollocks, maybe it's equally plausible to imagine corporate offices teeming with John Ashberys, Margaret Atwoods and other literary superstars. And yet, in the midst of this celebration of powerful new ideas, that same special issue of *The New York Times Magazine* reminds us bluntly that the old idea of traditional publishing and reading is pretty much dying. A tidbit describing a new trend to set literary fiction in the near future offers this deflating observation: 'The current wave of literary near futurism comes at a time when the printed book – and the very act of traditional reading – seems under siege by digital technology'. And what's notable about these authors, the piece goes on to say, is how much they mimic new non-literary forms of communication, from text messages to PowerPoint presentations (Schuessler, 2010: 34).

If publishing and reading as we know them are becoming extinct, then why would creative writing be thriving? On the surface, this academic field seems to be fully entrenched in traditional literary genres – students by and large choose courses and degrees in poetry, fiction or creative non-fiction, and within creative writing programs – especially at the MFA level – there's still reverence for print publishing as the primary method of building literary credentials and reputation. But why would all these creative writers want to publish if the audience for these traditional literary categories appears to be so small? And more importantly, given how unlikely the chances of any one creative writing student going on to a successful publishing career, any dream of actually finding a large literary audience would be, for most people, a profound delusion.

Creative writing students, however, are not nearly as deluded as some literary pundits make them out to be. Almost every undergraduate I've encountered in my creative writing teaching has either no specific literary ambition at all, or only the vaguest desire 'to publish a book someday'. Although from the top down, creative writing appears to offer pure professional training for writers of poetry, fiction and creative non-fiction, students themselves often enter the creative writing field with very little awareness of these literary genres and the world of literary publishing, almost no sense of what a contemporary poem, story or literary essay might look like, and even less experience as readers of contemporary literature. What students want from creative writing, I suggest, is access to a kind of cultural capital that's not specifically 'literary' but much more amorphously 'creative'. Like Jump and other purveyors of creativity, students understand that creative skills and experiences have enormous value in our current historical moment. Of course creative writing students do end up writing poems, stories and essays in their classes, but they're less attached to the literariness of these products than to what I call the 'creative literacy' that goes into making them.

As a field, creative writing needs to think about what creative literacy is, why it's so powerful right now, and what kind of effects it already has, and could have in the future. Given that the vast majority of creative writing students don't go on to follow a professional literary path – mostly because they have no interest in doing so, but in some cases because they aspire to literary success and don't achieve it – we need to consider what else these students are getting from creative writing, and how they're using it in their lives.

What is Creative Literacy?

Not just the ability to make literary works, creative literacy is the term I give to the skills and experience that students can gain from taking a creative writing class and that they can apply to a broad range of activities and jobs beyond the classroom. Creative literacy develops many proficiencies, including the ability to use language (along with visual images and many other media) to produce complex affective states in an audience; the ability to think and communicate in associative, metaphorical, non-linear, non-hierarchical ways; the ability to craft evocative stories with fully realized characters, personas, voices; the ability to manipulate or destabilize received meanings and to produce new meanings. Creative writing has become a primary site for accessing creative literacy because it's positioned conveniently in the liberal arts wing of most colleges. Plus, in return, students receive real academic credit towards a degree, and because creative writing appears to be a fun, playful alternative to the unpleasant work of traditional academic writing (whether these perceptions are accurate or not), many students find it very attractive.

Students can learn these skills in other fine arts academic fields like photography, film and music. And just as creative writing needs to think about transformations in the category of 'literary author', fine arts in general needs to think about how the label 'artist' has grown, for better or worse, much more flexible and ambiguous, particularly with the rise of new media and digital technology. It's now much easier for anyone without substantial technical training or resources to call herself, for example, a photographer, a filmmaker or a musician.

Perhaps even more noteworthy, there has been a dizzying proliferation of the means of distributing creative products or accessing an audience. Just about any artist or aspiring artist can create a website or use an existing website to display work, as long as it can be digitally reproduced. Etsy and other online brokers allow individuals to sell just about any artsy, crafty, handmade item imaginable. YouTube, whose rallying cry is 'Broadcast Yourself', offers anyone with simple video technology the chance to screen their little movie – often starring themselves – in a virtual theatre almost as large as the planet. Musicians use MySpace to promote and disseminate themselves. And Facebook, of course, has become everyone's stage on which to perform our witty, weird and wonderful personas, in the form of photos, video clips, status updates and so on.

Much of this new creative activity involves writing that's neither strictly functional nor strictly literary, and Facebook is currently the most obvious example of this kind of writing. Of course users can conduct practical business or post a poem that they've written on Facebook, but more likely their status updates or comments, no matter how mundane or uninterest-ing, will amount to a kind of creative writing that doesn't define itself in literary terms. Or consider Twitter as another delivery system for creative written expression, encouraging a poetic compression without calling itself poetry. And the entire blogosphere presents itself as a forum for a kind of private, journal-like creative expression turned public but without traditional literary ambition.

Whether you find any of this new creative activity to have artistic merit or not, it's hard to deny that a creative ethos now saturates the lives of many people living in the developed world, not only in our leisure time but also in our work. Those who have creative literacy have a skill set that's grown remarkably valuable throughout our 21st century post-industrial economy, exemplified especially in companies like Jump Associates. 'Think-ing outside the box' has become the corporate world's most celebrated product. Adding intangible value to tangible goods and services has become the primary engine of economic growth in the US and other developed countries. Consumers apparently demand – or they're encouraged to demand – the new, the innovative, the revolutionary, the unpredictable, the outlandish, the beautifully designed, etc., and in recent decades economic production has shifted largely toward satisfying that demand for creativity.

In his 2011 State of the Union speech, President Obama's central vision for economic revitalization was 'winning the future' through innovation. 'What we can do – what America does better than anyone – is spark the creativity and imagination of our people', he declared. 'In America, innovation doesn't just change our lives. It's how we make a living' (transcript of State of the Union, 2011). And not only in America, Obama should take note. In recent years in the UK and Australia, there has arguably been a greater willingness to build more collaborative relations between the arts and the economy, and you can find serious academic inquiry in journals and institutes devoted entirely to the study of 'creative industries'. Those who write poems and stories may claim a more authentic, artful kind of creativity than the kind that generates wealth, and they may argue that the near-impossibility of making a living purely through sales of literary works is proof of that difference. But all those other former creative writing students who don't pursue a professional literary career, or who pursue it only in their leisure time, are very likely applying their creative literacy in the workplace.

Perhaps the most well-known recent argument for creativity's economic power came in sociologist Richard Florida's book, *The Rise of the Creative Class*. Florida (2002: 44) says bluntly that our entire economy has become 'fundamentally a creative economy' – evidenced, for example, in the skyrocketing investment – an over 800% increase, adjusted for inflation – in research and development by businesses in the last half of the 20th century (p. 45). This new economic climate has generated a new 'creative class' of workers, says Florida, who work in fields of 'science and engineering, architecture and design, education, arts, music and entertainment, whose economic function is to create new ideas, new technology and/or new creative content'. In addition to this core group, Florida includes 'a broader group of *creative professionals* in business and finance, law, health care and related fields' who 'engage in complex problem solving that involves a great deal of independent judgment and requires high levels of education or human capital' (p. 8).

Clearly Florida's definition of 'creative worker' is flexible and can include just about anyone who's not in the diminishing manufacturing sector, or in the growing service sector, which is still significantly larger than the creative sector. But even if the Creative Class doesn't amount to a majority of workers, says Florida, it's still 'the most influential' class – a remarkable development given that only decades ago we used to associate creativity with the social margins. How creativity has become so central is largely a story of a major shift in values: whereas that mid-20th century 'organizational age' defined itself by 'homogeneity, conformity and "fitting in"', our creative age values 'individuality, self-expression and openness to difference' (Florida, 2002: 9). And while our forebears tended to identify themselves with stronger ties to family and local community or to institutions like churches, we now see ourselves functioning more independently, accumulating an increasing number of weaker ties over our lifetimes while striving to form our own identities. 'It is this creation and re-creation of the self, often in ways that reflect our creativity', says Florida, that define much of our social and economic lives (p. 7).

Although Florida is worried about certain aspects of the creative economy – especially how it tends to correlate with increased disparity of wealth – he's essentially a cheerleader for it, encouraging individuals, businesses, institutions and cities to embrace the creative ethos. Certainly not the first to have proclaimed this message, his name has nonetheless become synonymous with it, and in the last decade the message has been reiterated by a growing chorus of pop business writers, including Thomas L. Friedman, Daniel H. Pink and Seth Godin, whose recent bestseller, *Linchpin*, argues that excelling in the workplace now requires being 'an artist'. Says Godin (2010: 90): 'Everything from food to luggage to phones to pens to insurance forms is transformed by design and art and insight. If art is about humanity, and commerce has become about interactions (not stuff), then commerce is now about art, too'.

Consider for a moment how attractive a creative writing course might be to a typical undergraduate student who aspires, consciously or not, to join the Creative Class. As that student scans the typical array of course offerings and sees mostly a sea of conventional intellectual work that involves studying the information and theories of a given field, it's not hard to imagine that creative writing calls out to such a student as a beacon of opportunity. Even though creative writing can and should build critical and theoretical frameworks for that student, it's often perceived as offering a way to earn credit 'outside the box' of conventional academic fields. This student likely has little desire to make literary works in particular, having little experience reading contemporary literary works aside from the few titles slipped into the English literature courses she may have taken. But her desire for some vaguely-defined notion of creative practice is likely very strong.

From Consumer to Producer

'Literacy' is a slippery and flexible term. Most obviously it refers to a basic ability to read and write. It also commonly refers to specialized knowledge that certain people have access to; a football fan can be said to have football literacy, for example, or someone who has cultivated a discriminating taste for wine can be said to have wine literacy. This sense of literacy as a special taste or authority can also apply to literature: a 'literary literacy' might refer not just to basic reading and writing skills but to an advanced breadth of knowledge (historical perspective, critical ability, etc.) as a reader of poetry, fiction and drama. Referring to someone as 'literate' can mean that she has rudimentary reading and writing skills, but often it means more specifically that she has literary literacy, a strong aptitude as a reader of literature and a deep understanding of the literary field.

Literary literacy has long had social value, at least since Matthew Arnold argued that the best literature could be a means for social progress and advancing civilization. Janice Radway (1997: 5) demonstrates in *A Feeling for Books* how the Book-of-the-Month Club enjoyed enormous success largely because of the desire of the early-to-mid 20th century American middle class 'to present themselves as educated, sophisticated, and aesthetically articulate'. So members of the Book-of-the-Month Club were accessing through the marketplace a kind of informal training in literary literacy, 'a kind of social pedagogy for a growing class fraction of professionals, managers, and information and culture workers as well as for those who aspired to the status of this class, to its work routines, and to its privileges' (Radway, 1997: 15). The Book-of-the-Month Club offered cultural capital, then, to a new class seeking social legitimacy, but Radway also shows how it threatened to erode that pure 'highbrow' space for authentic appreciation of literary merit, helping to fuel a series of cultural battles between the defenders and detractors of 'middlebrow' forms. If literature can be so easily repackaged and sold to a mass audience, not unlike toothpaste and cars, then what is the real value of literature and other arts? So although the Book-of-the-Month Club's heyday in the mid-20th century signals a high point in the prestige of literary literacy, it also signals the beginning of its decline.

In *Cultural Capital: The Problem of Literary Canon Formation*, John Guillory (1993) examines a more recent cultural battle – the canon debates of the 80s and 90s, the clash between champions of the traditional Western canon and champions of multiculturalism – arguing that this battle is actually a symptom of a larger crisis in literary value, a shift in cultural capital away from literary reading in general. As Guillory says, 'the category of "literature" names the cultural capital of the old bourgeoisie, a form of capital increasingly marginal to the social function of the present education system' (p. x). Assertions about the decline of traditional literary value appear to be supported by the much-discussed National Endowment for the Arts (NEA) study that showed a dramatic drop-off in literary reading rates among

Americans (NEA, 2004). Although a follow-up study (NEA, 2009) showed a slight increase in the number of adult literary readers, from 47% in 2002 to 50% in 2008, that rate is still down significantly from the high-water mark of 57% in 1982, when the NEA first started conducting this survey.

If literary literacy no longer offers as much social currency to the middle class, I propose that creative literacy is claiming much of that lost cultural capital. While literary literacy derives from the reading and studying of literature, the reception and *consumption* of the canon, creative literacy derives primarily from *production*, from practicing skills for making not only literary texts but also a wide range of cultural texts. This emphasis on production, on using literacy as a means of making, I argue, is a central feature of a newly dominant cultural capital at the beginning of the 21st century. While the 'old bourgeoisie' could use literary consumption as a primary tool for self-construction, for making leisure time meaningful, for achieving social status, the new middle class often addresses these same desires by actively creating new texts and cultural forms. The new middle class claims authority not so much by reading and appreciating the great authors, but by *being* an author.

Should we be skeptical of this democratization of authorship? Is the role of the author being dumbed down and mass marketed? Many successful students and teachers of creative writing are indeed skeptical, and the field often frames itself as the lone protector of literary excellence, especially given that the folks across the aisle in academic literature departments are mostly no longer interested in evaluating literature as 'good' or 'bad'. We should certainly look critically at the rise of creative literacy, and there are certainly ways in which its democratic pretensions are false, but it's too easy to dismiss creative literacy and, more importantly, dismissing it will not make it go away.

Among the charms of Radway's treatment of middlebrow culture is her calculated ambivalence toward it. She acknowledges that the Book-of-the-Month Club 'uses sophisticated marketing techniques to sell not only individual books but the very idea of taste itself', and yet in a nicely intimate moment, she says:

> I have found myself unable to condemn the organization in any simple way for commodifying what I was taught in graduate school should never have been commodified by the market in the first place, that is, literature, art, and culture. Instead, in attempting to reconstruct the motives and intentions driving not only the club's founders but its subsequent judges, editors, *and* subscribers, I have continually encountered

not merely the insistent desire to rise socially through any means available but also deep-seated longings for the possibilities of self-articulation and the search for transcendence promised by education and art. (p. 5)

It turns out that the anxieties and desires surrounding the Book-of-the-Month Club are strikingly similar to those surrounding the creative writing field. Both institutions promise expanded access to literary experience, and both are accused of transforming literary experience into a mere commodity, stripping it of its authenticity and meaning.

If we suspend the legitimate impulse to critique these powerful institutions, we can see ordinary people using those institutional tools to fashion some sense of autonomy and meaning in their lives. The young man who posts a quirky description of his morning routine on his Facebook page may not be able to claim status as an elite author, nor can the young woman who submits a 'bad' poem to her creative writing workshop – nonetheless, both of these middle class figures are accessing an authorial experience that has real effects. Particularly in the midst of our current textual saturation – when information, knowledge, stories and images are penetrating our eyes and brains at every turn, when even the idle time spent pumping our gasoline can be infiltrated by a screen full of sensory stimulation and happy bargains – it can feel particularly powerful to assert a gesture of authorship, and whatever text one makes, no matter how insignificant or trite, that gesture can feel like a moment of freedom, a feeling of control and ownership over one's life and body.

This deep and widespread middle class desire to be creative and to claim some creative literacy has increased the cultural capital of creative writing, I suggest, much more than the specific desire to become a writer of poetry or fiction. Literary literacy may be losing cultural capital, but creative writing thrives because it promises (implicitly or not) to satisfy a more generalized aspiration among ordinary people to engage in a creative practice.

The Democratization of Authorship

The notion that everyone can and should become an author – or otherwise express themselves – is not new to the 21st century. A number of scholars have traced the historical forces that have shaped the creative writing field and allowed the idea of creativity to emerge as a widespread democratic ideal. In his compelling book, *Creative Writing and the New Humanities*, Paul Dawson (2005) highlights a few key moments in this transformation, pointing out that the term 'creativity', as we understand it, has roots in Romanticism. Prior to the 18th century, imagination was commonly framed as a more 'passive mental faculty' (p. 22) akin to memory, the ability to imitate what was already there in the world. But with the rise of Romanticism, the term 'creative' became more widespread with its connotations of originality, innovation, newness and individuality. This is a democratizing shift in that the source of art and ideas – inspiration – moves from an external, higher authority (tradition, God, etc.) to the human. Dawson points out that European Romantic theories of creativity, however, still tended to cling to an elite notion that relatively few humans had access to the 'genius' required to be creative in authentic ways. The American front of the Romantic project, on the other hand, articulated most notably in Emerson's essays, showed a decidedly more generous view of common creativity. Dawson quotes from 'The American Scholar', where Emerson asserts that books are meant to inspire 'the genius which is "not the privilege of here and there a favorite, but the sound estate of every man"' (p. 33).

This kind of democratic spirit similarly informed the progressive education movement that emerged in the US between the World Wars, and the significance of this movement as a shaping force for the creative writing field is explored by Dawson and others, including D.G. Myers, whose book, *The Elephants Teach: Creative Writing Since 1880*, was the first comprehensive history of the field. Although Myers (1996) looks mostly at developments within higher education, part of his account turns to a junior high school in New York City where, in the early 1920s, Hughes Mearns transformed the standard English curriculum into a student-centered space for creativity and self-expression (p. 101). A major figure in the progressive education movement and highly influenced by John Dewey's educational philosophy, Mearns was the first to use the term 'creative writing' to refer to a course of study in his widely read book, *Creative Youth* (Myers, 1996: 103). In the following couple of decades, the progressive education movement came into dominance, and creative writing was adopted in schools across the country, becoming 'one of the most popular subjects in the curriculum' (Myers, 1996: 104). Mearns and other progressives were driven by the belief that everyone has the capacity for artistic aptitude given the right guidance and circumstances, and they were less interested in upholding aesthetic standards than giving a broad range of students access to creative experience. Myers makes it clear that he's skeptical of such democracy of authorship, asking this pointed question: 'did not a culture also depend upon undemocratic distinctions between greater and lesser creative achievements? Wasn't *criticism* . . . unsparingly evaluative criticism – also necessary?' (p. 120).

For Myers, then, the ideal era of creative writing history comes later, in the 1930s and 40s, when higher education took up the field, most notably at the University of Iowa, tempering the Mearns' model of unrestrained and unrigorous expression with a reverence for standards and tradition (p. 135). Unfortunately, according to Myers, this golden age of creative writing was swallowed up quickly by another resurgence of those soft, standardless impulses, and as the field expanded in the late 20th century, it became a system of patronage for fat-cat writers and a misguided bureaucracy encouraging literary mediocrity rather than greatness. This anxiety about creative writing's abandoning of aesthetic ideals, similar to the kind directed at the Book-of-the-Month Club, has been recycled many times by literary pundits in recent decades.

Mark McGurl (2009) adds to this discussion in his ambitious book, *The Program Era: Postwar Fiction and the Rise of Creative Writing*, and while he's not interested in accusing creative writing of selling out, McGurl agrees with Myers that the field has carried a legacy of progressive values. McGurl emphasizes that progressive educators were reacting against what they saw as oppressive tendencies in traditional schooling toward rote learning, standardization and harsh discipline: 'Responsive to a growing concern that institutions, left to their own devices, make for problematically "institutional" subjectivities, progressive educators worked to re-gear US schools for the systematic production of original persons' (p. 83). This resistance to conformity and celebration of unique individuals becomes increasingly central to the US educational system and helps creative writing flourish.

Although this anti-institutional impulse may make progressive ideals sound removed from the practicalities of everyday life, McGurl shows how that focus on experiential and creative learning in a nurturing environment was conceived as a more effective way to socialize students from a wide range of backgrounds, preparing them for the practical demands of the workplace while supporting them in a friendly familial setting. Just as the progressive ideal of self-expression ripples out beyond the student and classroom, so too the creative writing field thrives within a broader milieu of creativity and reflexive attention to selfhood. Thus, in the postwar period, says McGurl, 'literary practices' take part:

> in a larger, multivalent social dynamic of self-observation. This would extend from the self-observation of society as a whole in the social sciences, media, and the arts, to the 'reflexive accumulation' of corporations which pay more and more attention to their own management practices and organizational structures, down to the self-monitoring of individuals who understand themselves to be living, not lives simply, but *life stories* of which they are the protagonists. (p. 12)

A profound implication of what McGurl says here is that the traditional category we call 'the literary' has taken on a much more central role in our social and economic lives, despite the chatter about the decline of literary reading, and despite the pervasive belief that the creative writing field is or should be simply a training ground for excellent writers of poetry, fiction and other literary genres.

Put another way, the literary is transforming, for better or worse, into a more general category I'm calling 'creative literacy', and this transformation is the real reason that creative writing has boomed. Students not only see themselves as protagonists of life stories, they see that life stories are being produced all around us, that much of the post-industrial economy is driven by life stories, that being able to tell your own story and help other people tell their stories has taken on enormous value. If authorship has become increasingly democratized, then, this doesn't simply mean that more people are writing literary works. Which begs the question: what is creative writing for? If many creative writing students are not particularly attached to traditional literary genres but seek access to a more general creative literacy, then what does this mean for an academic field that often sees itself in strictly literary terms?

The most practical implication is that creative writing can and does lead students to a much wider range of careers and professional paths than is often acknowledged, although outside the US – in the UK and Australia, for example – there have been more intentional efforts to link creative writing and other fine arts with creative economy fields like new media, TV, advertising, and so on. But the shift from a narrow literariness to creative literacy also suggests an aesthetic opportunity: creative writing can lead students (or perhaps students are the ones who can lead creative writing) beyond rigid definitions of what is authentically literary and what is an authentic literary genre. Much exciting, vital fiction and poetry being made in the 21st century doesn't look or sound much like fiction and poetry; instead, it sees itself collaborating with all kinds of non-literary texts (news reports, personal ads, word games, recipes, etc.) along with non-literary technologies (the internet, computer software, video, etc.). And as literary boundaries continue to open, creative writing can have a much more profound impact on what we call academic work.

Creative Writing and the Future of Higher Education

The rise of creative literacy has enormous consequences not just for one field called 'creative writing', but throughout higher education, and this is especially evident in the influence creative writing has had, and will continue to have, on the first-year composition course. I'm convinced that the traditional thesis-driven expository essay is less relevant than it once may have been, and many teachers are discovering that teaching creative literacy skills as a complement to critical literacy is an effective way to engage students more and invigorate their academic writing. This shift toward a more creative academic writing has certainly been fueled by the very mundane economic reality that an increasing number of people who've earned creative writing MFAs have become teachers of composition. But the shift should be seen in broader social terms, as well – as an effect of creative literacy's increasing cultural capital.

What kind of skills are students supposed to learn in the traditional composition course? The answer is not simply 'basic literacy' – that is, the ability to use correct grammar, punctuation, and so on, to communicate through writing. At least since the 19th century, a fairly broad swath of the American population has gained these basic literacy skills in primary and secondary schooling, and this population has been able to use this literacy in the workplace, as well as in their leisure to become authors of diaries, letters and other kinds of informal texts. The college composition course, however, is supposed to build on this foundation and provide a kind of advanced critical literacy that has become widespread in American society at least since the post-World War II boom in higher education. The conventional first-year writing course encourages students to assert their authorial intelligence about a wide range of topics through various disciplinary lenses. Students are trained to write a conventional academic essay that primarily uses analytical language and critical thinking, asserts a thesis about its topic, supports this thesis with concrete evidence, and develops a logical, hierarchical sense of organization and transitions.

The composition field has never been static or monolithic, and in recent decades the rise of an expressionistic approach to academic writing, promoted by folks like Peter Elbow, has given students access to a more personal, narrative-based mode of authorship, moving away from a drier, more disinterested mode. Nonetheless, composition courses still primarily teach students the fundamental communication strategies and structures of that thesis-driven academic essay. This kind of advanced critical literacy has provided college graduates with the ability to navigate the rote writing tasks of white-collar work, but it has also given them a certain kind of authorial experience, a claim to some unique critical perspective and an ability to assert this thinking within a vast marketplace of ideas and opinions, an ability to participate in democratic life as an educated and socially-mobile citizen.

John Guillory (1993) positions composition as the educational site where the new middle class of the late 20th century acquired its literacy:

> it is the speech of the professional-managerial classes, the administrators and bureaucrats; and it is employed in its place, the 'office'. It is not 'everyday' language. The point of greatest historical interest about this speech is that its production bypasses the older literary syllabus altogether. Students need no longer immerse themselves in that body of literature in order to acquire 'literary' language. In taking over the social function of producing a distinction between a basic and more elite language, composition takes on as well the ideological identity of that sociolect, its pretension to universality, its status as the medium of political discourse. (p. 79–80)

So composition has traditionally taught students to 'think inside the box' (inside the 'office') of blocky organization and linear argument, to fit into the highly rationalized and disciplined white-collar workplace of the 20th century. Traditional critical thinking privileges objectivity, clearly articulated evidence and explanation, reasonable interpretation and evaluation, sound solutions and conclusions.

Now in the 21st century, I propose, the new 'elite language' with its 'pretension to universality' is accessed increasingly through creative literacy. Those who aspire toward the American middle and upper class, both in their work and their leisure, are increasingly encouraged to 'think outside the box', to think of themselves not as machine cogs but as creative authors of new ideas and new content to provide to their audiences. Creative literacy privileges subjectivity and affect, storytelling and sensory data, ambiguity and contradiction, associative leaps and disruptions of conventional logic, doubt and uncertainty; it uses the strange and the unknown as productive forces rather than trying to overcome them. Moreover, creative literacy is more attuned to contemporary network thinking, globalization's manipulations of time and space, instantaneous connecting, and the digital production of information and performance. The traditional academic essay no longer reflects the profound difference in how language and ideas are organized and presented to us, and creative literacy can help composition bring academic writing into the 21st century.

I want to emphasize here that I'm not advocating that creative writing *replace* composition; I'm saying that these two fields are already collaborating and should continue to collaborate more intentionally, to develop more fruitful relationships between creative and critical literacy. Insofar as composition has traditionally functioned as the primary service course for post-secondary students, creative writing should also begin to consider how it can (and already does) provide the same kind of 'service' to students. At many elite colleges and universities, where students demand more and more sections of creative writing while the traditional first-year writing requirement is being phased out, creative writing is becoming a *de facto* service course, despite being framed as a kind of extra-curricular or 'elective' course. If students need both critical and creative literacy to survive and thrive in the 21st century, if academic writing needs to embrace creativity to remain relevant, then creative writing needs to see itself not simply as a training ground for literary writers, but as an essential point of access to creative literacy for the whole of academia.

Most academic fields, particularly those in the humanities and social sciences, don't see themselves only as providing direct, practical professional training, and I think creative writing should likewise be seen as more integral to the larger mission of higher education. Most students who take courses in anthropology don't become anthropologists, most history majors don't become historians, and so on. It's understood that these fields are not failing simply because their students are not all following a successful professional path in that field; instead, students gain a general overview of the field's theories and methods as part of a broader education in a variety of fields. Students in the humanities and social sciences are not expected to become specialists but to gain generic skills often lumped together as 'critical thinking' – the ability to question assumptions, to see a range of choices or perspectives about a given intellectual issue, to generate logical and efficient strategies for solving complex problems. Most students who take courses and even earn a degree in the creative writing field don't go on to become professional literary writers, but this doesn't mean that they gain nothing from that educational experience. What they gain is creative literacy, a kind of literacy that can and will become an important complement to the still dominant critical mode.

Creative Life Beyond Literary Practice

What do students do with creative literacy, if not forge a career as a poetry or fiction writer, or become a teacher of creative writing using their publication credentials? Just as the anthropology or history student can use that education as part of her training to become, for example, a social worker or a lawyer, so too there are a number of ancillary vocations associated with the creative writing field, including journalism, publishing, editing, arts administration and so on. But as I've suggested, creative literacy has much broader application for a range of vocations throughout the new knowledge economy. The ability to manipulate language, to produce powerful story, image and affect for audiences, is increasingly valued in marketing and advertising, product development and design, social media and internet services, along with many other post-industrial fields driven by a creative ethos.

By far the majority of fellow students I encountered in my undergraduate and graduate creative writing workshops have not become published literary writers and/or creative writing teachers, but many of them are likely using creative literacy in their work and leisure and social lives. I recently had conversations with two friends – all of us earned MFAs in poetry writing from UMASS/Amherst at roughly the same time – and while neither of them has pursued their literary writing after graduate school, both have been very successful in other fields, and both see strong connections between their current work and their creative writing education.

Eric Forst worked in marketing for a number of years, and has more recently joined a thriving start-up company that sells 'social intelligence technology', mostly to other companies who want to improve their use of social media. In all of this work, Eric said, he has used creative writing skills to help companies communicate with customers in engaging and effective ways, to 'quickly understand the narrative' of a company and then help it deliver that story to people. Liz Brixius transformed her literary ambitions into a career in TV writing, and her most recent project is the critically-acclaimed, Emmy-nominated Showtime series, *Nurse Jackie*, which she helped create and for which she continues to be an executive producer and writer. In our conversation, Liz was unequivocal about the strong influence of her creative writing training on her current work, emphasizing especially how the need to be very specific, precise and concise in poetry has served her well: 'Economy is crucial in television. And to economize well is an art form. Writing for television is all about constraints. A scene can only be so long, a character can only be assigned so much dialogue . . . it's not unlike adhering to a rhyme-scheme'.

Both Eric and Liz, it seems to me, are applying literary skills in what are traditionally considered non-literary work settings, and they provide a glimpse into the profound changes that have occurred in the post-industrial creative workplace. Not only are they developing uses for the literary outside of traditional literature, their success arguably depends on cultural consumers choosing to invest less leisure time reading literature and more time grazing on the internet and watching TV. I certainly don't advocate the death of literature, but setting up popular forms like the internet and TV in opposition to literature is far too simplistic, because these forms are capacious and complex enough to contain all kinds of provocative and artful literary impulses. The internet may provide a forum for inane, uninformed and uninteresting chatter, but that doesn't prevent it from also providing users with meaningful artistic exchange, encouraging political dialogue and social responsibility, etc. TV, too, offers lots of remarkably anesthetizing programming, and yet, particularly in recent years, there has been an enormous output of compelling shows with a kind of literary ambition. Certainly serial programs like *Six Feet Under, Deadwood* or *The Wire*, for example, can be just as aesthetically-sophisticated as a 'great American novel'.

So the spread of creative literacy as a dominant value can be a powerful opportunity. But it can also be seen as a component of an ongoing disaster that Marxist theorist Guy Debord (1994) calls 'the spectacle' – the total commodification of language itself, capitalism's system of illusion and images that pervades all of society. In *The Society of the Spectacle*, Debord defines the spectacle not simply as a veil or 'decorative element' that hides 'the real world' (p. 12); instead, it produces 'sham battles between competing versions of alienated power' (p. 36), between spectacular versions of reality and artifice, freedom and oppression. Creative literacy turns out to be an excellent tool for the spectacle, because commodified creativity so effectively presents itself as a liberation from the dehumanizing effects of capitalism. A number of notable theorists have picked up on Debord's concept of the spectacle and articulated strategies for reclaiming language without pretending to occupy some pure, transcendent space outside of the spectacle. In *The Coming Community*, Giorgio Agamben (1993: 79) suggests a paradoxical possibility that the spectacle, in so thoroughly destroying 'the common good', actually 'retains something like a positive possibility that can be used against it'. Because the spectacle so completely alienates humans from their language, that alienation itself becomes a commonality, and 'for the first time it is possible for humans to experience their own linguistic being – not this or that content of language, but language *itself*, not this or that true proposition, but the very fact that one speaks' (Agamben, 1993: 82).

Creative literacy is a set of skills and awareness that's not inevitably pure or impure, libratory or oppressive. No social position or job can transcend the forces of the marketplace, commodification and the spectacle, and certainly being a literary writer or creative writing teacher is no exception. But there is opportunity in every position and job to begin reclaiming language for the common good and to use creative literacy in ways that are ethical, compassionate, socially-engaged and aesthetically vital. Creative writing as a field needs to acknowledge that it's much more than simply professional training for writers of poetry, fiction and other literary genres

– it has become one of the primary institutional sites where people access creative literacy, an enormously powerful force in our current historical moment. Creative writing has this role whether it wants it or not, and the field now has an opportunity to develop more critical awareness of creative literacy and to take more responsibility for how it's disseminated throughout the academy and society.

References

Agamben, G. (1993) *The Coming Community* (Trans. M. Hardt). Minneapolis: University of Minnesota Press. (Original work published in 1990).

Dawson, P. (2005) *Creative Writing and the New Humanities*. New York: Routledge.

Debord, G. (1994) *The Society of the Spectacle* (Trans. D. Nicholson-Smith). New York: Zone Books. (Original work published in 1967).

Florida, R. (2002) *The Rise of the Creative Class, and How it's Transforming Work, Leisure, Community, & Everyday Life*. New York: Basic.

Godin, S. (2010) *Linchpin: Are you Indispensable?* New York: Portfolio/Penguin.

Guillory, J. (1993) *Cultural Capital: The Problem of Literary Canon Formation*. Chicago: University of Chicago Press.

McGurl, M. (2009) *The Program Era: Postwar Fiction and the Rise of Creative Writing*. Cambridge, MA: Harvard University Press.

Myers, D.G. (1996) *The Elephants Teach: Creative Writing Since 1880*. Englewood Cliffs, NJ: Prentice Hall.

Radway, J.A. (1997) *A Feeling for Books: The Book-of-the-Month Club, Literary Taste, and Middle-Class Desire*. Chapel Hill, NC: University of North Carolina Press.

Schuessler, J. (2010) Literary near futurism. *The New York Times Magazine*, 19 December, p. 34.

Segal, D. (2010) In pursuit of the perfect brainstorm. *The New York Times Magazine*, 19 December, 24–28.

Transcript State of the Union (2011) Obama's Full Address – ABC News. Accessed 28 January 2011.

US National Endowment for the Arts (2004) *Reading at Risk: A Survey of Literary Reading in America* (July), accessed 22 May 2011. Available at: http://www.nea.gov/pub/ReadingAtRisk.pdf.

US National Endowment for the Arts (2009) *Reading on the Rise: A New Chapter in American Literacy* (January), accessed 22 May 2011. Available at: http://www.nea.gov/research/ReadingonRise.pdf.

5 To Fill with Milk: or, The Thing and Itself

Katharine Haake

This essay investigates the question of genre, particularly as it can be useful in the creative writing classroom. Using analogies drawn from Mary Louise Pratt's work on autoethnography and Elaine Showalter's work on gender, and their complementary ideas of contact and wild zones, the essay examines how genre can frame questions about what writing is and how it moves through the world in such a way as to help students develop a greater sense of their own authority. Frequently understood by means of description, genre may also be generatively explored as a methodology (how it is written), a location (who is writing it), or a motivation (why it is doing what it is doing). The essay concludes with a discussion of interstiality as a mode of resistance that can further our understanding of both genre and its function, even as it opens new spaces for students to write themselves.

> *Either there were too few albums, or there were too many pictures. She couldn't decide or didn't know how to organize them. She had given up her struggle with genre from the outset*
> Dubravka Ugresic (2002)

> *Genres are not to be mixed.*
> *I will not mix genres.*
> *I repeat: genres are not to be mixed. I will not mix them*
> Jaques Derrida (1988b)

Do you remember the A-1 steak sauce commercial?

You know, the one where the man in the kitchen holds a bottle of it aloft and chummily asks, as if speaking to you: *what is hamburger, my friends – chopped ham?*

As a child, I never really got it. I don't like A-1 sauce and not even steak that much, although hamburgers were a big favorite, and the question seemed inane. But still it perplexed me, not the inanity so much as the *genre* of the question, which turns out to be a definition question. What, after all, *was* hamburger?

Later, I started out teaching, like most of us, the way I'd been taught. Write three stories, I told my students. There were due dates and workshops, rough drafts and revisions, and this went on for a couple of years, with varying degrees of success, until I began to understand that since my students really didn't know very much about stories, the assignment – to write one – was specious. So this is how it happened that I started asking first, what's a story? And every time I asked, I heard the A-1 steak sauce man's voice in my head: *what is a [story], my friends?*

It made me feel oddly close to my students, as if we shared a common purpose, as if their resistance to analysis and naming (wasn't this *creative writing?*) and my insistence that we analyze and name were not a source of friction, as if two small ironically intoned words (*my friends* – as if we *were* friends) could shift the balance of power between us.

The question of story – what something *is* and what it does, its genre – is critically important, but students don't always share this conviction. And yet their resistance has less to do with any credible objection than it does with a simple lack of familiarity. Students come to us amply prepared to talk about what a story is *saying*, but are less comfortable describing what it might be *doing* only because, or so they say, they haven't been asked it before. I had a hard time myself when I first started trying to frame the *idea* of story for precisely the same reason – it had not been framed for me before. And so, as a young person I'd set out to write, like most of us, well, *stories*, which seemed natural enough, and if my own trajectory was not without dead ends and diversions – some early years spent cobbling together a weird blend of what my dissertation adviser, Francois Camoin (1994), once called a 'horsily adolescent Jamesian' syntax with equal twists of American gothic and modernist/Western/feminist aesthetics, and then five more years wrestling minimalism – I'd read widely and had some sense of literature.

But student ideas of what stories are don't tend to come from literature, and although they have strong feelings about what they like, much of it is drawn from non-prose based media – movies and TV, even now, video games.

So questions lead to others: What is writing? What is language? What is genre?

And if we were to answer these questions, to define writing, language, genre, wouldn't we wonder what is a definition, anyway, but an impulse toward order, toward naming, toward categorization which we, being human, are dependent on to organize and even to know things?

In the interminable debate about whether creative writing can be taught, one recurring strand is that students learn writing by writing. But part of any education in creative writing needs also to extend beyond *doing* to seeing the practice itself – not just what we're making but what we are doing when we are making it and how it might move out, into, and through the world. And we begin with language as a critical analog of narrative, taking up, from Derrida, the long familiar (to us) idea that, 'From the moment that there is meaning there are nothing but signs. We think only in signs' (in Cohen & Shires, 1988: 19). If signs are capable of producing meaning not as some transparent representations of an external reality but only in relation to each other, the same can be said of stories, and successful creative writing teaching depends, as well and at least part of the time, on preparing students to become more active agents in this larger field of literary discourse. Until then, their stories will continue to refer not to other stories, but to their Aunt Clara's drinking problem and the latest sequel to the latest mega blockbuster thriller. Such stories are not really 'readable', in Roland Barthes' sense, but they're not really 'writeable' either. Neither belonging to nor working against any recognizable genres, they are what Derrida might call monstrosities. Or, as an ex-student recently wrote, 'They are like injured kittens I want to fill with milk'.

When I backed up years ago to the first question – what is a story? – I didn't really know I was talking about genre, and although I would go on for years adapting Gerald Graff's claim that to a large extent 'our ability to [write] well depends more than we think on our ability to *talk well* about what we [write]' (Graff, 1994: 40), when it came to genre, I found myself – and often still do – struggling and, more often than not, confusing students with such frustratingly ineloquent concepts as the story that is aware of the thing that it is even as it is the thing itself. It turns out I am not alone – genre is notoriously resistant to theory, and for this reason, contemporary genre theorists focus more on what genres *do* than what they *are*, their rhetorical affect, their function and modes of circulation. And these are critical issues for the creative writing classroom too. But we also know from Derrida's (1988b: 57) 'law' of genre that genre complicates itself by lodging 'within the heart of the law itself, a law of impurity or a principle of contamination'. Thus, whatever we *can* say of it, it will rapidly require us to say otherwise, for at least according to Derrida, while genre may generally be understood both as a set of conditions, prescriptions, prohibitions, limits and exclusions, as well as a practice used to legitimize and disseminate common knowledge or ways of knowing, it (genre) can be said to exist at least in part because it is transgressable. As in any discourse where 'a sign has the potential to *disrupt* as well as *facilitate* the passage of meaning because the relation of signifier to signified is unstable' (Cohen & Shires,

1988: 19), genre is both stable enough to hold together as its function and fluid enough to allow for its own transformation, existing not as a fixed and stable *idea* of such a category which we, being human, crave.

But when we say so to students, they say, 'You mean, like science fiction?'

Still, the idea of genre persists, powerful and vital to our pedagogical practice. And we know it exists – genre, or at least the idea of it – not so much because we can say here, this is what it is or even does, but because, as with all the elusive subjects, we find ourselves trying to define it, lured by its promise of organization and transmittable meaning, leery of its proclivity to limit and proscribe. This process, which may not exactly qualify as one of definition because it has no final outcome but constitutes instead a kind of intransitive inquiry, has value in and of itself, especially when we engage students collaboratively in it.

The first time I used the word *genre* after graduate school was at a 1993 CCCC's half-day creative writing pedagogy workshop. By then, I had been full-time teaching nearly seven years and yet, when the participants at one table started to chant, 'genre desire' I really had no idea what they could mean. But because I wanted to seem cool, I started chanting too, and the whole room was chanting. But what was desire for genre?

I knew, of course, what 'genre envy' was: an unpleasant jealousy I'd had for poetry ever since I first stepped in to the creative writing classroom and imagined verse to be somehow easier than stories – my own genre – to teach. Of course this was impossibly naïve – the desperate self-deception of a young teacher anxious to feel certain of at least *something,* for there is nothing easy in what any of us do. But poems were small and easily identifiable as self-aware artifacts, with clear forms and conventions – *rules* – rhyme schemes and scansions and line counts and breaks. With poems, it was easy for students to see that it mattered how the poem was made. Whereas stories, which were not small, had nothing clear about them at all – big and apparently shapeless things, it seemed to students, filled with nothing so much as intended meaning, especially with regard to real people, the very ones to whom the students seemed so haplessly to be related.

Either that, or the opposite – wild, and usually violent, fantasy narratives in which, as one student put it, they just wanted to 'blow stuff up'.

Stories, no less than poems or even words, mean 'only through convention and only as part of a communal system' (Cohen & Shires, 1988: 5), although students sometimes find this concept difficult to grasp. For them, stories seem completely natural, as if they are only about what they're about, pointing to a world outside the words of which they're made and replete with moral imperative and didactic meaning. But isn't this where we all begin when we first get the desire to write, and with a little hallelujah, find ourselves taken up with the idea that we have something to *say*?

Naturally, this is before we've learned famous quotations, like Robbe-Grillet's claim that 'real writers don't have anything to say, but only a way of saying it', or 'a poem should not mean/But be' in Archibald MacLeish's 'Ars Poetica' (1926), or before we've come across Richard Hugo's (1979) concepts of a writer's triggering subject (where the ideas come from) and his or her own idiosyncratic sense of language (where writing comes from), or Trinh Minh-Ha's (1989) critical distinction between writing 'about the self' and 'writing the self'. I want to say it took us years to take this in, to understand Francois Camoin's (1994: 5–6) exhortations not to think, or fully to appreciate his observation that 'the student who learns that he has no intentions worth talking about – that he has nothing to say when he sits down [to write] but only something to make – will make much better stories'.

But as I write this I'm taken back to the memory of writing my first story, lying prone on a brown ragged Santa Cruz couch and making sentences, one after the other, working them this way and that before I got the sound right and moved on. I knew something then that my own creative writing education would soon work out of me, and so my commitment to foregrounding the problem of making, not saying, and its immediate corollary – making what? – has always been highly personal to me. I came to my first writing program with a keen ear for sentences and an inarticulable interest in meta-consciousness and hybrid narration, but left two years later doggedly apprenticed to minimalism – a genre and aesthetic uniquely inimical to my sense of language and story – because I did not know to call it that. It would take years to find my way back to the storytelling strategies and long embedded sentences that better reflect my own sense of language and form. This first-hand experience with what happens not just to our writing but also to ourselves when we feel compelled to write the way we think we are supposed to write and are unable to write any other way, convinces me that students benefit when we help them develop those skills.

And so I begin not just with the idea of a story but with the idea of a story in relation to all other stories, a vast sea of stories to which students aim to add their own. I begin by introducing them to language itself, and how its arbitrary and conventional nature constructs meaning through relations of similarity, difference and placement. From here, it is an easy reach to see how stories construct meaning similarly and are 'readable' only by virtue of what they share in common with other like stories, as well as how they differ from unlike stories, and where they find themselves in which literary discourse or tradition. The same, of course, can be said of poems.

And while there are those who might still argue that this sounds a lot like theory and that theory is bad for writing because it interferes with what a worried student recently described as his 'writing mojo' – everything depends on how theory is presented in the classroom.

Before she died, Wendy Bishop took to calling theory 'thinking systematically' instead, and maybe that's good enough to finesse the paradox. But even the idea of systematic thinking can be fraught if students can't see the value of it – the *why*. Naturally, this *why* has multiple dimensions, but primary among them is student agency itself. It's been more than a quarter of a century now since my graduate seminar in feminist theory at the University of Utah where the professor, Karen Lawrence, once casually observed that 'a person never simply speaks but that there has to be context in which the person feels privileged to speak', and that lifted the veil – and transformed the world – for me.

Not that our business is world transformation, but why not? If we limit our objectives to the teaching of 'good writing', once somewhat vaguely defined as writing of 'publishable literary quality', we miss an important opportunity to raise larger questions about writing itself – what and how it is and what writing means and how it moves through the world. These larger questions are transferable, across disciplines and discourses, and for this reason alone they're important. But they also frame the context in which students may be encouraged to write not so much in imitation of the models we provide but in full conversation with them and other texts of their own choosing, self-aware and autonomous and sounding a bit more like themselves. Such a practice may be understood as a literary analog of the kind of autoethnographic writing taken up later in this essay, but for now it suggests how important it is that students be trained to think systematically about what they are doing when they're writing and the kinds of choices they are making, word by exact word, some evident, most not. The choices they can't see are the ones that conscript them; lifting the veil reverses that binary, a critical step in developing the 'poetics' that Rachel Blau DuPlessis (1990: 156) says 'gives us permission to continue'.

I didn't always think so, and in fact rejected outright Jonathan Culler's (1975: 134) claim that, 'If we do not want to stand gaping before the monumental inscriptions, the strange, the formal, the fictional must be naturalized, brought within our ken'. This was my first introduction to theory and, like so many others, I found it rough-going and disaffecting. And anyway, I *liked* to gape, I thought at the time, for wasn't gaping somehow part of the wonder – wasn't that *art*? And wasn't it *wonder* that took us up when we were young and whenever we lost ourselves in the pleasures of reading? Wasn't this what we were writing for?

Thus placing myself firmly with Susan Sontag (1966) against interpretation, it would be some time before I would learn to distinguish between that and description. For if interpretation treats writing as a kind of mirror image of Tvetzan Todorov's (1978) two activities of reading – 'projection' (which seeks to take the text back to an 'original' – the 'idea' or 'reality' behind it) and 'commentary' (which seeks to illuminate the 'interiority of the text') – description mirrors, instead, what he calls 'poetics'. Poetics does not assume an elsewhere and is not preoccupied with an interior, but instead links the text literature itself, its practicing being largely *descriptive* and looking to the general – to genre. 'Like other formalist schools . . .', Todorov writes, 'poetics seeks not to name the meaning of the text, but to describe its constitutive elements' (p. 236).

Culler locates this idea of the genre in the middle of a five-part taxonomy of convention and naturalization, beginning with the 'real' and ending with 'parody and irony' (p. 137). Describing genre as a 'conventional function of language, a particular relation to the world which serves as norm or expectation to guide the reader in his encounter with the text' (p. 137), Culler argues that this is the first level of naturalization that depends on a 'specifically literary intelligibility' (p. 137).

This idea of a literary intelligibility, once new to us, is almost always new – and potentially alienating – to students. But because in my own life, learning to see the shape and the context of a story not as natural but as a literary construct we only make to seem natural in our reading practice had been both difficult and vital to my survival as a writer, I would try from the beginning to engage students in such learning. But, again, the only words I had for describing 'genre' were 'the thing that (a story) is', and for parody and irony, the 'thing that's aware of the thing that it is'. If we need categories to organize and make sense of the *world*, we need genre to organize and make sense of *literature*. From the perspective of the creative writing classroom we can assume that students come to us intent on the former, and at least part of the time our job is to persuade them of the value of the latter. I didn't always think this either, as my early experiences in the creative writing classroom had led me to appreciate the wide range of reasons that bring students to writing.

'Students,' I wrote (though I can't remember where), 'just want to write, and we should let them'. Over time I've developed more of a both/and practice, where writing is encouraged as a positive value, but where we also work to locate it in relation to larger literary and historical trajectories. All the classes I teach, regardless of level or topic, share certain objectives in common. I want, first and foremost, for writing to function as a critical practice and primary experience ('intransitive act', from Barthes) in students' lives. I want to lay the groundwork for this practice to continue. I want students to recognize writing as a 'conversation' as texts engage other like texts that know themselves both through their similarities and through their differences, and so to be able to (or at least to move toward this) write texts that can teach the reader how to read them. I want them to begin to parse the ways these concerns are governed by a range of literary institutions that determine what writing can be and do and how it moves through the world. And then I want them to make their own decisions about the kind of writing they want to do and what they may want to do with it. And I want these decisions to be systematic and well informed.

Each of these objectives depends on some understanding of genre.

Poets understand this, the centrality of genre. Accustomed to thinking in forms, they recognize a sonnet as a sonnet; a villanelle as a villanelle; almost everyone knows what free verse is. These genres are at least partially fixed and, while certainly transgressable, nonetheless have features stable enough to be described with some certainty. But the novel, being, as Bakhtin (1988: 48) describes it, 'ever-developing', is different, its only stable feature that of mutability, a capacity to change that is, moreover, determined by its taking place in 'a zone of contact with the present in all its open endedness' (p. 46). In my mind, this links the novel – and fiction, in general – inextricably with Linda Nochlin's observation that, 'Nothing is more interesting, more poignant, and more difficult to seize than the intersection between self and history' (in Roth, 2000: 18). That intersection implicates another contact zone with important implications for the creative writing classroom as it works to reframe the lens students bring to writing and the process they go through as they attempt to claim it as their 'own'.

In an earlier essay, 'Re-envisioning the workshop: Hybrid classrooms, hybrid texts', in the collection *Does the Writing Workshop Still Work?* (Haake, 2010), I describe various attempts to work with hybrid narrative as a means of exploring the idea of contact zones – literary, social, cultural and historical – to render genre visible and so promote student agency. Although the essay describes a particular creative writing course on narrative hybridity, its procedures are widely applicable. In it, we draw on multiple strands of English studies – theory, literature, writing – to raise questions about a 'genre' – hybrid narrative – that resists the very idea of conventionality and defines itself, at least in part, by opposition to it. This potential is not limited to hybrid forms, and all the genres that define themselves by opposition or resistance – whether we imagine them as 'blurred' or 'multi-discursive', 'fused' or 'factional' – present exciting opportunities for the creative writing classroom.

Both the class and the collection's chapter rely heavily on Mary Louise Pratt's (1991: 34) essay, 'Arts of the contact zone', in which Pratt explores the idea of the contact zone as a 'social space' where people come together 'in contexts of highly asymmetrical relations of power, such as colonialism, slavery, or their aftermaths as they are lived out in many parts of the world today'. The idea of such a contact zone is notable not just because it echoes the two described above (Bakhtin and Nochlin), but also because it reflects the very nature of today's classrooms in which the social experience of multiple contact zones shares important parallels with the literary genres that might be forged in them.

Pratt spends some time discussing Guaman Poma de Ayala's letter to the King of Spain written in the aftermath of the fall of the Incan empire and extraordinary in many ways, not least because it had been composed by a person from a culture not thought to be literate and as an amalgam (hybrid) of Quechuan, a language not then believed to have had a written form, ungrammatical Spanish and line drawings. Titled *The First New Chronicle and Good Government,* this 1200-page document was lost for 350 years, surfacing in 1908 in the Danish Royal Archive but remaining largely 'unreadable' until the 1970s when Western scholars began to develop the multi-discursive literacy skills necessary for reading such a transcultural text.

This is what Pratt calls 'autoethnography', a genre that takes place in the margins where the so-called 'other' attempts to represent an experience of self that is at once authentic and autonomous *and* communicable. This genre is a complex rhetorical challenge that, just as Guaman Poma depended on an appropriated version of Spanish, depends on 'selective collaboration with and appropriation of idioms [and/or conventions] of the metropolis or the conqueror' (Pratt, 1991: 35) to merge with, infiltrate and intervene with the understandings the dominant group has constructed of this 'other'. Both as a genre and practice, autoethnography has important implications for our classrooms, where 'selective collaboration' can be used to mediate and frame the clash and struggle not just of students and the social groups they represent but also of the genres they produce.

Reading Pratt, it's impossible not to bring to mind yet another zone of contact described by Elaine Showalter (1981) in 'Feminist criticism in the wilderness', that attempts to represent the power relations between men and women, as shown in Figure A below.

No longer as monolithic as it once was, this paradigm, nonetheless, still resonates with students, in part because gender, and/or its complications, is an experience all of us share, and in part because it so vividly represents the idea of contact zones and their complex dynamics. First we note – and students are quick to point out – that the social space shared by dominant

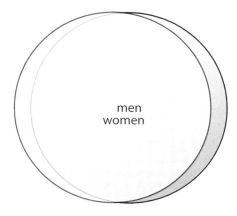

Figure A

and muted groups (in this case men and women) is much larger than the spaces they do not. In that shared space, women, as the muted group, may struggle even to know or recognize their own experience as they negotiate and adapt to the behaviors, ideologies, languages and discursive practices of men, as the dominant group. Self-narratives produced in that contact zone will always, for women, be at least double-voiced, if not circuitous, ambivalent, evasive – both themselves *and* something else, or neither/nor. But yet on either side of the contact zone, two spheres – small discrete crescents – remain that can be said to represent other spaces, neither shared nor contaminated by the infiltrations of the other. Showalter describes this space, again, for women, as a 'wild zone', a site of unfettered play exploration, and autonomous expression, what the French might call of *jouissance*, of pure invention – at least in part because it lies entirely outside the realm of men. And while men, too, may be said to have a separate sphere beyond the realm of women, Showalter views this space as the origin of myth, ideology and power, to which women may lack access but which they nonetheless know very well.

Leaving aside this problematic premise, Showalter's paradigm is helpful as a metaphor by which to frame the experience of 'self' and 'group' as both shared and discrete. As students so visualize themselves in relation to others, they begin to appreciate that their experience need not be fixed, and that it is precisely because gender has become so relatively easy to negotiate that it helps us acknowledge the function choice – men coveting 'freedom' can step inside the wild zone; women, 'power', can leave it. Gender also makes it relatively easy to see how such identity strategies and issues can apply to both writing and genre as well.

In the classroom, this discussion can be especially useful because it is both provocative and transparent. If students have a hard time seeing genre as a category, they have no trouble seeing themselves as gendered – female or male, gay or transgendered, or something more ambiguous, something between. And however they identify who they see themselves to be, their status as a speaking subject clearly marks what can be spoken and by them. Gender thus serves as a useful metaphor for genre, both of which are linked also in their origin and share the Latin root *genus* for 'kind', 'type' or 'sort'.

Another useful parallel to both teaching and writing can be found in Roland Barthes' (1977) distinction between 'readable' and 'writeable' texts – the one we can read because it's been written, and the other we long to write (but can't read) because it doesn't yet exist. The concrete nature of the Venn diagram clearly demonstrates what happens when the speaking subject is fixed entirely within a sector that does not overlap with any other. If writing from the 'wild zone', for example, can be said to be 'writeable', it's easy to see it, also, as incomprehensible precisely because it is detached from the very relations to other texts by which reading itself takes place. Whether by refusal or inability to conform to familiar genre conventions, its modes of circulation will be limited. I don't mean to imply the relation between gender and genre is anything other than metaphorical and some-times situational, but both are useful tools in the classroom. If genre seems mysterious and invisible to students, gender is something they can't miss.

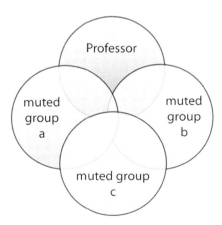

Figure B

But of course, according to Pratt, today's classrooms look more like this:

Pratt's analysis has arresting similarities with and critical differences from Showalter's. The 'muted' groups above can represent various categories of 'otherness' – race or class, or sexual orientation, or even age or ability, religious or national affiliation, even – in a place like Los Angeles – geography or immigration status. Most of these will be emerging from more violent historical trajectories and more contested cultural and individual experiences than those represented by gender difference, but the essential binary – power and its lack – persists.

Potentially in conflict with each other, at least double-voiced inside academe, students negotiate complicated classroom spaces on a daily basis. These 'contact zones' are multiple, alienating and charged, and for this reason Pratt advocates the use of what she calls 'safe houses', a kind of space beyond the contact zone where students who share similar backgrounds can come together without fear of conflict or censure. Roughly analogous to Showalter's Wild Zone, these safe houses are 'social and intellectual spaces where groups can constitute themselves as horizontal, homogeneous, sovereign communities with high degrees of trust, shared understandings, temporary protection from legacies of oppression' (Pratt, 1991: 40). Unlike the Wild Zone, however, these may not be spaces of exuberant expression (though perhaps, in time, they could be) but more of 'healing and mutual recognition . . . In which to construct shared understandings, knowledges, claims on the world that they can then bring into the contact zone' (Pratt, 1991: 40). Whether we think of them as 'wild' or 'safe', it is in these spaces that the organizing principles of autoethnographic writing – a genre with important implications for creative writing and clear affiliations with other transformative genres – can take root and flourish.

The complex and highly selective rhetorical strategies of the *New Chronicle* have twinned formal properties born of necessity and invention, two critical components of the writer's toolbox. And they merit special attention because this space beyond the contact zone is not merely a space of autonomous expression, but also a space of student agency in which novice writers may aspire to writing that matters both to them, by reflecting self and culture, and to us, by proceeding from a practice that is innately literary. Whether this writing is 'autoethnographic' in material, form or practice, at its best it can be said to share important filiations with what Gilles Deleuze, Félix Guattari and Robert Brinkley (1983: 16) describe in 'What is a minor literature?' not as the 'literature of a minor language but [as] the literature a minority that makes its way into a major language'. Minor literatures, too, grow out of contact zones and share as common traits, in addition to their political and collective natures, deterritorialized languages that proceed in opposition to dominant ones and a coming into knowing themselves only as 'stranger[s] *in* [the other] language' (Deleuze *et al.*, 1983: 26). How many people today, Deleuze *et al.* ask, live in a language that is not their own? For them, hating the literature of masters, the work of the minor writer is to 'push [the master language] to the point where no culture or myth can compensate for deterritorialization – absolute deterritorialization even if it is slow, viscous, coagulated. Slowly, progressively carry the tongue away into the desert. Use syntax to cry out; give syntax to the outcry. [For] only the minor is great and revolutionary.' (p. 26). And it's worth pointing out that such a minor literature can take place only in a contact zone, and that it therefore shares, at least in its material and practice, crucial similarities with autoethnographic writing, which, as a genre, can be understood as inherently hybrid, libratory and *minor*.

Here, again, the Venn diagram enables students to visualize their experience of writing as a stratagem of collaboration and resistance. By imagining themselves as speaking subjects with the ability to move in and out of spaces where languages, modes of knowing, forms of expression – of *genre* – are familiar and not, they can be motivated to develop sophisticated rhetorical and creative strategies precisely because of what's at stake – not what they think they're supposed to write about, but what they really want to; not how they think they're supposed to sound, but how they really do. When they get to talk systematically about their ambivalence and process, they take a first important step toward developing a poetics that gives them 'permission' to 'write what they know' (which turns out not to be such bad advice after all). Together, these two activities enable us to ask of this genre, in particular, and by extension, any genre: do we know it as description (what it 'looks' like and 'does', its 'constitutive elements'); a methodology ('selective collaboration and appropriation', furtive forays); a location (where it comes from – muted group, wild zone or safe house); or a motivation (to write the self, to subvert dominant modes of knowing and aesthetics)?

By the end of the nineties, my feminist theory and literature-based creative writing course would have run its course, but its various successes would lead me to experiment with other topics-based courses, first on the graduate level and subsequently on the undergraduate level as a permanent addition to our curriculum. To date, these are the courses I have taught under this rubric: (1) genres that problematize the distinction between what we believe to be true and what we're convinced we make up, (2) new wave fabulism, (3) contemporary international literatures, (4) hybrid narrative, and (5) interstitial fiction.

All these courses were, by definition, hybrid classes. They were hybrid not just because they brought together multiple discursive practices and modes of inquiry, but also because they were offered for credit in both our literature and creative writing options and so brought together students from diverse backgrounds. I picked the courses, or they picked me, in part because they interested me, but also because, although I wrote in the genres I taught, I had yet to 'think systematically' (theorize) about them. My own lack of conventional 'knowledge', coupled with my strong and personal investment in the subjects, shifted the balance of power in the classroom in interesting ways and provided an authentic model of motivated inquiry. This produced a strange result: the students engaged, wrote better – they even talked better. The language we used in class began to circulate among other writing students. You could hear them in the hall, talking 'faction', talking 'multi-discursivity', talking 'hybridity'.

One reported that the breakthrough work he did in the class was like 'stepping off a cliff'. Another confided that students were so over-stimulated by class discussions they'd have to go out and drink beer just to keep on talking. Nobody, of course, knew what, exactly, they were talking about, but they kept on talking, trying to figure things out, and perpetually ended up, as in the feminist classes that preceded theirs, concluding that whatever it was they were trying to describe, the best that they could do was: well, it's not really this, and not that either, not even yet – which turns out, after all, to be a surprisingly powerful logic. For if in each of these classes the most pressing student need has been for certainty, the most generative affects have always been produced by the inability to achieve it. Students want to know what to think, which often means they want us to tell them. What's the difference, they ask, between a 'hybrid' genre and a 'blurred' one or an 'experimental' one? Why won't I tell them? they complain.

'Let's get this straight', I found myself pronouncing in one exasperated term-end moment, 'a hybrid text is one that brings together writing from multiple discourses in order to tell or contain a narrative that otherwise cannot hold together', which at least sounded tenable to me. Students wrote it down, asked me to repeat. One bitterly complained that things would have been a lot easier (better?) if I would have said so at the start.

At the time I imagined that I had said as much all along, but that students simply had not been able to take it in until then; now, I'm not so sure. As with genre itself, I didn't have a clear definition of 'hybrid' narrative any more than I would later of the interstitial, and certainly not one that doesn't collapse in the very next breath. But the questions, vexed and contentious and highly contestable, are exciting.

I like to imagine the days when we saw writing as somehow 'natural' are in the past, but the attitude persists in creative writing's continued rejection of theory in the US, its ongoing commitment to publication as the highest measure of success, its deeply held conviction in the privilege of literary activity over other forms of writing. My own work in this field has tried to advance a both/and logic that seeks to develop – and teach – a broader range of frameworks and meta-consciousnesses with which to know writing not just as writing, but also as a product of its cultural and historical moment, its nationness, and its affiliation with its precursors, its genres. The work of the Interstitial Arts Organization, a multi-disciplinary project that promotes work in a variety of media and forms that resists easy classification, can help further this polysemic practice.

In my own life, this begins – or did, when I was a graduate student – with Virginia Woolf's (1989) *A Room of One's Own* and the intoxicating premise of a 'female sentence'. Like hybrid narrative or the interstitial later, the idea of such a genre – if indeed a sentence can be said to be a genre – was one to which I'd respond with an almost visceral recognition, and yet as right as it seemed on an intuitive level, I found myself hard-pressed to describe it, this 'female sentence'. Any attempts to do so clearly also applied to a range of male writers, never mind that the women writers in whose work I felt its presence most compelling – Woolf herself, for example (long, lovely, lyrical), as well as Jane Bowles (clipped, double-edged, acidly ironic) – wrote nothing at all like each other. Slowly, I began to understand the female sentence not as a stable form or set of features but as a stance or origin where, as with Pierre Menard, difference lay in the identity of its author – her motivation, her method, her location. However radically a male/(dominant) writer may break from convention, he starts, at least at one point, from the center. By contrast, the female/(muted) writer begins in the margins and, never (yet) at home with her patriarchal precursors, may write in ways that break with convention not because she rejects it but because she does not own it and cannot employ it.

Or so it seemed to me then. Attracted initially to feminist theory because it helped illuminate what *I* knew of difference, the real paradigm of interest has always been power. As I've tried to suggest above, the idea of the contact zone can be used to explore this paradigm and its vexed dynamics and is pedagogically powerful not just in its capacity to create classroom spaces where all students feel privileged to speak, but also in the way it can help us see and understand genre. The two are not unrelated. And yet, even if we define such difference as multiple and fluid, we're still working with binary assumptions. A both/and formulation depends on the original either/or, but maybe a neither/nor doesn't.

The idea of interstitial art is similarly powerful not because it takes place in or constitutes just such a contact zone but because it moves beyond it, or slyly aside. An interstice is a space between – not a shared space but a no-space, a space defined by none of its surrounding categories, but yet informed by them all. From what we know of difference, we can imagine it as a continuum, a line between two essentialist points – men/women, teacher/student, literary fiction/genre fiction – at the center of which lies another point, the point of binary opposition, where each category becomes what it is by becoming 'not' the other. Imagine, instead, that point as a gap – an opening out, an interstice; imagine the space that it opens out not as a continuum but as a plane, and a bit like the Derridean (1988a: 109) center – that very thing that is both itself and not ('the center is not the center') because it can be said to organize the structure while somehow lying outside the structure, and infinitely rich because of what is missing from it. And 'as always', Derrida (1988a: 109) reminds us, such 'coherence in contradiction expresses the force of a desire'. Taking genre as its origin, interstitial art expresses the force of that same desire as it emerges in a *separate* site, made contradictorily coherent by virtue of its dependence on and resistance to genre as proscription, and sharing, in this way, strategic affiliations with autoethnography as practice.

Heinz Insu Fenkle's (2007) introduction to *Interfictions*, an anthology of interstitial writing, is an important contribution to the developing poetics of the interstitial. Just as the contact zone can illuminate both the experience of students and the writing they produce there, Fenkle turns to Homi Bhabba's work on culture to reveal both important parallels and certain distinctions between it and the interstitial.

'It is in the interstices', Fenkle cites Bhabba, ' – the overlap and displacement of domains of difference that the intersubjective and collective experiences of *nationness*, community interest, or cultural value are negotiated', noting that much of what Bhabba observes about culture is 'just as applicable to the world of literature' (in Fenkle, 2007: iii). For if we substitute the word 'genre' for 'nation', Bhabba suggests, and 'cultural value' for 'community interest', we can begin to see more clearly the kinds of valuations we make between, say, such categories as literary fiction and fantasy. But while Bhabba constructs the interstice as liminal – a kind of threshold – Fenkle argues that the interstitial artist instead claims the space-between as a generative space of its own that is 'not transitory' and 'does not require reintegration', but is instead 'willfully transgressive' and 'noncategorical'. We don't enter the interstitial to get someplace else but rather to linger, and while we retain there a 'consciousness of the boundaries (we have) crossed or disengaged with' (p. iv), we view them not as limits but as, maybe, portals.

Cesar Aira's (2009) *Ghosts*, a strangely haunting small novel about a large Chilean family living in a half-constructed high-rise luxury Buenos Aires apartment – a building without skin also occupied by a host of genial, floury ghosts, all male and naked and with remarkable members – brilliantly exemplifies the power of the interstitial. The novel takes place on the eve of the New Year, coalescing around the celebration of the large family clan that lives in the unfinished building performing the function of caretakers. Throughout the long day and elaborate meal preparations, Patri, the novel's young adolescent protagonist who alone can see the ghosts, has multiple encounters with them as they follow and tease and gently amuse her with their light and ebullient play, until finally they invite her to their New Year's celebration. The novel takes place in multiple interstices – a vertical world between earth and sky, inside and outside, childhood and adulthood, male and female, family and social world, Chilean and Argentine culture, wealth and poverty, past and future, life and death – and interrupts itself dead center with a long disquisition on cultural anthropology and architectural theory creating yet another interstitial space of genre. And when, in the end, Patri accepts the ghost's invitation and steps off the top of the building (between sky and earth, life and death) just at the stroke of midnight (between the two years) students want to naturalize the ending as Patri's death.

But the novel ends, instead, not in the liminal space of a threshold, but in the interstitial space of something altogether else, like this:

> As she fell, Patri's thick glasses came off and went on falling, separately, beside her. A ghost, appearing suddenly from somewhere, caught them safely before they hit the ground, and rose, as if lifted by a gentle spring to the edge of the terrace, where he came to rest, in front of the family, who were stunned by the tragedy. He held the glasses out to Raul Vinas, who reached out and took them. Man and ghost stared at each other. (pp. 138–139)

Fenkle notes two other crucial features of the interstitial: the first is that it is what he calls 'bi-locational'. Mildly ironic in its innate self-awareness, the interstitial text strives to exist simultaneously in a space that is both a no-space (neither contact zone nor wild zone/safe house) *and* two spaces at once, telling a good story even as it acknowledges itself as an artificial construction of language – or what I once rather haplessly tried to describe as the text that 'is aware of the thing that it is even as it is the thing itself', and later as a 'text of seduction'. Such texts can be said to be radical in their capacity to alter the reader's experience of reading by luring her into the story without letting her forget that's precisely what it is, thus rendering its artifice visible even while retaining, on another level, all the pleasures of narrative illusion. And this introduces a political dimension to interstitial art, which can be distinguished from the pseudo-radical nature of, say 'experimental' texts that depend instead on readers already familiar with their intents and strategies. In its capacity to reconcile the contradiction between post-modern irony and plain old-fashioned storytelling, the interstitial, by contrast, is not confrontational but inviting, open to the widest range of readers, from novice to the most highly trained, even as it teaches its reader how to read it. In this way, its disruption of genre may work to transform not just the experience of reading, but also the reader and her reading practice.

Secondly, the interstitial is inherently self-negating: once it becomes reproducible and recognizable, it is no longer interstitial.

These features and their motivations and methodologies give rise to some important observations:

(1) Because the interstitial can be understood at least in part by its resistance to convention, it helps frame guiding questions about poetics.

In practice, this means that I require term-end 'creative/critical (hybrid) literacy autoethnographies/poetics/manifestoes' in which students must explicitly reflect on their own writing – and not just its formal conventions, but also its motivations, aspirations and filiations. Not surprisingly, students often find this assignment challenging as they struggle to identify, much less articulate, a generalized sense of their work as it might be identified by its constitutive elements, and its relation to other like texts and writing in general. The form, too, is challenging, since they must define it themselves and speak in it from multiple subject positions. And of course, students are accustomed to seeing reading and writing as natural and, therefore, invisible, but in the interstitial works we read, what their ears pick up first is what they don't hear – what really isn't there, the absence that defines the presence they've spent their lives steeped in and thus unable to see. In its capacity to move us into the gap and a little aside from yet another zone – our 'comfort' zone – the interstitial renders visible previously invisible constitutive elements and helps us name them and so begin to frame poetics. Importantly, this also helps us frame new questions – about what genres do, yes, but also where they come from. Because, of course, that does matter – it matters a lot – for whether the writing originates in a contact zone or safe house, a margin, a wild zone, a center, or interstice will determine not just its methods of composition – mimicry, contest, negotiation, collaboration, resistance – but also its medium – master discourse, deterritorialized language, or some other order of sentence altogether. What is this work *doing* by whom, and *why*? As we learn to ask 'why', we learn also to ask: why this, why now, why us?

And this – all this – is genre desire.

(2) Because the interstitial can be understood at least in part as both location (where it comes from) and motivation (what it aspires to do), it helps frame guiding questions about student agency.

Again we return to both the similarities and differences between contact zones and interstices, and in the clear and steady light of the one in the other, students may begin to see self, group, world and art as fully interconnected. Whether we call the writing that comes out of this interconnectedness autoethnographic, hybrid, or interstitial, naming it at all gives students permission to claim their own material both as subject and genre.

But as I've discussed above, this activity is not uncontested and students need their safe houses, which can be transformed to wild zones in the conditions that allow it. So let's re-imagine our Venn diagram as somehow three-dimensional, bending at its edges back in on itself so that the slender half-moons that represent difference are drawn, like magnets, toward each other, never touching but yet coming close, demarcating an open space – an interstice – between them?

Or Patri, in her long, suspended descent from the top of her skinless luxury building . . .

What might the writing that grows out of such a space look like?

(3) Because the interstitial enables just such speculation, it helps frame guiding questions about writing itself.

It's beyond the scope of this essay to examine the relation between writing and the Lacanian 'suture', but it is surely worth noting that this suture is also interstitial, marking as it does, the space between the imaginary and the symbolic. And for that matter Foucault's (1972) 'slender gap' of discourse is also interstitial. For wouldn't we all, as he has written, have 'preferred to be enveloped in words, borne way beyond all possible beginnings . . . a nameless voice, long preceding (us), leaving (us) merely to enmesh (ourselves) in it, taking up its cadence, and to lodge (ourselves), when no one was looking, in its interstices as if it had paused an instant, in suspense, to beckon (us)?' (p. 215).

The idea of the interstitial provides a concrete metaphor for the space that is neither signified nor signifier and not even both – the sign itself – but the space between. I always think of Italo Calvino's (1987) idea of 'combinatorial play', where the writer tosses words together until they make a spark that takes the writer down to the place where writing takes place. I do think of this as somehow happening in the suture – not being or meaning, but the space between. And it's here that we can come to know, but only when we're in it, what Barthes means when he calls writing 'intransitive'.

The paradox of writing, of course, is that it's also only here that it can exist as a primary experience, not dependent on derivative effects, where, even as we let go of the thinking of meaning, meaning truly takes place.

(4) And there is also this: because the interstitial is self-negating, it helps frame guiding questions about sustainable writing practices.

When writing is new, when it knows itself as a field of play and invention, it is ever exciting and we are happy to endure all its difficulties and frustrations for the pure pleasure of working them out. But of course this can't last because it *is* liminal – a threshold – and the instant we cross over from invention to convention – neither one of which can exist without the other – the instant we *know* what we're doing, writing is reduced to a kind of repetition and we begin to lose interest.

A long time ago when I was a child, people seemed to think it mattered if you got the facts straight, though in my family this was challenging for me. Don't stare, they used to say, your nose is growing. Thus chastened by this early strict construction of the 'truth' and convinced it was an either/or proposition, I spent years trying to keep my life, which I knew to be 'true', separate from my fiction, which I clearly 'made up'. And I suspect this would have proved the end of writing for me were it not for one long night of work that included a midnight intruder, a looming noon deadline, and my fervent magic thinking that if I did not stay awake (and writing) until dawn, something truly bad would happen.

I'd been stuck on that story for weeks, knowing too much about it – not just what was going to happen but also how. Terminally bored with what I already knew how to do, I didn't yet know how to do what came next, and so I found myself on the verge of giving up and going off to chef school, which might in fact have happened if I'd had that other glass of wine and gone to bed, as I most desperately wanted to, just before my intruder showed up and as I was writing the words, 'It doesn't matter who he is. He's here, he could be dangerous'. Still, it would take the next six hours (for a total of eighteen straight hours of writing – and you know, when you've been writing long enough at a single stretch, intent starts to break down as, really, you'll try almost anything), a pack of Mexican cigarettes, and the safety of dawn for me to finally notice a small scrap of autobiographical text on the corner of my desk, not anything meant for fiction (because it really happened), just something I had written in an introspective moment, unrelated to the story I was writing except it was 'I' who was writing the story and 'I' who had lived the moment I'd commemorated on the scrap. And so inspired to solve two problems at once – finishing the story (at last) and getting some sleep (at last), I stuck that fragment in my text and went to bed.

In the years between then and now, slowly I'd begin to understand – and find a form for what had happened in my writing throughout that long night of combinatorial play in which I worked my way into a kind of interstice where I could break off my allegiance to what I already knew how to do and, like Patri, what I did not. It's a small thing to know that this space depends at least some of the time on a kind of slippage between convention and invention, as fluid and as porous as a sentence or a lie. But it's a large thing to know that, in its absence, writing ends.

If at least one objective of a successful creative writing pedagogy is that writing should continue as a lifelong practice for our students, we need to begin by framing the structures in which they can discover for themselves how this might happen. Years ago, I accompanied my son's second grade class on a field trip to an artist's studio where the artist observed that 'art happens in the mistakes you make when you are doing what you don't know how to do'. Students, of course, crave certainty (and good grades) and so they resist this most essential principle of writing. But as they learn to appreciate the self-negating aspect of interstitial art, they can see clearly how it is that as soon as you arrive it is time to move on.

I want to end with the story of a bridge.
And not just any bridge either, but Redding's Sundial Bridge, my hometown's latest claim to fame and an unlikely work of world class architecture that spans the deep, broad, powerful Sacramento River above which I grew up some several miles below Shasta Dam (my hometown's first claim to fame) and the subject of my interstitial 'novel', *That Water, Those Rocks*. In no stretch of my imagination, when I was growing up, could my hometown

ever seem a probable place for a work of world-class architecture, for although I loved its river, nothing else was beautiful about it. Over the years, the strip of seedy motels that had once serviced its sad tourist industry and the remaining mill or two would be replaced by lowbrow chain motels along the freeway and a noxious sprawl of homogenized big box stores and a 25% poverty rate; my sons would come to call it 'skinhead heaven'.

The people in my hometown, where I no longer live but where my parents do, fought about the bridge for years. You wouldn't think a thing like that could stir up so much trouble, but even in my own family, we were split. My father, who used to take us to see dams being built, would now take us, when we visited, to the site from which we could view the bridge in construction. My sister, an environmental activist, sided with my mother: the bridge was a total waste and totally out of place – what was wrong with a simple concrete span? My father and I, though, would stand transfixed – gaping before the monumental inscription – as this exotic structure took shape. But I wanted to tell the story of this bridge not because I fell in love with it from the first instant that my father took me down to watch it being built the same way he once took me to see dams when I was still a little girl in a prior century, but because of what happened to the *river* in this process.

Years before, when I was that little girl in a prior century, people in my hometown could access the river I also loved only from the city park. Now, the extensive trail system of which the Sundial Bridge is a culminating part, has opened out a landscape I'd hardly have imagined as a girl and, like a work of interstitial art, completely transformed our experience of it. It brings us to the river, yes, and makes it visible, but it is also never not teeming with a strangely hybrid mix of people – locals and tourists alike – all enjoying a participatory sense of community, nature and art, which is just what I imagine a work of world class architecture should do.

I once heard a poet at AWP promote the idea of 'negative space', readings in which students present work with no expectation of commentary or response – a kind of safe house reading into silence. Though I can't remember who the poet was, such readings have proved hugely liberating in my own classes.

Maybe the Sundial Bridge is powerful because it creates a kind of negative space where we can finally see the river, and through it, the Bridge, and on it, each other, and, taken all together at once, art. Or maybe it is powerful because it brings together elements that would not normally be found together – big art in a small town, affluent (even foreign!) tourists with local skinheads and unemployed loggers.

Either way – or both – it's kind of interstitial.

Also, there is this: just the other day I received the following email from a student, Matthew Waldeck:

> I like making unauthorized collaborations. Mostly I do this with stories I've received in workshops, as is the case here, but it is not my only method. In workshop, the bad stories do not distress me, the good stories do not distress me, but the mediocre stories do distress me. They are like injured kittens that I want to fill with milk. I feel guilty saying so, but I believe I can secretly heal them . . . and so I revise these stories myself. Perhaps this is unethical; I've made sense of it enough to serve me. In my defense, I do always at least double the length of the story, so that it is not a total lie when my name is on it . . .

And then he attached a story so charged with play and invention *and* evident affection for its origin that it seemed to me to be, well, also interstitial.

I hadn't yet thought of it quite that way – of the interstitial as an antidote for the mediocre, a rescue for injured kittens.

It's the narrator's mother in Dubravka Ugresic's *The Museum of Unconditional Surrender* (see epigraph at the start of the chapter) who gives up her struggle with genre, unable to organize family photographs; her daughter, the narrator, threads and weaves. Carrying in it its own contamination, genre is marked by and marks the binary opposition between 'inside' and 'outside'. But these other activities – surrender, resistance, blurring, braiding or simply feeding with milk – proceed from the in-between where while we can never really know what's coming next, the one thing we can know for certain is that it's going to keep on coming.

References

Aira, C. (2009) *Ghosts* (Trans. C. Andrews). New York: New Directions.

Bakhtin, M.M. (1988) Epic and novel. In M.J. Hoffman and P. Murphy (eds) *Essentials of the Theory of Fiction* (pp. 48–69). Durham: Duke UP.

Barthes, R. (1977) The death of the author. In R. Barthes (1977) *Image Music Text* (Trans. S. Heath) (pp. 142–148). New York: Hill & Wang.

Calvino, I. (1987) *The Uses of Literature*. New York: Mariner Books.

Camoin, F. (1994) The workshop and its discontents. In W. Bishop and H. Ostrom (eds) *Colors of a Different Horse:Rethinking Creative Writing Theory and* Pedagogy (pp. 3–7). Urbana, IL: National Council of Teachers of English.

Cohen, S. and Shires, L. (1988) *Telling Stories: A Theoretical Analysis of Narrative Fiction*. New York: Routledge.

Culler, J. (1975) *Structuralist Poetics: Structuralism, Linguistics, and the Study of Literature*. Ithaca, NY: Cornell UP.

Deleuze, G., Guattari, F. and Brinkley, R. (1983) What is a minor literature? *Mississippi Review* 11 (3) Essays Literary Criticism (Winter/Spring), 13–33. Available at: http://www.jstor.org/stable/20133921.

Derrida, J. (1988a) Structure, sign and play in the discourse of the human sciences. In D. Lodge (ed.) *Modern Criticism and Theory: A Reader* (pp. 107–123). New York: Longman.

Derrida, J.R. (1988b) The law of genre. *Critical Inquiry,* On Narrative, 7.1 (Autumn 1980): 55–58.

DuPlessis, R.B. (1990) *The Pink Guitar: Writing as Feminist Practice*. New York: Routledge.

Fenkle, H.I. (2007) *Interfictions: An Anthology of Interstitial Writing*. Boston, MA: The Interstitial Arts Foundation.

Foucault, M. (1972) The discourse on language. In R. Swyer (trans.) *The Archaeology of Knowledge & The Discourse on Language* (pp. 215–237). New York: Pantheon Books.

Graff, G. (1994) Disliking books at an early age. In D.H. Richter *Falling into Theory: Conflicting Views on Reading and Literature*. Boston: Bedford/St. Martin's.

Haake, K. (2010) Re-envisioning the workshop: Hybrid classrooms, hybrid texts. In D. Donnelly (ed.) *Does the Writing Workshop Still Work?* (pp. 182–193). Bristol: Multilingual Matters.

Hugo, R. (1979) *The Triggering Town*. New York: Norton.

Minh-Ha, T. (1989) *Woman, Native, Other: Writing, Postcoloniality, and Feminism*. Bloomington: Indiana UP.

Pratt, M.L. (1991) Arts of the contact zone. In D. Bartholomae and A. Petrosky *Ways of Reading* (5th edn) (Trans. R. Howard). Available at: http://www.nwe.ufl.edu/~stripp/2504/pratt.html.

Roth, M. (2000) Of self and history: Exchanges with Linda Nochlin. *Art Journal* 59 (3) (Autumn), 18–33.

Showalter, E. (1981) Feminist criticism in the wilderness. *Critical Inquiry* 8.2 (Winter), 179–205.

Sontag, S. (1966) Against interpretation. Available at: http://www.colbacon.com/writing/sontagagainstinterpreation.html.

Todorov, T. (1978) *The Poetics of Prose*. Ithaca: Cornell, UP.

Ugresic, D. (2002) *The Museum of Unconditional Surrender* (Trans. C. Hawkesworth). New York: New Directions.

Woolf, V. (1989) *A Room of One's Own*. New York: Mariner Books.

6 Creative Writing Research

Graeme Harper

Both creative writing as research and creative writing research are taking place more than ever, most often in and around our universities and colleges. Creative writing draws on many areas of knowledge and understanding, yet it is distinctive not only in how it uses these areas, incorporating them into creative writers' actions, and into the artefacts that emerge because of these actions, but also in how it negotiates between our personal and public human worlds. While some knowledge about creative writing has been exchanged, a focus on creative writerly action and creative writerly understanding has not yet occurred to the point where the growing community of creative writing researchers is globally connected and developments are occurring in good knowledge of what has come before, and what might come in the future. How creative writers proceed with research has not yet been as widely explored as could, and should, be the case. We need to undertake this work now, and urgently.

Questioning and Defining Research

Inquiry, investigation, closely studying or examining: these are all forms of questioning. Definitions of research begin at us questioning, and proceed by assuming we will question, and potentially challenge established knowledge, or that we will create knowledge anew. There are connections between these two modes, of course, and even research that could be said to have created something new begins with the challenge that something is not known that could or, indeed, *should* be known.

From inquiry, from investigation, and from the close studying or examining of something, our research proceeds and it is seen to be successful if it considers and confirms or challenges what is already known or, noting the proviso above, if it creates knowledge that did not previously exist. How then can the undertaking of creative writing not be a form of research; after all, doesn't it always involve inquiry, an investigation of some kind, an examination of something?

Well, yes, but it is *not* a form of research if it simply repeats or recalls what is already known and makes no inroads into investigating its validity or if it fails to develop any new knowledge. It has to do one or the other of these things to be considered research. In a public sense at least, creative writing can sometimes do neither of these things.

Relatively recently in the UK a distinction was drawn, in many Higher Education institutions, between research and scholarship. Research was, indeed, defined much as it has been defined here. Scholarship, alternatively, was frequently defined as maintenance of knowledge rather than a challenge, extension or further development of knowledge. Here, for example, from Scotland's University of Strathclyde:

> Scholarship is activity that updates or maintains the knowledge of an individual; or adds to their skills and experience. The knowledge base already exists elsewhere. Scholarship is therefore different from Research. (University of Strathclyde, n.d.: 1)

This kind of guidance to UK faculty and staff emerged from manuals entitled the 'Transparent Approach to Costing Teaching' or TRAC manuals, issued by the Joint Costing and Pricing Steering Group (JCPSG), 'a representative group, bringing together members from universities and colleges, from the funding bodies for UK higher education and from Universities UK, Standing Conference of Principals, Universities Scotland and Higher Education Wales' and initiating a project 'to develop effective costing and pricing approaches for Higher Education Institutions, and to encourage their implementation and use across the HE sector' (JCPSG, n.d.: 1). That JCPSG project concluded in 2005.

How much influence such costing related analysis had, or has, on broader thoughts about what is and what isn't research in the UK is obviously open to debate. That debate is outside the scope of this chapter. Furthermore, others around the world use the words 'research' and 'scholarship' in different ways and the kind of contrast suggested in the UK's TRAC manuals does not map directly onto all the ways in which these words, and concepts, are currently being used elsewhere. However, what is important about the definitions suggested by TRAC, and implemented in the name of costing and pricing research, is that they provide a starting point for thinking about what research might be, and they thus provide a way of thinking about how creative writing, and investigations of creative writing, can be defined as research, and in what senses.

Creative Writing *as* Research

Creative writing incorporates both creative practice and critical understanding. I am using the term 'creative writing' here to refer to the actions that constitute creative writing, not to the material artefacts that emerge from the human activity of creative writing. Those artefacts take many forms, including final works, drafts, auxiliary or complementary works, notes, diary entries, doodles and a great deal more. They are a significant part of the landscape of, and around, creative writing. But creative writing is first, and foremost, human action.

Using that distinction between research and scholarship, with research as an investigation and/or challenge to established knowledge or a development of new knowledge and scholarship as a maintenance of what is already known, it is hard to imagine that any creative writing could be defined as scholarship. Even if the structure or form of a piece of creative writing defined the human actions of creating it, the subject matter, the themes, the subject or subjects would surely make it new. The creative writer would acquire new knowledge, even if new knowledge was not acquired by the reader or audience from works that emerged from the creative writing. A creative writer would have to seek to *both* use *no* new mode of presentation and explore *no* new theme or subject to produce something that could not be defined as research. That scenario is unlikely.

The more complex, and more significant problem, lies in how this research is located within our human world. In other words, if a creative writer had nothing new to offer an audience on a subject or theme, on a situation, a description, a story, a viewpoint, and presented this 'not new' material in a similarly not new form, could this still be research if the creative writer themselves investigated something they did not know, questioned something they did know, or produced knowledge that was entirely new to them?

In answering this question we are faced with the difference between public and private knowledge, and with how individualized the popular human practice of creative writing might be. We can return to that interesting expression in the University of Strathclyde's TRAC documentation in which scholarship is said to be different to research in that, with scholarship, 'the knowledge base already exists elsewhere'. Given its often highly individual nature, and given the relative lack of current public research on creative writing, how much of the knowledge does *not* exist elsewhere? That is to say, most of this knowledge base exists in varying degrees and in an infinite variety of ways and forms and by varying means in *each* individual creative writer. For every one of us, therefore, a good portion of the knowledge base always 'exists elsewhere'.

Sometimes, such as in the case of a creative writer teaching or taking a creative writing class, this individualized knowledge is shared with others. However, as can also be seen in the teaching and learning of other creative arts, the high degree of individuality involved in these human actions means that exchanged knowledge is frequently reduced to aspects of artistic form, function, appearance, dissemination/communication strategies, textual, cultural, economic or social context. The fuller extent of a writer's individualized knowledge is never exchanged.

This ensues because even when comments are made on such things as emotions, feelings, intentions, behaviours, reasons, physiological and psychological responses – all of which influence much that occurs in creative writing, and indeed much of the artefactual evidence and completed work that emerges from the activities of creative writers – even when these things are referenced, this kind of exchange is not undertaken in an analytical way. Almost always it is offered anecdotally.

Of course, let's not avoid the fact that much of this knowledge might not be easily accessible by the techniques, types and disciplines of analysis we have easily available to us at the moment. It might not be reachable, not yet, not today, not with the tools or modes of consideration we have so-far developed and so-far employed. It might well be that creative writing, as a synthesizing human activity, a bringing together of many different aspects of human creative practice and human critical understanding, involves such a range of knowledge types, forms and undertakings that to suggest any one creative writer, or any group of creative writers, would currently be able to analyze each contribution to a project is to understate the complexity of creative writing in the first place. Given the relative lack of attention given to date to the many contributions and components that make up this complex human activity, this means we do not yet know all that there is to explore; or, indeed, entirely how to explore it.

Such a statement nevertheless rightly indicates that there is something (in fact, many somethings) to discover; and such a statement suggests, because human beings do communicate and human beings do share many common features of life no matter where we are in the world, that the individualized nature of knowledge creative writing entails does not prevent us undertaking creative writing research, and it does not prevent us supporting exchanges of knowledge that will be to the benefit of each and every one of us.

We can best start this by defining what is currently public knowledge about creative writing versus what is currently (or can currently be assumed to be) private knowledge about creative writing. On the one hand, what has been shared between creative writers, between creative writers and the world, between creative writers in different historical times or in different places? What elements of this might well be further explored and knowledge about these things further developed and exchanged? On the other hand, taking into account what we do know, creative writing synthesizes much that humans think, feel and do that has not yet been fully articulated and certainly not researched.

None of this is to say that our individualized knowledge is not reasonably accessible to us personally, of course. That, as is obvious, is each creative writer's primary entry point to the development of our own notions about creative writing. Nor is this to say that individualized knowledge cannot be exchanged between people, ultimately even analytically considered, if it is made accessible to analysis, and if the tools of analysis exist. But it is to say that creative writing is strongly situational and the knowledge that it contains, explores, employs and creates is also strongly situational, based in the individual creative writer's needs, desires, feelings and reasons as that writer undertakes creative writing.

Situational knowledge, just to ensure we also keep this clearly in view, is not necessarily knowledge that is only applicable to one instance, or one person, to one circumstance, but it is knowledge that is generated by and applied to the situation or circumstance that ensues. It might well be informed by an individual writer's memory as well as by immediate sensory stimulus, but its primary aspect is that related to pursuing the task at hand. If a creative writer is pursuing the completion of a task, whatever knowledge they explore, employ or produce will be defined by that aim of completion or, at very least, the aim of being able to feel that task has been concluded or can be abandoned.

Creative writing as research constantly negotiates this territory as is required, in different ways at different times, by the creative writer. If not universally recognized at present, this certainly can be explored by creative writers as a research community in our universities and colleges. This distinctive, writerly research community is already globally recognized, not least because of the considerable growth of graduate study (particularly doctoral study), in creative writing over the past 20 years. Already collaborative senses of the known and the unknown in creative writing are being shared at conferences, in journals and in new books on creative writing – in the same way that such exchanges occur in many longer established university research communities and graduate research communities. Understandably, different countries have higher education histories that are at different points in these graduate developments. They might also have some diverging points of view on the directions such research is taking.

Returning to the role of Devil's Advocate and saying again 'but, perhaps not all creative writing is truly research', it is possible to counter such a statement by saying that while creative writing might not always be investigating current public knowledge or not be producing new public knowledge it is always producing some form of personal, and situational human knowledge which an individual creative writer possesses and seeks to possess, sometimes challenges, maybe sometimes laments in its absence, and sometimes even celebrates.

Researching Creative Writing

Creative writing as research is increasingly accompanied by researching creative writing. The growth in this kind of research has been stimulated by the global increase in the number of creative writing graduate programmes, many launching in the latter part of the 20th century, and it also reflects the ways in which creative endeavours have been more widely distributed in a direct person-to-person way, using online and mobile technologies emerging in the latter 20th and early 21st centuries. This form of exchange has meant that more opportunities exist now than ever before for discussing creative writing as a practice, across an incredibly diverse and diversely located range of individuals, regardless of whether these individuals ultimately release their creative works through mainstream avenues of publishing or performance or not.

Researching creative writing means exploring the actions, artefacts and contexts of creative writing, though not necessarily always undertaking creative writing itself. Even if the researcher is not using the activities of creative writing to undertake such research, such research begins from the point of view of creative writing. This makes researching creative writing different to researching literary artefacts or aspects of literary culture, and to researching creative writers who become well known (that is, biographical research of literary and/or cultural icons) and to researching publishing or performance histories or contexts. The purpose of researching creative writing might or might not be related to the researchers' own creative writing.

So, for example, a researcher in creative writing might seek to compare the compositional strategies of a number of contemporary poets; another might explore the impact of reading on a particular creative writer. A researcher in creative writing might begin with what might be considered in literary terms as ephemera (e.g. writer's notes, diary entries, personal objects) and explore what these represent as evidence of writerly practice and how they impacted on such practice. Another might seek to explore subjects, themes, forms or structures employed in creative writing and to do so across cultural or linguistic boundaries, differences of gender, race or sexual orientation. A researcher in creative writing might investigate the impact of different tools on a creative writer, or different disciplines of employed knowledge, such as History, Anthropology, Biology, Sociology, or an association with one of the other arts.

Because creative writing draws from as many areas of human knowledge as the creative writer requires to undertake and, most often, attempts to complete a creative writing project, and because creative writing combines contemporary action as well as memory, the event of doing creative writing as well as the creation of evidence or artefacts created in doing it, research in creative writing possesses a wealth of areas of investigation.

Terms and Contexts in Practice-Led Research

Over the past dozen or so years, the expression 'practice-led research', used in relation to arts practice research including that in creative writing, has gained considerable academic currency, particularly in the United Kingdom, Australia and New Zealand – though other nations and realms of academe have used the term. The latter includes developments in Asia and Europe mostly, with the expression growing more prevalent at academic gatherings globally, if somewhat less so at present at those in North America.

Much debate has occurred on the subject of practice-led research and a number of studies have already been written. Some examples include Barrett and Bolt's *Practice as Research: Approaches to Creative Arts Inquiry* (Barrett & Bolt, 2007), Dean and Smith's *Practice-Led Research, Research-Led Practice in the Creative Arts* (Dean & Smith, 2009) or the more disciplinary specific work by John Freeman, *Blood, Sweat and Theory: Research Through Practice in Performance* (Freeman, 2010). Consider also the articles in the *Journal of Visual Arts Practice* special issue (ed. C. Smith) on practice-led research, published in 2008, or the articles and interviews in the special issue of *The Creative Industries Journal* (ed. G. Harper), published in 2011.

In addition, many recorded and unrecorded practice, policy and exploratory events have been taking place, adding further to the growing number of published examinations. For example, in the UK from 2005–2008 a committee brought together by the government's national arts and humanities research funder, the Arts and Humanities Research Council (AHRC), in collaboration with representatives of the Council for Higher Education in Art and Design (CHEAD), talked about practice-led research across many of the arts practice disciplines. Committee representatives were funded to explore, with their constituents, their particular disciplines' ideas and interests in practice-led research. The idea was to gain a sense of the ways in which different creative practices in academe were encountering and discussing arts practice research.[1]

Before considering this further, it has to be acknowledged that although it is one of the more popular expressions, the term 'practice-led research' has not stood unopposed, and expressions such as 'practice-based research',

'research-led practice', 'research though practice', 'practice as research', are some of the variants that have their proponents and, indeed, their strong advocates – each aiming to best describe how arts practice contains, explores and produces knowledge.

Readers here will already recognize how these broader considerations of practice-led research (to choose this expression, though not to suggest the irrelevance of any of the others) have a direct connection to creative writing research and creative writing as research. Creative writing as research and researching creative writing both point toward practice-led research as a mode of enquiry, or a collection of modes of enquiry, but it might be expected that only the former of these would be widely viewed as practice-led research, because it is located primarily in the practice of writing. However, this would be an unsound assumption.

Commentators on practice-led research often refer to modes of 'reflection' or 'reflexivity' that incorporate, or are fundamentally driven by, some form of critical engagement. Creative practice is rarely considered to be the end of practice-led research. So, for example, this outline offered by Monash University in Australia with regard to its Doctor of Philosophy (Creative Writing):

> Candidates will be required to submit a piece of their own creative writing together with a critical commentary both of which must be produced during candidature and under supervision. For the purpose of this course, 'piece of creative writing' will be understood to be constituted by a novel, a group of short stories, a play or a group of plays, a sequence of poems, or a portfolio of works of various genres. The critical commentary will be a piece of critical writing focused on the student's piece of creative writing, the writing of which will itself be considered as an act of research into the nature of literary creativity. The critical commentary will involve thoroughly researching the various aspects of the creative writing project: the characteristics of the genre, the influence of the context and the shaping elements in a work of art. (Monash University, n.d.: 1)

This Monash University statement is typical of the kinds of creative writing doctoral degree formats employed in countries such as the UK and Australia. Terms such as 'commentary', 'reflective', 'reflexive', 'response', 'critical component' have become commonplace in relation to the critical aspects of these degrees, while the word 'exegesis' has become notably well known in Australian academe, in relation to that critical element.

Each of the terms carries both literal and suggested meanings, and it is likely that practice-led research exponents will continue to explore these terms, what they are indicating or attempting to indicate, and which of them works best for creative writing, to bring out the most valid and productive relationships between creative writing practice and critical understanding in and through creative writing practice.

Meanwhile, some of those teaching creative writing express concern about whether there is, or ever should be, a need for 'practice-led', 'practice-based', 'research through practice' researchers to include an overtly critical element to any of their work. In other words, if such a critical endeavour is truly required at all. Their argument is that the creative works speak for themselves and should, in themselves, be work enough to justify (or not) the awarding of a degree and/or the work's acceptance as research. Other commentators on practice-led research speak of practice-led researchers 'identifying' themselves as both creative practitioners and researchers, such as outlined here by Chris Rust, who has written frequently on the field of Design:

> Those who wish to be regarded as researchers – as well as being artists or photographers or designers – must 'own' their research in several important ways. They must declare the subject of their inquiry and their motivation for investigating it. They must demonstrate that they have a good understanding of the context for the work and what has gone before. They must have both methods and methodology and they must set all these things out in ways that the rest of us can recognise and understand, although we need not be prescriptive about the actual means of doing that. (Rust, 2007: 75)

Quite obviously, there are aspects of personal preference and of personal identity in all this. What might we choose to call ourselves, how would we each like to be identified, and in what ways our identities relate to occupational categories. Equally, many creative writers might choose not to 'set all things out in ways that the rest of us can recognize and understand', in that the individualized nature of their research, and the situational development of it, is seen to take precedence over more general exchange. The question becomes whether such a choice effectively removes these creative writers from the contemporary university or college, whether it should, or whether choosing not to 'declare' and 'outline' their research is part of the nature of their practice in the first place.

While not offered as an address to this particular issue, but related to it, thinking of the critical elements of such practice-led research in creative writing as a *response* greatly aids discussions. Such a definition opens up opportunities to get closer to the considerable variety of writerly acknowledgements, reactions and propositions with which creative writers as an occupational or recreational group tend to be most familiar.

While 'reflection' and 'reflexivity' can limit the potential directions of critical exploration, response does not. That is, reflection must, by its nature, be static – suggesting a moment or moments during which the writer pauses. This is not an accurate depiction of ways in which creative writers combine creative and critical thought or action. Reflexivity, alternatively but similarly, suggests a turning back upon the work undertaken and while creative writers undoubtedly turn back upon, or can turn back upon previous work the significant aspect of continuing as a creative writer is responding in order to move onward, in order to continue.

Notions, terms and definitions such as 'exegesis' or 'commentary' are also inadequate, in that they suggest the creative writer performs an interpretation of the work that has been undertaken. While this might not be a simplistic endeavour, reduced to the narrowest definition of interpretation, the suggestion nevertheless remains that a form of interpretation occurs and that this is based on what *has occurred*, and what has occurred *as represented* by the artefacts that are now present before the creative writer and, in the case of graduate work, frequently also that are present in front of a supervisor and, ultimately, in front of an examiner. But neither exegesis nor commentary can adequately address new critical knowledge the creative writer now possesses through the undertaking of a recent creative writing project, because they both rely on representational reflection or reflexivity. Neither can articulate the full extent of established and new knowledge, given that some of this knowledge is based clearly in feelings, emotions, memories, in the writer's disposition, physiological engagements as well as psychological ones, and that all of this is applied to a situational undertaking that is only barely seen in the creative writing artefacts most commonly placed before any audience.

At best, an exegesis or commentary can offer some post-event notes on an event of creative writing, observations after the fact on a range of human actions that are represented (but not encapsulated) by the most commonly exchanged artefacts produced by creative writing. At worst, both of these potentially create a patina of academic credibility while simultaneously falsifying the nature of creative writing knowledge, the shine of such institutionalized artefacts overwhelming the less shiny but decidedly more real practices with which creative writers engage, and through which creative writing emerges and continues to emerge.

Most importantly, for all creative writers, terms such as 'commentary', 'reflective', 'reflexive', 'critical component', 'exegesis' and 'critical commentary' suggest that those who might choose to be 'regarded as researchers', as Chris Rust put it, are choosing to be something other, something alternative, to the creative writer who does not choose to be so regarded. This creates a division in our writerly communities that is neither productive nor accurate. Rather, all creative writers, in all environments, respond to the world around them in some fashion, all respond to their previous endeavours, all respond to their readers or audience, in one way or another, even if writing only for themselves, all respond to the stimulus of sensory perception and of memory, and all in some way respond to the fact of being creative writers and of engaging in creative writing. It is for these reasons that the critical aspects of creative writing, which are often melded with the practice itself, and which are often referred to when discussing practice-led research in creative writing, should be seen as a response. In research generally, and in the construction and examination of graduate research degrees in creative writing, this should be the case.

Creative Writing in Research

A brief mention is needed of research in which creative writing is incorporated, but which is not creative writing as research or creative writing research. In other words, research that is most accurately seen as located in other areas, subjects or disciplines, but into which creative writing is incorporated. Perhaps the most intriguing of these is research in literature or literary culture where the outcomes are primarily to do with the final artefacts produced by creative writers, the published or performed works, or the cultural conditions that surround or influence this, but where creative writing practice is referenced, even closely examined, and where some discoveries are made that have relevance for creative writing and creative writers.

Academic territorial disputes aside – and over the past century these have been many in this particular landscape – there is little legitimate argument to be made against the potential in collaborative research that such endeavours can promote and develop, and little valid argument to be made that suggests anything other than possible new knowledge that can emerge. The problems that have occurred – and these can indeed be described as territorial – relate more to who might drive this research and who might own it. Simply, this is not creative writing research – creative writing research I have covered elsewhere throughout this chapter. Alternatively, this is literary research in which creative writing and creative writers can usefully take a part, and acknowledgement of this might well resolve any questions of ownership or where research territory might be located.

Creative writing is also seen within a number of other research areas and disciplines, from education to computer science, from sociology to geography, from anthropology to the medical humanities. And more! These disciplines are mentioned here in their university or college designation, but only so as to give some shape to these interests. They could just as easily be described as avenues of human knowledge which include learning and teaching, technologies, social forms, structures and practices, and so on. These disciplines, and others, have incorporated creative writing into their research methodologies, and in relation to their aims and objectives. Most often they have done so because researchers in these fields have recognized the ability of creative writing to reach individuals, to empower individuals to undertake actions that bring together their creative and critical understandings, and that creative writing produces artefacts that potentially represent at least a portion of these human undertakings and bring to the researchers something invaluable.

Conclusion

I began with questioning so it seems appropriate at this moment in our understanding of creative writing research and creative writing as research that I end with questioning.

What, therefore, does any of this mean for any us? Adopting the role of sceptic, if creative writing knowledge is always likely to be individualized and situational, and if the tools we have in front of us and might, by some estimates, always have in front of us, cannot reach its true nature or even begin to approach and articulate what creative writing is, what it does, and how it contributes to our world, can there ever be a viable research community associated with creative writing? Surely, a research community of this kind is a falsehood because the research base of such a thing cannot be anything other than 'located elsewhere' for each individual creative writer, and the varieties of synthesis that are brought about by us cannot be replicated by others or even fully explained to others? For these reasons, creative writing knowledge cannot be exchanged in any way that might be seen as developmental, one piece of knowledge building on another. Therefore creating a community of researchers is impossible, because each individual and each situation will be different, in its moment and in individual memory, and only will be truly approachable by the creative writer undertaking it.

Such criticism seems to me frighteningly logical and frighteningly strong. However, we might recall here that individual knowledge is exchanged between human beings every second of the day, otherwise we could not exist in any social or communal sense, nor could we have evolved the types of shared knowledge that define societies, groups, organizations or nations. Situational knowledge is also widely exchanged, otherwise we could not enter a crowded space without bumping into each other, drive a car on a roadway where others were driving, or expect to learn anything from exposure to other opinions in a classroom, online or elsewhere. The answer to how we progress creative writing as research, and creative writing research, is therefore not located in whether it is possible (because it is). It is not located in the predominance of individual and situation (both of which are core in creative writing). Rather, it is located in the development of modes, methods and ways of recording such research and, at present, we have some way to go in doing exactly that. Onward!

Notes

(1) I was the National Association of Writers in Education (NAWE) member representing the subject of Creative Writing on this committee. While the committee did not contain representatives of all the arts practice disciplines, it interestingly brought together several disciplines, including Music, Fine Art, Dance, Drama, Architecture, Design and Creative Writing. While some ideas about arts practice research were similar, others were identifiably drawn from specific disciplinary perspectives that contrasted with those in other disciplines. The question of whether Creative Writing is close to all or some of the arts disciplines in the ways and means by which practice-led researchers approach their investigations remains an area in need of further investigation.

References

Barrett, E. and Bolt, B. (2007) *Practice as Research: Approaches to Creative Arts Inquiry.* London: Tauris.

Dean, R. and Smith, H. (2009) *Practice-Led Research, Research-Led Practice in the Creative Arts.* Edinburgh: Edinburgh University Press.

Freeman, J. (2010) *Blood, Sweat and Theory: Research Through Practice in Performance.* Faringdon: Libri.

Harper, G. (2011) Special issue on practice-led research, *The Creative Industries Journal,* 4(1), Bristol: Intellect.

Joint Costing and Pricing Steering Group (n.d.), accessed 18 May 2012. Available at: http://www.jcpsg.ac.uk/index.htm.

Monash University (n.d.), accessed 21 May 2012. Available at: http://www.monash.edu.au/pubs/handbooks/courses/3940.html.

Rust, C. (2007). Unstated contributions – How artistic inquiry can inform interdisciplinary research. *International Journal of Design,* 1(3), 69–76.

Smith, C. *Journal of Visual Arts Practice,* Bristol: Intellect.

University of Strathclyde (n.d.), accessed 18 May 2012. Available at: www.strath.ac.uk/media/ps/finance/fec/media_78706_en.doc.

7 Creative Writing Knowledge
Dianne Donnelly

With the aim to further explore creative writing as a field of intellectual inquiry and as a practice-led academic discipline committed to the advancement and expansion of knowledge in its field, this discussion seeks answers to the following inquiries: (1) In what ways has creativity been associated with knowledge theories? (2) What constitutes academic knowledge in creative writing programs? (3) In what ways has creative writing drawn epistemologically from the theories and practices of other subject domains, and in what ways is creative writing epistemologically different? Moreover, in considering what we know about the range of creative writing knowledge areas and the bodies of evidence that exist for knowledge exploration, (4) how might knowledge discoveries in creative writing be further developed?

> *Literary works 'are the products of a demanding process' which 'involve intellect-, research-, observation-, recording- and knowledge-related skills, equivalent to those demanded by normal research practice'*
> Nigel Krauth and Tess Brady, 1997 (in Dawson, 1999)

Introduction

This chapter explores a range of creative writing knowledge areas, considers the breadth and depth of creative writing knowledge, and investigates whether we can usefully begin to explore where discoveries have been made in this area and where knowledge discoveries might be further developed. Beyond the creative writers, writer-teachers and writer-teacher scholars in the academy who are invested in such a discussion, there exist beyond our concentric core, colleagues in other research domains, university/college administrators, and officials within governing bodies to whom we might also share the ways in which creative writing advances as a knowledge-based discipline.

Universities and colleges do vary in their research requirements, and the degree that these disparities impact ideas associated with knowledge and investigations of knowledge are evidentially proportionate to local, national and global initiatives. For example, the research activity associated with creative writing programs in the United Kingdom and Australia is a critical exegesis, a study which situates the creative work within a body of scholarly knowledge and contributes, through its theory and practice, new disciplinary knowledge. These programs are governed by university and funding initiatives to advance new knowledge to the creative writing domain through academic research practice. The Master's and doctoral academic equivalency of research output in the United States is the creative dissertation. As such, the creative output is viewed by funding and accreditation bodies as a legitimate study that advances knowledge. While funding imperatives and university requirements do not compel the US discipline to integrate practice-led research into their programs, there are still cogent and persuasive claims for investigating and discovering practices that will reveal new modes of knowledge to the writer and to the discipline, and there has been considerable dynamic movement to situate creative writing with its own identity and scholarship.

With the aim to further propel creative writing as a field of intellectual inquiry and as a practice-led academic discipline committed to the advancement and expansion of knowledge in its field, this discussion seeks answers to the following inquiries:

(1) In what ways has creativity been associated with knowledge theories?
(2) What constitutes academic knowledge in creative writing programs?
(3) In what ways has creative writing drawn epistemologically from the theories and practices of other subject domains, and in what ways is creative writing epistemologically different?
(4) Considering what we know about the range of creative writing knowledge areas and the bodies of evidence that exist for knowledge exploration, how might knowledge discoveries in creative writing be further developed?

With the goal to broaden our site of knowledge and strengthen global interest in knowledge discoveries in creative writing, Graeme Harper (2009: 93) reminds us that 'there is more important work to do, answers to seek'. And so we begin.

In What Ways Has Creativity Been Associated with Knowledge Theories?

Long before creative writers entered the academy, there were challenges to the notion that creativity could be linked to research and knowledge. But that is not to say that creativity did not have its own history, its own 'intellectual path that was for two centuries independent of the institution-alization and conceptualizations of research' (Albert & Runco, 1999: 17). To note that creativity was independent of research (and knowledge) accounts for the fact that these concepts were not seen in alignment or even considered relatable to one another for most of their histories. Robert Albert and Mark Runco (1999: 17), who surveyed the history of research on creativity, tell us 'it took another 150 years after research was a recognized and widely encouraged institutional undertaking before the concept of creativity was sufficiently sculpted out of the many debates regarding the meaning and eventual separation of such competing ideas as imagination, originality, genius, talent, freedom, and individuality'.

Ancient philosophers, beginning with Plato and Aristotle, spoke of the arts as an imitation of nature – the aim of creativity, the ideal, was in the truth of the replication. In fact, Plato viewed poets as full of false knowledge and envisioned creativity, in general, as the antithesis of the search for knowledge, 'entirely opposed to that reasoned discourse that seeks understanding' (Dye, 1986: 93). He perceived creativity as being 'on the opposite end of a line diagramming our mental functions' and as 'undermining intellectual culture, and ultimately the whole society' (Dye, 1986: 93). Platonic views eschewed that the discovery of knowledge was in the hands of scientists and philosophers, who were deemed authorities in 'the relation between human beings and the objects of their inquiry' (Rorty, 1997: 390). The belief was that only scientists, as 'true inquirer[s]' could use *words* 'to obtain a vision of real existence' (Dye, 1986: 93). (Certainly, this view is diametrically opposed to what we now know about the inquiries associated with creative processes and how these critical investigations lead to the acquisition and production of original knowledge.) Plato's viewpoint was followed, in classificatory rhetoric, by Aristotle, who categorized what he saw as rules for productive activities, the skills or *techne* associated with creativity acquired through practice.

Interesting connections between creativity and knowledge theories since the Renaissance period bear import on socio-historical perceptions relative to the times. Yet, while such connections suggest a long history of creativity's subjugation to reason as the primary impetus for the making of new meaning, there exist some markers that connect creativity to the development of ideas associated with knowledge theories. During the Renaissance, cultural and artistic movement (consider Shakespeare, Ben Johnson and Christopher Marlowe) coexisted with a focus on knowledge (e.g. an individual's intellect, the scientific method and detailed observation). For the duration of the Enlightenment, imagination was linked with reason, sometimes as reason's helpmate in the development of ideas.

In other words, in the context of discovery, creativity might have helped to generate new ideas, but in the context of justification, any hypothesis was validated empirically through observation and experimentation. Cartesian doubt put all truths in question as uncertainty stacked creativity against reason as an intuitive process that could not be scientifically investigated.

Sometime later, Nietzsche, operating under the flow of determinism, reasoned nothing should limit the creative powers of the gifted because 'creativity as the purposeful expression of the will to power, [was considered] the highest value' (Weiner, 2000: 84). What followed was the Romantic opposition to the supremacy of reason, and a perspective that elevated, instead, the imagination as the primary faculty for creating all art. In opposition to the reasoned imitation of nature as it had once been, Wordsworth positioned poetry as 'the spontaneous overflow of powerful feelings'. Shelley called poets the 'unacknowledged legislators of the world'. Blake asserted the creative freedom of the imagination and the duality of creation as a necessary tension toward resolution. Coleridge united both reason and feeling with the paradoxical phrase 'intellectual intuition'.

The epistemological shape of creativity did not take form until the late 19th century, in part, as Darwin's evolution theory spilled over to his view of creativity as part of the natural process. Creativity, as a knowledge-based concept, transcended the growing technical domain. The modern view situated creativity and knowledge theories in more positive ways. Any 'suddenness' of creative insight was predicated on longer periods of cognitive processes. There was a shift from product to process – to formalism and technique, to characteristics, capacities and properties. Robert Paul Weiner (2000: 86) reports that 'the artists concerned themselves with technique, and the technicians concerned themselves with aesthetics, and all were concerned with the new'. By the early 20th century, the social sciences entered the conversation as J.P. Guilford catapulted the study of creativity within the field of psychology, and Lynn White (1963: 273) went so far as to say that 'the analysis of creativity [became] one of the chief intellectual commitments of our age'. Studies since then have varied in terms of perspectives on the relationship between creativity and knowledge theories to include the following areas: historic (Albert & Runco, 1999; Dye, 1986), psychoanalytic (Brophy, 1998; Csikszentmihalyi, 1997; Kaufman & Kaufman, 2009), scientific (Boden, 2004; Bohm & Peat, 2000), socio-economic (Bereiter, 2002; Florida, 2002; Friedman, 2005; Godin, 2010; Landry, 2000; Nonaka & Takeuchi, 1995; Pink, 2005), and political (Nagel, 2000).[1]

The cultural concerns of the 21st century shaped universities' attention to the research of creative practices. Universities became centers of knowledge creation by which a global knowledge-based society and economy still depend, as creativity was/is fundamental to human experience and essential to the development and advancement of economic interests.

Creativity is now seen as an integral element in the discovery of new knowledge. Its association with knowledge theories has been better understood in the creative writing discipline within the broader scope of practice. 'If creativity is valuable enough to be studied', Albert and Runco (1999: 81) remind us, 'originality is to be valued as well'. Creative writers' reflections of their creative processes and the research efforts that coincide with their practice lead writers to new insights and to original contributions which have value to the creative writing domain.

What Constitutes Academic Knowledge in Creative Writing Programs?

First, to make headway with this particular question, it seems reasonable to begin with some broad representation of what is meant by 'knowledge' and then narrow down an understanding from there to the ways in which knowledge is (1) new to the creative writer – and the ways in which writers acquire and produce new knowledge, and (2) the ways in which knowledge is new to the creative writing domain and the body of human knowledge – and, in the end, the manner by which this knowledge is communicated and justified.

'Knowledge', according to the Merriam-Webster Dictionary (n.d.), is defined, in part, as (1) 'the fact or condition of knowing something with familiarity gained through experience', (2) an 'acquaintance with or understanding of a science, art, or technique', (3) 'the range of one's information or understanding', and (4) 'the body of truth, information, and principles acquired by humankind'. The Oxford English Dictionary (n.d.) adds that 'knowledge' includes the 'mode of knowledge acquisition to reach new conclusions, [and/or to] discover new or collate old facts', [as well as knowledge which is] the 'nature of newness, new to the world, new to the body of human knowledge'.

These words and phrases demonstrate the broad range of knowledge applications associated with creative writers as learners and with the study of creative writing as an academic discipline. Part of the challenge in defining the knowledge of creative writing rests with the many knowledge models associated within academia that don't quite fit what really happens in the creative writing process. Philosophical debates surrounding epistemology generally concern these primary arguments: (1) skeptics argue that we cannot know anything at all – they believe that nothing is justified true belief; (2) empiricists and rationalists deliberate as to whether knowledge acquisition comes through the senses or through critical thought and deductive reasoning. Each position can certainly be moderated – there are gray areas and pluralities. As such, efforts to define and articulate the foundations of knowledge (its acquisition, production, communication and justification) become paramount for our discipline if we are to build on and draw from our own substantiated body of understanding, if we are to render for others our methodology for meaning-making, and if we are to contribute to the larger conversation about knowledge production with other academic disciplines.

It proves challenging, for example, to characterize creative writing in terms of propositional knowledge, knowledge which is true, evident or justified. Creative writing cannot be defined in such absolutes. However, we might suggest that there exists propositional *language* in creative writing in that creative writers need the syntactic sense of vocabulary and the linguistic sense of how to use this vocabulary, the schematic awareness of genre differences and a variety of writing strategies from which to choose. Creative writing offers a certain skill set that is particular to its domain. Writers begin with knowledge, which is embedded in individual experience; more specifically, this is tacit knowledge that is internalized and practiced through immersion in creative writing acts and actions. Consequently, all of these cumulative elements lead writers to the 'knowing' or the 'knowing *what*' of creative writing. What begins as the practice of craft skills and writing conventions, combines with the acts and actions of creative writing, and these components build on the understanding of constructionist elements of writing such as the choices writers make and the consequences of these choices and the ways in which writers synthesize and rework this new knowledge into their own writing practices.[2] Such activity is the methodology of creative writing (the studying of writing through writing) – the mode of knowledge acquisition that leads to new conclusions. This practice is also supported by a writer's immersion in the history of creative writing (e.g. genre, discipline, culture), or as T.S. Eliot (1965: 24) suggests, in writers absorbing what the past 'knows'.

The 'knowing *how*' is less clear in creative writing as little practical or procedural knowledge is available to the creative writer. The 'how-to' texts that exist mostly in the US may suggest practical guidelines for writers, but there is no set formula for how to proceed in the development of a creative work. Each piece, through the process of technique and discovery, yields a different start, approach and direction. As Alice Munro (1982: 224) insists, 'There is no blueprint for the structure. It's not a question of, "I'll make this kind of house because if I do it right it will have this effect"'.

There is, however, no doubt that one of the ways creative writers gain knowledge is through empirical research as acute observers of the world, as human beings who not only know about the human condition, but who also 'contribute enormously to the production, building and development of knowledge about human beings, human society and the world we inhabit' (Webb & Brien, 2006). Chekhov (1886: 151) tells the creative writer, 'you will bring life into nature only if you don't shrink from similarities that liken its activities to those of mankind'. Faulkner (1949) talks about the 'necessary verities and truths of the heart'. Tolstoy (1897: 797) addresses art as 'an organ of human life', that which transmits 'man's reasonable perception into feeling'. The accuracy of observation is, for Wallace Stevens, the equivalent of accuracy of thinking. Joseph Conrad (1897: 193) notes that the writer, like the philosopher or the scientist, 'seeks truth and makes his appeal'. More specifically, writing ('art'), for Conrad, is a:

> single-minded attempt to render the highest kind of justice to the visible universe, by bringing to light the truth, manifold and one, underlying its every aspect. It is an attempt to find in its forms, in its colors, in its light, in its shadows, in the aspects of matter and in the factors of life, what of each is fundamental, what is enduring and essential – their one illuminating and convincing quality – the very truth of their existence. (p. 193)

In fact, as Harper (2010: xi) reminds us, it is 'because of human action that Creative Writing exists, but . . . it is [because of] human understanding that Creative Writing has evolved and continues to evolve as both an art and communication'. Brian Castro (2011: 5) insists that 'research through observation, through interlocutory practices . . . is every bit as scientific and ethical if one wants to case the issue under an empirical light'. To demonstrate what writers gain from this empirical study, Castro points to Virginia Woolf, who understood 'the language of relationships, of the family, of social class, of men and of women', as well as 'the tensions within her language'. She made these tensions 'foreign', Castro explains, 'the better to glimpse them in their awkward spaces and elastic time-frames when reflected upon'. While Castro admits '[t]his may sound intuitive', he asserts, 'it is research nonetheless'. Consider that Nabokov rode school buses to learn the language of teenage girls; Raymond Carver observed the dynamics of ordinary people; James Baldwin understood the boundaries between racism and sexuality. Zora Neale Hurston, who said, 'you have to go there, to know there', recorded slave narratives. Wallace Stevens explored poetry as a synthesis of creative imagination and objective reality.

Rather than associate knowledge with certainty as traditional models might do (e.g. validation through replication), the knowledge in creative writing is in the discovery that takes the writer beyond the routines of writing, in the questions that arise and that are answered through the writing process. Gilles Deleuze (2003: 101) refers to this turning point in painting (though the transference is easily made to writing) as 'the chaos or catastrophe' in which 'a rhythm emerges'. Barbara Bolt (2004) explains that the '"new" emerges through process as a shudder of an idea, which is then realised in and through language'. For Toni Morrison, it is the 'What if?' that 'squeezes' an image forward. The writing that seeks the knowledge is represented in the creative work and contained as well in the reflection of the creative writing. Such processes teach Morrison, for example, that she 'can't just reach some little plateau and say that's it, this is the place. It is always a search' (in Houston, 2009).

In addition to the influences of reading and the theories that underpin our process, the site of knowledge that supports the creative work, also includes research, 'not just in gathering information but in gathering texture; that is, in putting together the kind of information [writers] need to create an "insider" sense of foreign, unfamiliar, past or future environments' (Meehan, 2010). This research lends credibility to creative works and the intentional 'disguise . . . [of] anything like research has ever taken place' (Meehan, 2010). Jon Cook (2005: 198) clarifies that '[w]riting is usually regarded not as a research method, but as a means of presenting the results of research'. As writers and readers, we all value the depth and verisimilitude of a well-researched body of creative work.

Knowledge, as a dynamic process, involves not only complex cognitive processes but also generative and transferrable skills that impact the ways creative writers approach their writing (and reading), the ways instructors design and teach their courses, and the methods by which creative writing scholars research and discover new meaning. Knowledge then, in creative writing, can be tacit, emergent, empirical, experiential, aesthetic and sensory – and certainly, this list is not inclusive – but knowledge that is new to the creative writing domain and the body of human knowledge can also be made explicit.

Through the generation of an original creative work, writers acquire new understanding and insight. Knowledge which is acquired by the creative writer through her writing practices is, however, difficult to communicate in the often narrowed essential ideal of quantitative scientific analytical methods and measurable outcomes generally associated with traditional academic research. Writers may share their knowledge with other writers within academia and at conferences, in writers' self-reports, in scholarship and through global exchanges. Does this practice advance knowledge? Yes, to a significant degree in that those new understandings can translate to new ways of thinking about writing and the teaching of writing. Knowledge is made explicit from this pedagogical perspective. Yet, while the Excellence in Research for Australia (ERA, 2011) initiative recognizes that creative works use existing knowledge 'in a new and creative way', such works, according to ERA and other such governing bodies, cannot stand alone in their representation of 'new concepts, methodologies and understandings' for research purposes. More specifically, the knowledge that is new to the creative writer and contained within the creative writing is distinguishable from knowledge which is new to the domain if the *aim* of the creative production is to view the work as art for art's sake or if the intent is for the 'advancement of scholarship and creativity rather than new knowledge and understanding' (Scrivener, 2009: 72).

Creative works as research products in United Kingdom and Australian tertiary institutions are predicated on a relationship between the creative work and the exegesis as the explication and elucidation of 'potential knowledges, or interventions in knowledge, to which the work gives rise' (Nelson, 2008). As such, the complementary critical study positions the work within broader practice and theory realms, frames the creative work in terms of its methods and its questions, offers a reflective role in relation to the creative work, and forms the basis by which the critical study is subject to peer review. Although the relationship between the creative work and critical study has been somewhat challenging in the past – as the discipline's practice-led activities juxtapose more traditional university research practices – there has been substantiated progress over the years. For instance, Harper (2008: 164–5) indicates that creative writing in the United Kingdom may have begun 'with basic notions connected to knowledge, knowledge investigation and knowledge acquisition', but creative writing research now 'proceeds by the recognition of the evidence for both empirical and theoretical research' (Harper, 2008: 164–5). Moreover, in surveying the first decade of *TEXT* (the online refereed journal published by Australasian Association of Writing Programs which features debates on creativity and writing), Webb and Brien (2006) conclude that:

> [i]t is possible to trace a shift, over this period, away from pedagogical issues and towards research-oriented questions that explore the role of creative writing in the academy and the world, and demonstrate that as a discipline writing is capable of combining conventional academic rigour with creative thought.

Some Australian higher education institutions' (HEIs) research guidelines even suggest a shift to a stronger symbiosis between the creative and critical parts, with a claim 'that the relationship between the two parts contributes to the originality and creativity of the whole' (Kroll, 2004), and as such, original knowledge can be asserted when the outcome is the creative product (Scrivener, 2009).

We can take a more macrocosmic view of the ways in which tacit knowledge is made explicit in creative writing by looking at the flow of knowledge from the individual writer to the larger creative writing domain. We can apply, for example, the 'knowledge spiral' concept, adapted by Ikujiro Nonaka and Hirotaka Takeuchi (1995) in their book *The Knowledge-Creating Company*, to the ways in which creative writers acquire knowledge and situate this knowledge within academic creative writing communities. At a quick glance, organizational knowledge creation begins with the individual and spirals up to become organizational knowledge. While Nonaka and Takeuchi's theory on organizational knowledge creation relates to value creation for organizations, their model of innovation process has epistemological and ontological applications for the ways knowledge creation begins with the individual creative writer and spirals upward to become knowledge in the creative writing domain. Creative writers begin with tacit knowledge, but this knowledge is made explicit when writers reflect, communicate and justify their creative works as research products. In the United States, often this process is advanced through conference forums (presented by writers, writer-teachers, writer-scholars and/or interdisciplinary cohorts) which are related to pedagogy and program development and forged through scholarship written by the many craft critics who investigate and interrogate writing practice through research activities. More insidiously, but critically important, are the gains that resound in creative writing classrooms today: (1) the discussions that push the boundaries of traditional writing workshops and welcome intellectual analyses that reveal new theories and operational significance to the field, (2) the variable lenses from which to view history in a different light, as well as (3) the practices that investigate genre, negotiate writing spaces, integrate polyculturalist[3] approaches and merge theory, inquiry and practice in new epistemological ways.

If we return then to Nonaka and Takeuchi's theory of spiral knowledge, we see similarities to the knowledge creation flow in creative writing. Knowledge begins with the individual and his or her creative practices; this is knowledge that is new to the creative writing academic. Knowledge creation spirals upward to the creative writing domain when individual practice leads to research insights and when new understandings are communicated and justified through research methods. Of critical importance, however, is the recursive and fluid path of the spiral knowledge. While knowledge creation spirals upward from the individual to the larger writing community, new knowledge also flows back to creative writers and knowledge creation transforms pedagogically. As new insights inform the discipline, new theories are developed and new skills are taught to creative writers in the academy. In addition, such knowledge creation stimulates new research initiatives.

In What Ways Has Creative Writing Drawn Epistemologically from the Theories and Practices of Other Subject Domains and in What Ways is Creative Writing Epistemologically Different?

Because each domain has its specialized knowledges and research methodologies, the answers to questions about epistemological similarities and differences should be contextually framed by the ways in which knowledge is represented in specific domains and the ways in which knowledge is understood. While an overarching view is more complex and heterogeneous than what is presented here, the conclusions drawn suggest particular signifiers that each subject domain places at its center of meaning-making.

In the generation of work (e.g. poetry, fiction, drama), creative writers undergo a series of creative processes. They gather anecdotes, bits of conversation, observations, field notes, reflections, research. They synthesize material, flesh out details, make connections, draw conclusions, remediate or reshape images and text. These creative processes lead to insights – discoveries that occur through the active practice of writing and problem solving. Scientists proceed through similar creative processes: preparation, incubation, illumination. In fact, Garth Boomer (1987: 9) asserts 'human beings are born scientists'. More specifically, Joe Moxley (1989: 35) adds, 'scientists, artists, and writers don't sit around coffee shops hoping for inspiration, [as] effective problem solvers are committed to understanding what they perceive to be an incomplete gestalt'.

A systematic study of inquiry and investigation drives the methodology by which scientists seek new meaning. Scientific writing, Charles Bazerman (1988: 503) reports, 'is often treated apart from other forms of writing, as a special code privileged through its reliance on mathematics (considered a purer symbolic system than natural language)'. Meaning-making differs among creative writers and scientists in that the processes of creative writing are not associated with certainty, with exactness, with a formulaic methodology of systematic questioning and replication that is located in the scientific realm. The generation of creative work may begin with inquiry, but the direction and order of questions and the kinds of questions posed might change throughout the process. As such, the methodology for making implicit knowledge explicit in creative writing is different and specific to the ways in which writers approach and engage in meaning-making activities.

Creative writing and composition share epistemological parallels. Both disciplines emphasize writing processes and engage in linguistic manipulation, modeling, invention and a broad range of pedagogical approaches to student learning. Writing processes are plural, fluid and recursive in nature and concern purposeful, interactive learning environments. As such, creative writing has drawn epistemologically from composition studies, particularly as it relates to process theory. Writers in composition studies, in part, seek truth by placing rhetoric at the center of meaning-making. The primary differences between creative writers and rhetoricians exist in the arrangement and aim of the writing. While a poem or story may have rhetorical properties inherent in its delivery, the primary aim of the creative work is not often to persuade its readers to take action. That is not to say that creative works do not inform communities, advance perspectives or adjure causes. In fact, Patrick Bizzaro (Bizzaro & McClanahan, 2007: 89) insists on the necessity that we 'use writing in the civic arena to understand the terms of our lifestyles and to express our views concerning when those lifestyles must change'. However, creative writing does not *typically* offer a thesis that drives the creative work; it does not *generally* integrate evidence that propels the writer's claim forward, or *necessarily* call its target audience to action. The kind of thesis-driven essay argued by composition writers is more explicit than the creative work.

Creative writing shares similarities with the other practice-based disciplines, incorporating, in its theories and practice, interpretations of the world and human condition. Like creative writers, musicians, painters, sculptors, dancers, graphic designers and other performance-based artists emphasize the practices associated with the doing or making of art. There is a symbiotic relationship between writing and performance – and practice-based and practice-led disciplines learn to value the juxtaposition, interposition and remediation of elements, techniques and possibilities that exist when textualities merge with other dynamics.

In literary studies, the reading of literature has historically been considered a hierarchal function. As such, knowledge is represented and understood through the interpretation of literature. The fundamental difference between literary studies and creative writing is located in the ways in which literature is read. Literary studies centers on the ideological or historical analysis of a text while creative writing approaches the text in more specific readerly ways. Creative writers consider the text from the inside, constructing theories driven by questions of 'What if?' R.V. Cassill (1962: 94) clarifies our readerly distinction from the determinism of literary studies when he insists that '[a]bove all, [creative writers] are interested in how texts are made – how the parts fit together to form a whole – which means [they] are committed to the view that a text might have been made otherwise than it is'. The discipline's writing practice is epistemologically different than writing produced in literary studies in that creative writing focuses on writerly processes, not discussions of the goals or methods of particular literary camps. These distinctions lead Harper (2009: 93) to conclude that 'the investigation of, in, and through the practice of Creative Writing is not the same as the critical study of Literature (English Lit., American Lit. or otherwise)'. Sue Roe proposes that because we experience writing as performance, our fluid form resists such shaping. Roe (2010: 196) suggests that since 'we know that an imaginative piece of writing might be informed as richly by painting, music, dance or theatre as by an in-depth knowledge of literature we have always been reluctant to hook the study of creative writing in a rigid or inflexible way to the study of English literature'.

While creative writing's 'markers of professional difference'[4] situate the study as an epistemologically-independent discipline, there remains widespread activity which intersects, plaits and merges creative writing practice with other academic domains.

In What Ways Might Knowledge Discoveries in Creative Writing be Further Developed?

In the past, assessment of a 'successful' creative writing program weighed heavily on post-event artifacts, rather than on the discoveries associated with the acts and actions of creative writers. While the products of creative writers (substantiated research events in their own merits) might be juried by readers and/or interpreted/deconstructed by various literary camps, the processes and practices of creative writers have only recently been recognized as critical evidence of the 'work' of creative writing and its contributions to knowledge. Subsequently, official responses like that from the UK Arts and Humanities Research Board (and similarly from governing initiatives in Australia) began to emerge, defining for the discipline of creative writing, 'research primarily in terms of research processes rather than outputs' (Candy, 2006: 2).

As a practice-led discipline then, what evidence suggests the research processes of creative writing? Referentially, beyond the performance of writing and the cognitive abilities associated with problem-solving and the sundry other critical elements, new insights can lead into and from writers' pretexts and post-texts, the kinds of texts which may be 'peripheral' and 'complementary' to completed texts (Harper, 2009: 93). Harper extends the evidence of creative writing to include work on 'writer or writers'; 'personal, cultural, sociopolitical and economic relations', 'craft instruments and objects', 'central results and attached results', and all other such 'documents of Creative Writing exchange' (p. 93).

How then might we build on the discoveries of our creative writing body? What other evidence might our discipline explore in its research practices? And if knowledge discoveries are to be further developed, how might creative writers in the United States, United Kingdom and Australian networks contribute to this conversation? We might begin to explore inquires such as these by formulating more specific questions that (1) drive our research initiatives, (2) lead to new insights, and (3) advance creative writing as a knowledge-based discipline.

Questions that drive research initiatives

(1) We know that the acts and actions of creative writing cross-pollinate with the activities of other university programs. How might the knowledge of creative writing link with other disciplines? How have 'hybrid learning styles [drawn] on the strengths of varying discourses'?[5] 'How might the modes of thought that students develop in other classes inform the making of their own poetry, fiction, creative nonfiction, drama and screenwriting?'[6]

(2) Creative writing connects with the public sphere in ways that other academic disciplines do not. What measures are in place to extend new insights beyond the academy to community interfaces and outreach programs? What new learning is to be gained from such efforts?

(3) Higher education institutions have long been the privileged site and codifier for many different kinds of knowledge. What other knowledge sources beyond HEIs bear import on creative writing's knowledge acquisition and production?

(4) How might we extend what we know about creativity and knowledge theories, conditions for enhancing creativity and innovation, and the relationship between creativity and development of new ideas?

(5) How has the digital culture of the university and more expansive digital literacies impacted the ways in which creative writers read and write? What new insights emerge as writers negotiate these new writing spaces and interact with multimodal textualities? How is learning complicated and/or enhanced with this emergence in mind? What can we discover about genre hybridity in the digital environment? What can we understand regarding concepts of audience and authorship given these online modalities? In the same light, what is the relationship between creative writers' blogs and the advancement of knowledge?

(6) What can be derived epistemologically from the metacognitive nature of writers who comment on the nature of writing as more creative writers engage in craft criticism?

(7) What is the relationship of knowledge acquisition and knowledge sharing that may result in creative writing study abroad and international exchange programs?

(8) How is knowledge acquisition and production distinguished between undergraduate and graduate programs as well as between varying universities and degreed programs?

(9) Webb and Brien (2006) agree that 'Any widening of our local frame of reference, interests and discussions can only add to the collaborative scholarly, professional and creative opportunities across the whole field of writing, and make our research efforts more viable' as well as advance and extend our site of knowledge. In this regard, what kind of data collection might prove effective in mapping global knowledge-building efforts? What would we do with such data?

Questions that lead to new insights

(10) How might research-led practice complement practice-led research and suggest new approaches to writing processes?

(11) What opportunities exist for collaborative work to share knowledge, and how might collaborations – writers and sociologists, philosophers, techno-rhetoricians, psychologists, historians, scientists, physicians, or artists (to get the list primed) – lead to more understanding of the writing process and suggest how new approaches to writing might be developed? How might other disciplines learn from creative writing?

(12) What is the relationship among kinesthetic intelligence, kinesthetic writing and problem-solving?

(13) In what ways can qualitative, quantitative and conceptual research lead to new understandings in creative writing?

Questions that advance creative writing as a knowledge-based discipline

(14) As creative writers explore the ways in which their practices and processes lead to new insights and as more evidence reveals the field's growing body of understanding, how might we best communicate creative writing as knowledge to others – to our colleagues in other research domains, to university administrators, to officials in governing bodies, and to international coalitions?

(15) Moreover, while international conferences provide some wide-reaching points of contact as do journals, scholarship and forums, how else might new global and international gateways facilitate a better understanding of creative writing's particular modes of research?

(16) Carl Bereiter (2002) argues that 'the emergence of the knowledge society has given rise to a view of knowledge as a thing that can be systematically produced and shared among members of a community'. If this assumption holds true and if it includes the discipline of creative writing, what then is the relation of creative writing knowledge to culture and how might we best create and advance a knowledge-based community for creative writing?

Conclusion

Nike Bourke (2007) is 'reminded of, and surprised afresh by, the refusal of creative writing as a discipline to be knowable, complete, and bounded'. Is this response a paradoxical theorem? In other words, can creative writing refuse to be knowable and yet also contain a repository of data that supports creative writing research as knowledge? Can the discipline resist movements to be complete and bounded even as we frame its epistemological shape?

Yes – and yes.

As an academic field of study, creative writing *is* always in motion; it *is* a 'fluid and inventive field of research', but it *is* also a discipline which 'continues to be informed and articulated by strengthening global interest and a commitment to the development of further knowledge' (Harper, 2009: 171). As creative writing builds on the knowledge discoveries of its creative writing body, as it enters new spaces, pedagogically spiraling in its knowledge creation; yet continuously outbound in its unfettered spaces, there is, *indeed*, more important work to do, answers to seek. And so we begin – again and anew.

Notes

(1) This list is modified from Jeri Kroll's original overview of creativity studies. (See 'Creative writing as research and the dilemma of accreditation', *TEXT* 6.1 (April). Available at: http://www.griffith.edu.au/school/art/text/april02/kroll.htm.)

(2) Nigel McLoughlin refers to something similar as poesis, process and praxis in his 2008 essay (see 'Creating an integrated model for teaching creative writing – one approach' in Harper, G. and Kroll, J. (eds) *Creative Writing Studies: Practice, Research, Pedagogy*. Clevedon: Multilingual Matters).

(3) See http://www.arc.gov.au.

(4) The term 'markers of professional difference' originated with Kelly Ritter (see 'Profession writers/writing professionals: Revamping teacher training in creative writing Ph.D. programs', *College English* 64 (2) (November), 205–227). The dialogue related to creative writing's markers of professional difference has been extended by Patrick Bizzaro in 'Research and reflections: The special case of creative writing', *College English* 66 (3) (January), 294–309 and by Dianne Donnelly in her introduction to *Does the Writing Workshop Still Work?* and in *Establishing Creative Writing Studies as an Academic Discipline*.

(5) This is an idea presented by Chad Davidson and Greg Fraser in 'The expanding role of creative writing in today's college curriculum', *The Writer's Chronicle* 42.3, 67–89.

(6) As above.

References

Albert, R. and Runco, M. (1999) The concepts of creativity and research. In R. Sternberg (ed.) *Handbook of Creativity* (pp. 16–34). Cambridge: Cambridge University Press.

Bazerman, C. (2009) The problem of writing knowledge. In S. Miller (ed.) (2009) *The Norton Book of Composition Studies* (pp. 502–514). New York: W.W. Norton.

Bereiter, C. (2002) *Education and Mind in the Knowledge Age*. Hillsdale, NJ: Erlbaum.

Bizzaro, P. and McClanahan, M. (2007) Putting wings on the invisible: Voice, authorship and the authentic self. In K. Ritter and S. Vanderlice (eds) *Can it Really be Taught?* (pp. 77–90). Portsmouth: Boynton/Cook.

Boden, M. (2004) Creativity in a nutshell. In M. Boden *The Creative Mind: Myths and Mechanisms* (pp. 1–10). London: Routledge.

Bohm, D. and Peat, D.F. (2000) *Science, Order and Creativity* (2nd edn). London: Routledge.

Bolt, B. (2004) The exegesis and the shock of the new. *TEXT* Special Issue 3, accessed 28 April 2011. Available at: http://www.textjournal.com.au/speciss/issue3/bolt.htm.

Boomer, G. (1987) Addressing the problem of elsewhereness. In D. Goswami and P. Stillman (eds) *Reclaiming the Classroom: Teacher Research as an Agency for Change* (pp. 4–13). Upper Montclair, NJ: Boynton/Cook.

Bourke, N. (2007) Passionate diversity: Review of *Creative Writing: Theory Beyond Practice*. *TEXT* Review 11 (2), accessed 12 February 2011. Available at: http://www.textjournal.com.au/oct07/bourke_rev.htm

Brophy, K. (1998) *Creativity: Psychoanalysis, Surrealism and Creative Writing*. Victoria: Melbourne University Publishing.

Candy, L. (2006) Practice-based research: A guide, creativity and cognition studios. University of Technology, accessed 13 January 2011. Available at: http://www.creativityandcognition.com.

Cassill, R.V. (1962) *Writing Fiction*. New York: Pocket Books.

Castro, B. (2011) Teaching creative writing in Asia: Four points and five provocations. In J. Camens & D. Wilson (eds) *TEXT* Special issue, Creative Writing in the Asia-Pacific Region, (April) 1–8, accessed 11 February 2011. Available at: http://www.textjournal. com.au/speciss/issue10/Castro.pdf.

Chekhov, A. (1886) Natural description and 'The Center of Gravity' (Trans. I. Prishvin). In D. Gioia and R.S. Gwynn (eds) (2006) *The Art of the Short Story* (p. 151). New York: Pearson.

Conrad, J. (1897) The condition of art. In D. Gioia and R.S. Gwynn (eds) (2006) *The Art of the Short Story* (pp. 193–194). New York: Pearson.

Cook, J. (2005) Creative writing as a research method. In G. Griffin (ed.) *Research Methods for English Studies* (pp. 195–211). Edinburgh: Edinburgh University Press.

Csikszentmihalyi, M. (1997) *Creativity: Flow and the Psychology of Discovery and Invention*. New York: Harper Perennial.

Dawson, P. (1999) *Creative writing in Australia: The development of a discipline. TEXT 5 (1), accessed 19 January 2011. Available at:* http://www.textjournal.com.au/april01/dawson. htm.

Deleuze, G. (2003) Francis Bacon and the Logic of Sensation, trans D.W. Smith, London: Continuum.

Dye, J.W. (1986) The poetization of science. In M. Amsler (ed.) *The Languages of Creativity: Models, Problem-Solving, Discourse* (pp. 92–108). Newark: University of Delaware Press.

Eliot, T.S. (1965) Tradition and the individual talent. In J. Hayward (ed.) *Selected Prose* (p. 24). Middlesex: Penguin Books.

Excellence in Research for Australia (2012). Australian Research Council, accessed 8 September 2012. Available at http://www.arc.gov.au/era/faq.htm.

Faulkner, W. (1949) Banquet speech. Nobelprize.org 5 September 2012, accessed 8 September 2012. Available at: http://www/nobelprize.org/nobel_prize/literature/ laureates/1949/faulkner-speech.html.

Florida, R. (2002) *The Rise of the Creative Class*. New York: Basic Books.

Friedman, T. (2005) *The World is Flat*. New York: Farrar, Straus and Giroux.

Godin, S. (2010) *Linchpin: Are you Indispensable?* New York: Portfolio/Penguin.

Harper, G. (2008) Creative writing: Words as practice-led research. *Journal of Visual Arts Practice* 7 (2), 31–52, accessed 17 January 2011. Available at: http://dx.doi.org/10.1080/ 14790720708668958.

Harper, G. (2009) Creative writing? *New Writing* 4 (2), 93–96, accessed 24 January 2011. Available at: http://dx.doi.org/10.1080/14790720708668958.

Harper, G. (2010) *On Creative Writing*. Bristol: Multilingual Matters.

Houston, P. (2009) A conversation with Toni Morrison. *O, The Oprah Magazine*, accessed 3 March 2011. Available at: http://www.oprah.com/omagazine/Toni-Morrison-on-Writing/3.

Kaufman, S.B and Kaufman, J.C. (2009) (eds) *The Psychology of Creative Writing*. Cambridge: Cambridge University Press.

Kroll, J. (2004) The exegesis and the gentle reader/writer. *TEXT* Special Issue 3 (April), accessed 7 March 2011. Available at: http://www.textjournal.com.au/speciss/issue3/ kroll.htm.

Landry, C. (2000) *The Creative City*. London: Earthscan.

Meehan, M. (2010) Researcher of the month (April). *Research in the Faculty of Arts and Education*, Deakin University Australia, accessed 11 December 2010. Available at: http://www.deakin.edu.au/arts-ed/research/profile/mmeehan.php.

Merriam-Webster Online Dictionary (n.d.), accessed 12 December 2010. Available at: http://www.merriam-webster.com/dictionary/knowledge.

Moxley, J. (1989) Tearing down the walls: Engaging the imagination. In J. Moxley (ed.) *Creative Writing in America* (pp. 25–45). Urbana: NCTE.

Munro, A. (1982) How I write short stories. In D. Gioia and R.S. Gwynn (eds) (2006) *The Art of the Short Story* (pp. 661–662). New York: Pearson.

Nagel, S. (2000) (ed.) *Creativity: Being Usefully Innovative In Solving Diverse Problems. Hauppauge:* Nova Science Publishers.

Nelson, C. (2008) Research through practice: A reply to Paul Dawson. *TEXT* 12 (2), accessed 14 November 2010. Available at: http://www.textjournal.com.au/oct08/nelson.htm.

Nonaka, I. and Takeuchi, H. (1995) *The Knowledge-Creating Company*. Oxford: Oxford University Press.

Oxford English Dictionary Online (n.d.), accessed 8 April 2011. Available at: http://www.oed.com.

Pink, D. (2005) *A Whole New Mind*. New York: Riverhead Books.

Roe, S. (2010) Introducing masterclasses. In D. Donnelly (ed.) *Does the Writing Workshop Still Work?* (pp. 194–205). Bristol: Multilingual Matters.

Rorty, R. (1997) *Achieving Our Country*. Cambridge, MA: Harvard University Press.

Scrivener, S.A. (2009) The roles of art and design process and object in research. In N. Nimkulrat and T. O'Riley (eds) *Reflections and Connections. On the Relationship between Creative Production and Academic Research* (pp. 69–80). Helsinki: University of Art and Design Helsinki and authors, accessed 12 January 2011. Available at: https://www.taik.fi/kirjakauppa/images/f5d9977ee66504c66b7dedb259a45be1.pdf.

Tolstoy, L. (1897) The moral responsibilities of art (Trans. A. Maude). In D. Gioia and R.S. Gwynn (eds) (2006) *The Art of the Short Story* (pp. 797–798). New York: Pearson.

Webb, J. and Brien, D.L. (2006) Strategic directions for research in writing: A wish list. *TEXT* 10 (1), accessed 2 January 2011. Available at: http://www.textjournal.com.au/april06/webbbrien.htm.

Weiner, R. (2000) *Creativity & Beyond*. Albany: SUNY Press.

White, L. (1963) The act of invention. In C. Stover (ed.) *The Technological Order: Proceedings of the Encyclopedia Britannica Conference* (p. 273). Detroit: Wayne State University Press.

Part 2

.

8 Teaching Toward the Future
Stephanie Vanderslice

In today's collaborative digital world, there is no such thing as a passive user. Users can be, are virtually expected to be, creators of blogs, wikis, videos, games, web applications, interactive texts, e-books. The possibilities are endless and the boundaries have all but vanished. Still, if we cannot predict the ways in which technology will evolve, how can we teach our creative writing students with a nod toward the digital future? What skills should we teach writers to encourage them to meet the new challenges of making art in the 21st century? This chapter considers the ways in which digital competency, industry awareness and initiative, and resilience lead students to mapping their own career pathways in the face of inevitable changes.

> *We're living in the time of the most significant change in human expression in human history*
> Richard Miller (2008)

One thing that frustrated me as a creative writing graduate student in the early 1990s was that my teachers seemed to be preparing me more for the creative writing landscape *they* had graduated into rather than the one *I* would be graduating into. Certainly, they were strong teachers of the craft itself – although their learning objectives were fuzzy (this was the pre-assessment, pre-pedagogy era), they were accomplished writers who nonetheless knew good creative writing when they saw it and had some sense of how to lead their students in that direction. But the creative writing world they had entered was a pre-digital, pre-writing-program-flooded-writer-inundated terrain which was quite different from the one I was entering. I received very little if any advice about publishing my work, securing a teaching position or simply sustaining myself as an artist after I graduated. One of my professor's typed her letter of recommendation for me on a typewriter which must have had one of the oldest ribbons in history – so faded was the ink on the letter. Entering the professoriate myself four years later, I swore that I would work to prepare my creative writing students for the world *they* were entering; not the world I myself had entered less than a decade before. I strove to make visible the learning objectives for my courses and settled on a group of core 'concepts' in creative writing that I felt my students needed to learn, tweaking this list for each course and genre I taught, concepts that I believed would serve them well as creative artists outside my classroom (more about this later).

My intentions and my efforts were good and for the first several years this was enough. Then, all at once it seemed, the terrain shifted. The century began anew and with it emerged Web 2.0. I remember my confusion when I first began hearing the term: Web 2.0¿ What was Web 2.0¿

It was the game changer.

Suddenly, whereas teaching with technology had once been about content delivery (and, as such, relatively easy to keep up with) it was now about the student writer as the explorer *and* creator and how well she could write *and* how well she could navigate new media as a collaborative producer. Suddenly, in this collaborative digital world, there was no such thing as a passive user. Users could be, were virtually expected to be, creators of blogs, wikis, videos, games, web applications, interactive texts, e-books. The possibilities were endless and the boundaries had all but vanished. The publishing world struggled to evolve with the new normal as previous boundaries disappeared and I struggled with how to help my students find their footing when I could barely find my own. It was tempting to hide from this new technology.

The confusion I felt was profound; so profound I almost abandoned the idea of keeping up with changes in publishing and new media, falling prey to the very temptations I had so disliked in my professors. How could I possibly keep up with the steady flow of web applications available to my students (Prezi, YouTube, Gimp, Glogster, Wix, Nixty and the list goes on – and will probably be obsolete by the time this book is published) well enough to teach *them* how to use them¿ Meanwhile, new 'apps' kept streaming in, replacing the previous 'new thing', at an almost constant pace. I had enough trouble just keeping up with the sea changes in the industry that affected *me* as a writer.

My salvation first came in the form of a collection called *Teaching the New Writing: Technology, Change, and Assessment in the 21st Century* edited by Anne Herrington, Kevin Hodgson and Charles Moran. It is easy, Herrington *et al.* (2009: 200) point out, to be overwhelmed and negatively 'influenced by the vocabulary of catastrophic change where the archdeacon of Victor Hugo's Notre Dame de Paris is right in his assessment of the powers of a new technology: "ceci tuera cela" – this will kill that – the book will kill the cathedral, the computer will kill the book, television will kill film' and so on.

That has not exactly happened, however. The e-book exists alongside the hardcover. Herrington *et al.* remind us that 'The cathedral, the book, and film are all still alive and well. Technologies do not supersede one another but coexist, combine and overlap in ways that futurists can't predict' (p. 200). Still, if we cannot predict the ways in which technology will evolve how can we teach our students with a nod toward that future?

The short answer is: we can't. That is, according to Alanna Frost, Julie A. Myatt and Stephen Smith in 'Multiple modes of production in a college writing class' (2009: 183) in the above volume, we can't expect to 'learn all the software and applications prior to creating assignments that involve said mysterious tools'. Students often know this technology better than we do and what's more, most of it is relatively easy for them to learn, in part because they are 'digital natives', a term popularized by Marc Prensky to describe today's students, the first to have grown up surrounded by digital tools and toys, whereas we who teach them, are 'digital immigrants', (Prensky in DeVoss *et al.*, 2010: 26) who learned digital technologies in adulthood and 'retain certain "old world" ways of seeing and interacting with their current reality' (DeVoss *et al.*, 2010: 26). It is also relatively easy to learn because students have access to an abundance of tutorials to teach them (via such sites as instructables.com, YouTube, the application site itself and so on).

The long answer is: we shouldn't. We aren't teaching technology; we're teaching creative writing and composing. We must focus on the important aspects of craft that remain remarkably stable regardless of how they are delivered. However, our students, as writers in the digital landscape must be aware of the ways in which new media changes and of their need to learn it as they see fit and accommodate to it in whatever ways that benefit their work. We must teach them this awareness, an awareness of the digital environment they grew up in and to which they must continue to adapt as they forge their careers as writers. As artists, their responsibility for understanding the digital world and its impact on them and their audience must go beyond fluency with their smart phones.

We must also teach a greater awareness of the industry in which they will work. It is no longer tenable to graduate students from creative writing classes with the limited publishing experience I described from my own student days. Even as late as 2008 Nick Mamatas wrote in the AWP *Writer's Chronicle* that 'It's not unusual for a student to collect her MFA and after two years of intensive study have no idea how to even format a manuscript or where to submit it for publication'.

Given the sea changes in publishing, specifically the rise of collaborative new media, the e-book and publishing on demand, encouraging our students to hide from publishing realities is simply irresponsible. Do I think we should be teaching students to be slaves to the market – absolutely not.

It is a basic tenet of any course I teach that the act of writing and the business of writing must be completely separate. In fact, students are so used to me asking, whenever I bring up an industry-related question, 'Again, is this something we think about when we're composing?' – my subsequent pause is met with an enthusiastic 'No!' But students must nonetheless be taught that an *awareness* of that business is the responsibility of any artist. Fortunately, with the accessibility of information online, seeking that awareness is easier than ever before. Students need to have the initiative to seek it, however.

How does this new knowledge find expression in my classroom? What skills do I teach my students to encourage them to meet the new challenges of making art in the 21st century? Like most professors, I teach a wide variety of courses such as Introduction to Creative Writing, Forms of Writing for Children, Writing for Children Workshop, Teaching Creative Writing, The Creative Life and Into Print.[1] Introduction to Creative Writing is a concepts-based, multi-genre course centered on teaching students to understand a core group of concepts that are common to any genre of successful writing. Early on, I relied on my own list of concepts; however, when I discovered writer Heather Seller's concept-based multigenre text, *The Practice of Creative Writing*, I decided I preferred hers (which she calls 'strategies'). These strategies are Focus, Energy, Images, Tension, Pattern, Insight and Structure (divided into elements and forms). Sellers explores these concepts deeply in such a way that any student who gains mastery of them is also gaining mastery in the foundations of the craft regardless of genre.

Aside from Introduction to Creative Writing, however, which is a foundational course required of all of our majors and frequently taken by non-majors as well, the rest of my courses require that I teach a diversity of elements of craft: Forms of Writing for Children, for example, introduces writers to the multitude of (relatively strict) forms of that genre while the Workshop course looks closely at student work in a particular children's genre in ways that are informed by both the introductory course and the forms course (both of which are prerequisites). Teaching Creative Writing, The Creative Life and Into Print are necessarily even more distinct in the concepts that I teach. Nonetheless, all of the courses I teach, and those I plan to teach in the future share several common objectives, objectives to which I refer explicitly in each syllabus/course plan so that students will understand exactly the skills I intend to teach and expect them to learn. While they may in fact be skills, moreover, I think they are also habits of mind. These are digital competency, industry awareness and initiative, and resilience.

Digital Competency

How does one teach digital competency without turning the creative writing classroom into the technology classroom? Simply put, what I teach remains the same, that is, the *craft* of creative writing as it relates to the genre specifics of the course. However, I require that students deliver *at least* one course assignment via digital media, as illustrated from the section reprinted from my syllabus/course plan noted below (the same section appears in the plan for all my courses). In the past, *I* chose the new media I wanted students to use: assigning students in one class to keep a blog while asking those in another to create a digital story based on a text they have written. However, I have since decided that allowing the student to select the digital form that best suits the project gives them more choice.

Syllabus: Digital competencies

Because digital literacy is cross-curricular, digital competencies are the same for each of my classes. They are based on preparing you to live and work in the 21st century and taken from an article in Inside Higher Education (www.insidehighered. com) on skills every college graduate needs to master. While the content of your assignments will be centered on reaching the objectives of the individual class, the form one of these assignments will take will be based on the digital competency you feel is best suited for the content.
10 Digital Competencies for Every Graduate as guided by Joshua Kim (2010)
Graduates should be able to . . .

(1)   *Start a Blog*
(2)   *Buy an Audio Recorder and Learn to Use It*
(3)   *Start Editing Audio*
(4)   *Post an Interview (or Podcast) on Your Blog*
(5)   *Learn How to Shoot, Crop, Tone, and Optimize Photos (And Add Them to Your Blog)*
(6)   *Learn to Create Effective Voice-Over Presentations with Rapid Authoring Software*
(7)   *Tell a Good Story with Images and Sound*
(8)   *Learn to Shoot Video*
(9)   *Edit Your Video with iMovie, Windows Movie Maker or Windows Storyteller*
(10) *Publish Your Video on Your Blog*

Initially some students may balk a bit at the idea that they may have to teach themselves a new technology in order translate their creative work into it.[2] I explain it to them this way: at the rate that technology changes, those who are going to be the most successful in the 21st century will be those who can identify when a new technology might be useful to their work (either in creating, delivering or promoting it) and then take the initiative (a key word which will appear again soon) to teach it to themselves. While their formal schooling is finite, in the digital landscape where they will live and work for the rest of their lives, informal learning is both infinite and necessary.

Industry Awareness and Initiative

I should admit up front here that I currently teach more traditionally-aged undergraduate students than mature graduate students and I have learned though experience that a certain amount of initiative, as well as industry awareness, must be taught. It might be a generalization, but many members of the current millennial generation are also children of helicopter parents who have taken the lead in mapping out virtually every aspect of their children's lives, to the extent that the concept of initiative, of taking charge of one's own future, can sometimes seem a bit foreign to students. For a number of years, for example, students who wanted to attend graduate school for writing would simply appear in my office in the latter half of their senior year with the hopes that I would tell them exactly what to do. One student, in fact, expected me to research programs for her and tell her where to apply.

While the latter student was a relatively extreme case, it is easy to say that natural selection will take care of those students who lack the initiative to take charge of their own futures. However, given the influence their parents have exerted on their lives (as well as the fact that, in my case, many of them are first-generation college students), I began to realize that rather than expecting them to sink or swim I should at least explain that pursuing any art requires independence and initiative, especially in learning the industry, and then require some evidence of this learning in my courses. After that, as with most endeavors, the most motivated would continue to use what they had learned and the least motivated would fall off, typical of any natural selection process. But I felt it was my responsibility to give my students at least some sense of the publishing industry that surrounded them and the tools to understand it.

Industry knowledge is perhaps the least emphasized in my introductory multi-genre course. Naturally I want beginning writers to focus wholly on developing their burgeoning craft. Nonetheless, towards the end of the course I might discuss ways to become more aware of what it means to write and publish today, explaining the rudiments of how to send something out for publication, describing the industry journals that are important to read like the book reviews of major newspapers (*The New York Times* and *The Guardian* are my own favorites), *Poets and Writers* and the *AWP Writer's Chronicle* (fortunately, our department carries an institutional membership in AWP and receives 75 issues of the *Chronicle* when it comes out, so there are always plenty around for students who want to avail themselves), in addition to suggesting that they start subscribing to some print literary magazines and reading some online as well, if they are serious about developing as writers. But that is as far as any introduction to the publishing industry goes.

In upper level courses, however, the circumstances are completely different. After all, I explain to my students, there are so many resources available in the online realm to teach them about the publishing industry that there is no excuse for pleading ignorance – which doesn't serve any writer very well. Students in these courses are expected to read blogs and follow the tweets of writers, editors, agents and other publishing insiders and summarize what they are learning on a semi-monthly basis, sometimes on their own blog, sometimes in a simple typed response, but always in our class 'blogosphere' discussions. In a genre specific course, such as Forms of Writing for Children, I might assign a few of the more well known blogs, such as Editorial Anonymous, Blue Rose Girls and A Fuse 76 Production, to ensure that we start out on the same page in our discussions, but I also encourage them to go out and find a few more to follow that pertain to their specific interests. In my Teaching Creative Writing course, students might follow Cathy Day's The Big Thing or Tom Kealey's MFA Blog, while in a course like Into Print, they might follow The Best Damn Creative Writing Blog, Nathan Bransford or the Guide to Literary Agents. None of these is firmly set in stone; moreover, my students know that nothing pleases me more than when they bring in a Twitter feed, blog or website that they think is a 'must-follow'.

Resilience

> *Writing is a war of attrition. Don't attrish.*
> Fred Lebron (2010)

The word 'resilience' is frequently invoked in psychological or educational settings to describe people who succeed in the face of severely compromising odds. It is difficult to imagine a career with longer odds than one in the arts, but students who cultivate the skills I have described here, digital competency, industry awareness and initiative, and finally, resilience, certainly have an advantage.

Educational psychologists Robert C. Pianta and Daniel F. Walsh caution that teaching resilience does not involve teaching a specific set of skills to respond to each challenging situation but rather it involves teaching resiliency as a holistic habit of mind (1998: 416). Such a habit of mind is especially important for the writers I teach who are first generation college students for whom the bottom rung of the economic ladder is dangerously close. Anyone reading this essay knows what it's like to persist in the face of families and friends who want to know when they're going to get a 'real job'. For students like mine, the pressure can be even more intense. After working hard to enable their children to attend postsecondary education, many parents don't see a career in the arts as plausible, so they encourage their children to pursue more practical careers such as those in business and law. For example, one of my students, 'Anne', desperately wanted to major in writing but her parents would only pay for this degree if she then agreed to attend a two-year nursing program immediately after she graduated. Even parents who see the benefit of allowing their children to follow their passion may not realize that success in this field is usually a long-term process fraught with ups and downs.

In fact, most *students* don't understand the challenges of a career in writing, especially to the ego. Over the years I've observed that those who understand it the least are most likely to quickly give up in the face of those challenges. As a result I've realized that I have to teach a certain amount of resilience and persistence tempered with realistic expectations.

According to Carol Lloyd (1997), author of *Creating a Life Worth Living: A Practical Course in Career Design for Artists, Innovators and Others Aspiring to a Creative Life*, Americans especially tend to have an either/or view of a career in the arts, that is, *either* you reap the rewards of Jodi Picoult or Stephen King *or* you will be flipping burgers – unless you finally take Dad's advice and go to law school. My job, as I see it, is to teach my students that there are, in fact, a lot of opportunities *along* the artistic spectrum to sustain themselves in creative lives whether they snag that 'big publishing deal' or not. In fact, in many of my upper division courses, I often bring in past students who have pursued creative paths and are on their way to success so that they can see what such success looks like: pursuing unpaid and paid internships, waiting tables in order to work on a local production that ends up premiering at Sundance, founding a new literary magazine. I also lead students in mapping their own paths, asking them to describe what their pursuit of their art in the next five, 10 or 15 years might look like and how they intend to make this possible, especially in the face of inevitable challenges.

Finally, taking a cue from Fred LeBron and from what I know about my own writing life and that of friends, colleagues and mentors, I relentlessly tell them not to give up. For a time I used to print the words, 'Never give up' along with my email address on slips of paper and hand them out at the end of the semester. Once I found an online source of cheap business cards (www.vistaprint.com, for those who aren't already familiar) I had 1000 printed up with those words, my email and a graphic of Abraham Lincoln – a well-known failure until his first presidential win – in the corner. They fit well in most wallets.

Who knows what will come of this practice, but it is part of my desire to give my students the best tools I can for the world that faces them today and that waits for them in the future. And I am still learning. After all, I still have about 900 cards and over 20 years of teaching left.

Notes

(1) Dianne Donnelly tells me that at the University of South Florida, students remediate a text by changing its method of delivery into another form (i.e. multimedia, graphic arts, song, performance) to see how the new space is negotiated and how the context/language/images and such may change in unexpected ways.

(2) I owe a debt to Mimi Thebo and Steve May at Bath Spa University for introducing me to the last two courses.

References

DeVoss, D.N., Eidman-Aadahl, E. and Hicks, T. (2010) *Because Digital Writing Matters: Improving Student Writing in Online and Multimedia Environments*. San Francisco: Jossey-Bass.

Frost, A., Myatt, J.A. and Smith, S. (2009) Multiple modes of production in a college writing class. In A. Herrington, K. Hodgson and C. Moran (eds) *Teaching the New Writing: Technology, Change and Assessment in the 21st Century Writing Classroom* (pp. 181–197). New York: Teacher's College Press.

Herrington, A., Hodgson, K. and Moran, C. (2009) (eds) *Teaching the New Writing: Technology, Change and Assessment in the 21st Century Writing Classroom*. New York: Teacher's College Press.

Kim, J. (2010) '10 digital competencies for every graduate', *Inside Higher Ed*, 16 March, accessed 31 August 2012. Available at: http://www.insidehighered.com/blogs/technology_and_learning/10_competencies_for_every_graduate.

Lebron, F. (2010) MFA Programs Panel. Association of Writers and Writing Programs Annual Conference. April 7–10, 2010, Denver, CO, USA.

Lloyd, C. (1997) *Creating a Life Worth Living: A Practical Course in Career Design for Artists, Innovators and Others Aspiring to a Creative Life*. New York: HarperPerrenial.

Mamatas, N. (2008) Pulp faction: Teaching 'genre fiction' in the Academy. *The Writer's Chronicle*, October/November, 2008.

Miller, R. (2008) The future is now: Presentation to the Rutgers board of governors (video), accessed 31 August 2012. Available at: http://www.youtube.com/watch?v=z65V2yKOXxM (statement at 1:45).

Pianta, R.C. and Walsh, D.F. (1998) Applying the construct of resilience in schools: Cautions from a developmental systems perspective. *School Psychology Review* 27:3, 407–417.

9 Holding On and Letting Go

Indigo Perry

The ways we teach creative writing and the environments and spaces we make available for the teaching and learning of creative writing at universities may well be ripe for change. In university creative writing courses, what we have been teaching all along is the art of balancing a delicately intuitive and entwined process of holding on and letting go that is the fusion of theory and practice. The future for teaching and learning creative writing, however, will be more about space and spaciousness for the dynamic energy of creativity, the dynamic energy of practice. This chapter contextualizes the history of creative writing in Australia and positions the future possibilities and opportunities for the discipline.

Part 1: Holding On and Letting Go

In university creative writing courses, what we have been teaching all along is the art of balancing a delicately intuitive and entwined process of holding on and letting go.

At a simple level, the *holding on* is about the theory of practicing creative writing, which might include technique, style, genre, form, perhaps some analysis of published literary texts, maybe studying the theories of creative practice itself in addition to further literary and cultural academic theory. At a similar level, *letting go* is about practicing – walking the talk – creative writing. Essentially the entwined process approach is not likely to change much in the future, nor has it ever changed much in the history of university teaching of creative writing. It is, after all, how the process of creating writing *works*, within or without a university setting: there is always that intertwining of theory and practice, how-to-do and doing. How the process is arranged, varied, added to and subtracted from, is what differs, and that is not just dependent on the individual artist, institution or location: it also depends on the specific moment of process; the individual artwork in progress. Australian novelist Peter Carey once commented that whenever he begins writing a new novel, he must learn to write all over again. And this is, after all, what we all do as writers. We learn as we create. There is a scene in *Hilary and Jackie*, the 1998 film based on the life of world-renowned cellist

Jacqueline Du Pre, in which the child Jackie, frustrated and clumsy in her struggle to learn the fingering of notes for the instrument, finally 'gets it' and begins to play with joy and abandon. She moves from a dogged, painful *holding on* to the technical foundation learning to *letting go* and actually creating the music almost as though she has known the technique all along or is inventing it as music itself. I see this is an apt and beautiful illustration of how the entwined process we practice in creative writing, or indeed any discipline of the creative arts, and perhaps even any skilful practice in our lives: we need to know how to do it – we need to equip ourselves with particular skills, particular basic knowledge – yet it's almost as though we can't do it until we forget *how* to do it and simply do it.

The ways we teach creative writing and the environments and spaces we make available for the teaching and learning of creative writing at universities may well be ripe for change. And I see the way of the future for teaching and learning creative writing as being about space and spacious-ness: around aspects of academic discipline; creative arts disciplines and practices; and – particularly within our creative writing course design, teach-ing and assessment – around genre and form. This concerns the recognition of what we already know: that most boundaries are illusory and that we do well to consider allowing more spaciousness around thinking about teacher/student, professional/amateur and producer/consumer binaries. This in turn leads to thinking and imagining, dreaming, perhaps, of the possibilities for spaces, environments, habitats for the teaching and learning of creative writing in the university. What do these look like now? What may they look like in the future? And out of all this, what future possibilities are there for research practices in creative writing, and how may we nurture those in the way we design courses and environments for creative writing in the university?

First, I will outline a brief historical perspective of creative writing university courses in Australia. In Australia, creative writing courses at universities burgeoned in the 1990s, following 1980s amalgamations of universities with the former technical institutions known as colleges of advanced education; this was part of what was known as the Dawkins reforms. Prior to those developments in the tertiary sector, creative writing was taught in two main ways that were not always or necessarily mutually exclusive. In the first way, universities usually incorporated creative writing tuition into generalist English units and/or majors. It was rare for creative writing to be offered as a specialist subject in its own right at those universi-ties before the amalgamations. The studies of the practice of creative writing within English subjects were mixed with the study of and analysis of literary texts and there was little focus on writing as a vocation or profes-sion, and limited links to or engagement with industry such as professional writers outside the academy, publishers and/or professional organisations such as writers' fellowships or centres. In the second way of teaching creative writing, colleges of advanced education were generally strongly focused on the technical aspects of creative writing and the related areas of editing and publishing. Courses included little focus on the critical analysis of literary texts, but instead concentrated on the practice of writing. These courses usually maintained strong links with industry and had a distinctly vocational or professional bent. Before the amalgamations, the two different types of creative writing courses offered in the different types of institutions had few connections or interactions with one another, at least not formally.

The amalgamations brought about considerable changes to the tertiary offerings of creative writing in some institutions. At first, particularly throughout the 1990s, the changes were present and meaningful for a limited number of institutions, as I will discuss further shortly, but as the demand for creative writing courses grew steadily, these changes began to affect most universities in the country, and provided a colourful if not somewhat foreboding foundation for what has come to be in today's university creative writing courses and what those may look like now and in the future.

When the amalgamations took place, only a small number of universities came to be offering specialised creative writing courses with majors in creative writing as opposed to those that offered only units or subjects in creative writing or perhaps modules or components in creative writing studies within more generalised majors such as English. The few universities that did begin to offer specialised creative writing studies following amalgamations with colleges of advanced education that had existing creative writing courses were perhaps the ones that set up future situations, challenges, conundrums, opportunities.

In those institutions, the strong emphasis on practice and on vocational and/or professional links seemed to be maintained. At the same time, the existence of complementary disciplines such as English and Literary Studies provided opportunities for students in the creative writing courses to incorporate more study of critical analysis of literary works into their degrees. This appeared, and perhaps still appears, a healthy situation for the writing courses and their students: the prior scenario of university creative writing courses having heavy emphasis on study of literary texts and less on writing practice and industry engagement, and the CAE courses having the opposite scenario seemed set to become more balanced. In some cases this may have worked perfectly, but in others a great deal of clashing of ideologies took place, and quite often through that first decade, creative writing and English or Literary Studies courses and pedagogies frequently smashed up against one another. Of course volatility may be a good thing for a university discipline and perhaps especially for those disciplines involving the making of creative artworks.

I was a student in such a course, beginning my undergraduate studies with a Bachelor of Arts with majors in Professional Writing and Literature, in 1991, at Deakin University in Melbourne, Australia. I continued my studies over the next eight years, eventually completing a PhD in 2001 at the same university, where I am now employed as a Senior Lecturer in a different iteration of the same course in which I enrolled back in 1991. If I think of that course that I studied when in my early twenties as an ocean, then it is the same ocean yet always changing water, currents, levels, temperatures, boundaries, colours and textures, and so also a completely different ocean to the one in which I am now a teacher aged in my early forties. In preparation for projecting into future possible understandings of what we may do in the academy, it is useful to reflect briefly on the past and how it is that we have come to where we are now.

Obviously the ways of teaching creative writing, at universities, or elsewhere, have always been varied and often as quirky and eclectic as those who teach and study the discipline. But there are trends, and in the early 90s, in the few Australian university courses with specialist majors in creative writing, workshopping was very popular. While the structure and design of workshops also varied considerably, most basically consisted of drafts of student creative writing being copied and distributed to all students in the class and to the tutor, and those drafts being read by all workshop participants either prior to the workshop or in dedicated reading time in the workshop, and the draft then being discussed and critiqued in the workshop by all participants, with the intention of helping the draft's author to improve the draft's worth as a piece of creative writing. (Although subsequent publication of the draft (in a professional site such as a literary journal) was not a required outcome for a course assignment, there was usually an implied intention for the work to reach a standard suitable for publication in such a site, and this is used as a kind of benchmark for standards of work both in workshop discussions and later at the assessment stage of the work.) Following the workshop, the draft's author would take away the draft and revise it, perhaps over a period of several weeks, possibly taking on suggestions made in the workshop, although this was never mandatory. The workshop as described just now formed a spine for most offerings in creative writing courses at the time. The workshops were complemented by a limited amount of theory and teaching that related mostly to the techniques of specific genres of creative writing, but it couldn't be said to be limited to technique. Indeed it's difficult to imagine how a discussion of creative writing techniques could not branch out to encompass content, ideas, imagination, maybe in a similar way that the study of music notes and chords could not be taught without the sound of the music and the meaning and purpose and potential of music infusing the study. We were directed to read and/or watch examples of great creative writing, and often we read and watched them together and discussed them in terms of technique, ideas, effect and affect, significance, imagination, possibility. At times, especially in the early weeks of a subject's duration, theory-teaching was presented in lectures or strongly teacher-led tutorials. But the teaching of creative writing theory – the theory of practice – essentially also took place in less formal ways throughout the courses, and often these ways appeared more vibrant. As we workshopped one another's drafts, for instance, we would learn much about the workings of techniques such as point-of-view, voice, character, dialogue, structure, by a kind of osmosis by feeling our way through rough, raw drafts of writing, sensing and experimenting for ourselves what made a piece of writing work and what seemed to break it, disable it. The teacher, too, had lively ways to teach theory in the workshops, using the student work in question to explain and illustrate aspects of the workings of language: the languages of creative writing. There was a sense, maybe not so prevalent in lectures or semi-formal, teacher-led tutorials, that the teacher too was learning and exploring; in a sense we were all inventing and dreaming up the 'rules' of creative technique in the moment – or probably we were discovering that there were no rules, but only possibilities and opportunities.

The classes were smaller then than they are likely to be now, 20-odd years later. The teachers were employed full-time and they generally taught all students enrolled in the subjects co-ordinated by each teacher, rather than being supported by sessional staff as most full-time university lecturers are now in 2011. Class hours were generous: for each third-year subject, for instance, a weekly three-hour tutorial was held. This meant that we had the luxury of time to participate in an intensive style of workshop. Fewer students allowed for only two drafts to be discussed in each of those three-hour sessions. And we even had time to read the drafts while sitting in class.

There was a very strong emphasis on genre and form. Subjects were clearly sliced up: Fiction, Creative Non-Fiction, Scriptwriting, Poetry, Editing. Even in other then-contemporary courses that did not offer separate subjects or units for each of these genres/forms, there was nevertheless a clear delineation between them, and crossing the boundaries of those was rarely actively encouraged or recognised. Likewise, exploration into other genres or forms other than these was rarely seen in the courses: song lyrics, comics, graffiti, texts in paintings, improvised spoken word, writing in public art. They were not mentioned in class, and would not have met assignment guidelines if any students had wished to create those forms.

What did I learn from the course, as a writer? It is hard to separate the learning done in the course itself from that done in my own continuing writing practice and in my other life experiences outside the course. But I believe I benefited most from the learning that took place somewhere between teachers (who were also practicing writers), class and myself; i.e. in that space and process described earlier where we discovered and created possibilities for writing by working on raw drafts in the workshop always augmented, perhaps fed; nourished; by the focus on great classic and contemporary works of literature, and the outlined theory of practice imparted at various moments of the course. Further, I was immersed in a world of writing, meeting and talking with writers both professional and experienced and new and emerging. I learned about the profession of writing, about publishing and the ways writing was measured, esteemed and recognised, such as through awards and fellowships. I also began to see the potential value of being part of a community of writers, even if just for a time. Yes, during my studies, I learned a lot about the more formal aspects of the theory of the practice of writing. But this was not what was of most direct significance or use to me. Neither was my learning and continuing to learn through my own extensive reading (and watching, listening, etc.) and even more so, through my own writing practice. No, what was of greatest value to me as a writer was learning about and experiencing spaces for exploration and discovery of practicing creative writing, and of having the opportunity to engage in the communities of creative writing, both at the personal level in meeting and working with other writers, and at a professional level in gaining understanding of how writing interlinked with publishing and the more general community and world.

And now, as a teacher of writing, my previous studies have brought me very similar things. The value of explorative and experiential space for creative writing practice and the opportunity for creating and/or engaging with communities as a writer tend to most effectively and usefully drive my creative writing teaching, and it is these that inform my concepts; my envisaging of what we might be teaching now in creative writing and what the future may hold for that teaching. Out of those aspects, I also suggest a moving away from the past, and this relates particularly to genre and form in creative writing, and how these have so often directed the structure and teaching of creative writing courses in Australian universities.

Part Two: Space and Spaciousness

Australian writer and creative writing academic Jeri Kroll has written a fascinating article on exploration and imagining across genre and form, in which she observes:

> Certainly the disciplines of creative and professional writing interpenetrate. Take a topic called creative nonfiction or simply nonfiction, which could easily be taught as part of either writing program. The teachers and students involved have multiple identities that might merge at points; they might be undergraduates, postgraduates, journalists, essayists, memoirists, novelists, poets and, more recently, bloggers, a group who are the fastest growing population of aspiring authors ... (Kroll, 2010, n.p.)

Here, Kroll is identifying the artificiality of generic boundaries, yet, strangely, in most Australian university creative writing courses we cling on to those boundaries in our course design, teaching and assessment. Also, in referring to bloggers, Kroll invites in – or acknowledges perhaps that it has already well and truly let itself in (to the academy) – the notion that beyond the university course structures, writers are already creating and recreating notions of genre and form, although the courses seem slow to adjust themselves to these developments. In predominantly theory courses such as Literary Studies, burgeoning genres, sub-genres, forms, sub-forms may be mentioned, but it's rare for them to be accommodated in any way that could be called whole-hearted in the teaching of creative writing – however, they are quite likely to turn up in the work of advanced students completing work for PhD programs.

In fact, the issue of creative practitioners working outside, over, between traditional boundaries of genre and form, and institutions not developing fast enough to encompass that work effectively, is examined in an article by Marcus Westbury about arts funding in Australia. Westbury writes:

> Australia is blessed with an abundance of talented and enthusiastic young writers, video artists, performers, media makers, musicians, designers, publishers, painters, sculptors, poets, cartoonists, animators, dancers, photographers, illustrators, creators, curators and catalysts. A small number of them work within our well-funded arts institutions. The majority do not. Most operate and create in ways and at scales that are very different from the ones that our arts agencies were designed for. (Westbury, 2009: 36)

And:

> Australia's funding agencies are divided between, or internally organised around, archaic art-form definitions. True innovation often takes place outside and between categories and happens quickly while funding bodies respond slowly. (Westbury, 2009: 37)

Very similar observations can be made for the organisation and practices of university courses in the creative arts, including creative writing. Many more genres and sub-genres exist in addition to Fiction, Creative Non-Fiction, Scriptwriting and Poetry. Places to publish or otherwise expose creative writing work are countless, and range way beyond journals, books, scripts, websites. We can be less rigid about the structuring and assessment of our creative writing courses and make considerably more room for choice and fragmentation – for ideas driven by students. It is time to move away from teaching writing primarily by segregated genre and form, and to allow in the space for greater possibility and opportunity. But what is it that is happening now? What appearance does the teaching according to genre or form have?

Considering what has changed in the nature of Australian university creative writing courses in the past 20 years, and how one might look at the future of the teaching of those courses, the word fragmentation comes to mind.

Now, many, many more creative writing courses are offered, and many more students are enrolled in those courses. In the university where I now work, we often hear from current, graduating and prospective creative writing students of the course that they desire greater choice: choice in the subjects they study and when they study them, and choice in complementary majors and sub-majors and electives. But, like most other creative writing courses, Deakin University courses still offer specific, quite segregated genres of writing in separate units or subjects. As in all earlier iterations of the undergraduate degree course, the genres and forms of Fiction, Creative Non-Fiction, Scriptwriting, Poetry and Editing are offered.

In terms of what is taught and how, very little appears changed from 20 years ago.

Some current Australian courses centre almost entirely on the idea that teaching a creative writing student to read well will encourage them to write well. Such a course or subject would consist of reading and discussing works of literature, and doing no or little creative writing practice in class, and would include no workshopping of student writing drafts. In terms of assessment, students would submit manuscripts of creative writing, perhaps accompanied by a theory assessment item such as a critical or analytical essay. For the creative assessment item, there would be an assumption that technique and style are absorbed mostly through analysis of published literary works and not through specific tuition in those aspects of writing practice.

Then there is the type of course driven strongly by the teaching of writing technique and style, usually divided into such generic subjects as those mentioned above (Fiction, etc.). This course might be heavy with lectures, complemented with a small amount of student writing exercises in tutorials or in set homework exercises. Assessment would usually be carried out in the form of creative works, most often workshopped at first draft stage and then revised prior to submission for assessment.

There is the currently very popular approach of workshop classes in which predominantly student-led workshops take place. Here, students and tutors give verbal and/or written feedback on works in progress, on drafts of student writing. The student is then given the opportunity to revise the draft before submission for assessment. Mostly, this type of workshop set-up will involve the students and tutor reading a first draft of a student-authored manuscript prior to the allocated workshop class. One, or more often, two or more, drafts are workshopped in a single workshop class session. There are variations on how discussion of each draft will unfold, but perhaps the most common scenario involves the author being asked to listen without verbally contributing to the discussion for a set period of time, so that fellow students can make suggestions and constructive criticism. The tutor may sometimes participate during this period, but often it's preferable and practical for the tutor too to remain silent as the students discuss the work, to avoid directing the discussion too much. The tutor may however interject a comment if the discussion gets off-track or stuck. Then, at the end of that set period of student discussion, in which all students in the class apart from the draft's author are expected to contribute, the tutor will make their suggestions and criticisms on the work. After that, the draft's author is invited to speak, and will usually thank the contributors to the workshop, perhaps ask a few questions, respond to queries that came up during the discussion, mention any issues of concern with the draft that were not canvassed during the discussion, and maybe outline plans for the revision of the draft. The workshop ends after that point, and the student will usually be given written comments by the tutor and perhaps by the other students, for use in the revisions that will take place before the rewritten draft is submitted for assessment at a later date.

Another type of workshop is the one that I call the hands-on workshop. This, I liken to workshop sessions that may take place in tactile and performing arts discipline courses, in which the students actively carry out practice of their art form in the space of the classroom or studio. Painters paint in such a session; dancers dance; writers write. In such a creative writing workshop, students will usually work on writing exercises on topics set by the tutor, perhaps relating to particular topics of discussion that have taken place in earlier classes, or to readings completed in readiness for the class, or maybe they will be related to a particular style or technique of writing on which the class has been recently focused. The students write for set periods of time, after which they are usually asked to verbally share their writing experience, whether that be through reading out what they have written, or talking about what they achieved during the period of writing, or both.

Yet another possible form of writing workshop occurs to me now, although it's not one I've often seen carried out in university creative writing courses, and that would be a kind of freeform hands-on workshop, whereby students are allocated time and space to simply come and write, free of instruction or set exercises or tasks. The students would then verbally share aspects of the writing experience at the end of the session.

But in most courses, whatever approach is taken to teaching and learning, it's usual that at least after the first, foundational year, the studies are divided into genre, mostly encompassing the very conservative array of choices already mentioned. But this limited array of thinking about, and thus offering, genre no longer seems particularly applicable and desirable now. The expansion of that array could lead into ideas for what we might be teaching instead or in addition.

We could focus our courses, now and into the future, on creative writing without the slicing up into genre and form that now seems *de rigeur* for most of those courses. Why not teach creative writing courses that whole-heartedly encompass the freedom of questioning boundaries. Students could certainly be taught about different genres and forms, and may practice writing in each of them. But we could also make room for those students to experience the *letting go* that comes with writing what they will. If it looks like poetry mixed with memoir with a bit of street art thrown in, well and good. If it's a film script that is designed to be cast – as-is, in the form of script rather than film – onto a wall in a gallery, then so be it. If it is fiction but it also seems to be a moment of improvised dance, then let it be. If it's an essay that is also a sestina, terrific. And if it's a short story that seems to be a short story, that's perfect too.

As far as space, environment, habitat for such courses, I suggest a studio-like space with a lot of emphasis on writing practice and on the sharing of what emerges in that practice. So, workshopping continues, in some of the forms I have described above: students and tutor commenting on drafts of creative writing; students carrying out writing practice in class, and sharing the experience verbally with the rest of the class. There could be some formal sessions, probably best placed early in the course's duration, in which aspects of theory, *holding on*, are taught.

In regards to assessment, at the moment most of us talk of the implied quality benchmark of publication-standard work as being what we expect from students in our courses. But this can become problematic when we question those binaries mentioned earlier, particularly the producer/ consumer binary. If the student's writing is to be self-published on the web, or perhaps form part of a piece of street art, or a zine, or a painting, then that benchmark is not necessarily appropriate. And we can continue to enforce particular paradigms such as literary-journal-standard of writing (assuming even that can be seen as stable and recognisable), but then it seems we are buying into a similar situation to the one Westbury describes: the bureaucratic institution lags significantly behind developments in the wider creative community and risks shutting out development and innovation; ideas; energy and excitement. At the same time, if we drop all benchmarks of quality, then I wonder if we are serving the students effectively: surely nobody wants to study a course that does not value excellence in some way. But writing that is excellent – that is powerful, effective, affective can take on many different shapes and myriad appearances. Sometimes it will be in the guise of perfectly parsed and punctuated elegance. Sometimes it will be in the punchy dialectical grunge of, say, Irvine Welsh. And so on. And that is not even beginning to take account of writing that veers wildly across discipline and mode: Paul Carter's sparse poetic fragments carved into stone on the floor of Melbourne's Federation Square district, for example; or a single word of writing scrawled across a painting, or a blog of scathing political satire in hypertext. But although these examples give some hint of the variety of assessment situations, we may encounter now and in the future, as teachers of creative writing, there may be creative ways to address the variety; the spaciousness.

Whatever the form or genre, whatever the site of publication/performance/exhibition/ exposure of the piece of writing, there will be some implied expectation of good quality, even if that benchmark may at first instance seem an example of anti-quality by some standards. But that anti-quality will have its own integrity, its own set of expectations. A particular writer may not care, for example, for perfect grammar, or discernible narrative arcs, or for the beauty of a subtle metaphor, but they will care about some aspect of what the work achieves; what it is or what it does; or perhaps the writer will have antithetical purposes that are just as valid. And so, part of the work for that writer/student in the university course may be to suggest those benchmarks for quality assessment. Quite recently, in readiness for the development of a research quality framework in the Australian higher research sector, many creative arts, and indeed creative writing, academics were asked to create quality assessment benchmarks for their disciplines of practice. We drafted discipline-specific criteria, which will hopefully allow our creative practice to be recognised appropriately in terms of research measurement now and into the future. But in our courses, too, if we are to encompass many more genres and forms than those we have recognised before, then we need ways and means to assess them on their own terms, and yet still maintain the integrity by ensuring the merit and significance of the work, and I suggest that we ask the writers/students/producers themselves to help with that task. And one way that this represents great opportunity for learning and achievement on the student's part is by linking in with the discourses of *practice-led research*: that is, research that is carried out in the process of producing the creative work itself. And this leads to how we might better establish pathways for research that develop quite organically out of coursework itself – and out of the creative environments that ideally we will set up for our university courses of now and into the future.

It could be argued that a strong focus on practice might include some theory on practice-led research: should this be incorporated from the early years of the courses, or presented later, say, at honours level as part of providing a research pathway? I envisage it as being part of the coursework from an early level, such as at first-year, so that students are aware that what they do when they practice creative writing may have intellectual merit in and of itself: that process itself, production itself, has knowledge discovery inherent in it. It could be argued that students need be taught no theory at all apart from the technical aspects of writing, but then it could be asked why the student is at the university: the technical aspects can be learned at a technical, non-university institution, for instance. But a university course might allow far greater intellectual engagement. Also, by studying at the university, the potential for continued study in the form of higher research degrees is available, and a student wishing to follow a research pathway, which among other things offers opportunity for advanced, applied creative practice work to be completed, will find it difficult if they have no grounding at all in academic theory discourses. However, if a course offers no teaching in the discourses of practice-led research, but there are studies, either within the offerings of the creative writing course itself or perhaps within complementary studies in, say, English or Literary Studies, then it's likely that most of the focus will be on the analysis, criticism and theory of published or otherwise produced literary works. That is, the study of literary artefacts. At the time of writing at least there is little to no encompassing of practice-led research theory into most English or Literary Studies courses. Therefore, if this approach is taken, the student will still have little formal tuition in the theories of practice by the time they complete the undergraduate degree, even though they will have just completed a course in the practice of creative writing. This sets up an odd scenario, in which a great deal of the student's years of study will have been devoted to learning the practice of creative writing, but other than learning practical skills and the practical application of techniques of creative writing, the student may not actually be aware of the depth of what they have learned *in process* of making their works of creative writing. For a student not wishing to follow a research pathway, it could be said that it doesn't matter. So what? The student knows how to write a poem; why do they need to know what they have discovered, learned, revealed in the making process and how they might articulate that? But I ask again why study in a university course if one doesn't want advanced intellectual engagement? It seems logical that if one spends a lot of time doing a particular thing (practicing creative writing) during university studies, that it is desirable to have an understanding and comprehension of what one is doing and what its possible outcomes may be, other than or as well as the artefact itself. And if the student does choose to follow a research pathway, and intends to complete creative writing as a component of that, as is common in creative writing higher degrees now, then they will have a foundation in understanding what they are doing when they practice their art form and how that artistic process may link in with wider discourses in the world. It is my suggestion, then, that we do teach our students to appreciate what they do in their creative writing practice, from the early stages of study.

I believe that what we will be teaching into the future of university creative courses will involve allowing more space and spaciousness for the dynamic energy of creativity – the dynamic energy of practice. We will continue to support that delicate entwining of holding on and letting go that is the fusion of theory and practice, but greater emphasis will continue to fall upon understanding what happens when we practice creative writing.

References

Kroll, J. (2010) Living on the edge: Creative writers in higher education. *TEXT* 14 (1) (April).

Westbury, M. (2009) Evolution and creation: Australia's funding bodies. *Meanjin* 68 (2).

10 Programme Design and the Making of Successful Programmes

Nigel McLoughlin and Patrick Bizzaro

Building a Better Elephant Machine: A Case Study in Creative Writing Programme Design

Nigel McLoughlin

The first part of the chapter that follows examines pedagogical issues and concerns related to creative writing programme development using a case study of the development of the creative writing degrees at undergraduate and postgraduate levels at the University of Gloucestershire, UK. It also considers what indices might be used in order to measure successful programme design, and examines how the programme design addressed issues of pedagogy, assessment and development of apprentice writers. The chapter also explores the nature of knowledge in the discipline, how that knowledge is manifest and how it might be most efficiently and effectively delivered within structural and resource-based constraints.

When seeking to address what makes a successful programme design, there is a danger of slipping into legislative mode and pontificating about what 'should' be considered in making new programmes. I prefer to offer instead a case study of what may be considered a successful programme design and explain why it emerged the way that it did, what factors were considered in its development and what that design offered that other models did not. This is preferable because it offers the reader an exemplar of one type of successful programme design, and can examine the philosophies and reasons behind the design, while also recognising that others may choose to do things differently.

Defining Success

Successful programmes at both graduate and undergraduate levels may be defined in many ways depending on who defines what success is. One benchmark is that students who complete the course go on to be published writers. Unfortunately, this is not possible for all students, and publication success is often more related to marketability of the work rather than to the quality of the work. For example it may prove much more difficult for an experimental novelist to publish than one who writes more mainstream texts. Some students publish the year after they graduate; others 20 years after. Given the fact that graduates tend to take several years to publish and begin to establish significant reputations as writers, and given that the number of these graduates will be added to year on year, this means that longer established programmes are more likely to demonstrate success by that criteria than new programmes which have only had a few such graduates in the years they have been running.

Success may be defined by recruitment or competition for entry. But recruitment and level of competition for entry may be affected by economic factors, marketing budgets and geographical location. Yet another definition might be related to economic success. However, the most cost-effective delivery may not be ideal for the student experience. Student satisfaction may be used as a measure, but this has the drawback that one might wonder what the students are comparing their experience against. One might use external comment, which has the advantage that the external advisor or examiner is able to compare across the sector in terms of what is innovative and the standard of the work produced, but it should also be recognised that the external may have been approached to be an advisor or an examiner because their philosophy was a good fit to the programme's ethos, or because they currently run or have previously run programmes which had a similar pedagogical basis.

While recognising the problems with the various criteria for success outlined above, I believe it is possible to achieve triangulation and define success in terms of a combination of the following key demonstrable factors: firstly, a successful programme regularly produces graduates who are writing to a standard that one might expect to see in good journals and at the higher levels of achievement, they may be expected to produce work which is publishable in book form. The students will possess the skills and knowledge to market themselves as writers and to operate effectively within the writing industry and the creative industries more broadly.

Secondly, I believe successful programmes are built on a framework which recognises and teaches the broad base of knowledge inherent in the study of creative writing and that there is coverage of domain relevant skills, creativity relevant skills and transferrable skills, and a recognition that motivational factors are important in creativity and in the pedagogy of creative subjects (Amabile, 1996). This knowledge includes critical reflective knowledge of the apprentice writer's own poetics and writing practices as well as craft-based and technical knowledge inherent in making verbal art.

Thirdly, the students should be engaged and motivated by what they are taught and how they are taught. However, one cannot shirk teaching difficult (and thus sometimes unpopular) material. Key also is the opportunity for students to be able either to specialise, or remain more generalist in their approach to writing, and to experiment with mixing genre, while being asked to engage with a varied and balanced diet of assessment. Fourthly, I believe successful programmes offer opportunities for the student to become a part of a community of writers as well as a community of learners. Lastly, I think a successful programme should be cost-effective without compromising standards. This involves working smarter rather than harder using large and small group methods appropriately and in a balanced way. This is likely to be a key driver in future, given the competitive market on fees, teaching quality and contact time.

The programme at the University of Gloucestershire has been in operation for six years now, and has produced several writers who are published or who have had work accepted for publication in book form. Others have published work in literary journals of national importance and several have been shortlisted for or won prestigious competitions. The programme has garnered external praise for its innovative design from all four of its current and previous external examiners on the BA and MA degrees and from those writers and academics consulted during the development process. This has been echoed by a number of colleagues informally when they hear about the programme structure and what we teach. It is run quite cost effectively through using a balance of large and small group teaching methodologies. It recruits well and our student evaluations and National Student Survey results year on year indicate that the students are motivated and challenged by the programme and are generally happy. So if a combination of all of the above indicators can be used as a measure of success, then it is a successful programme.

Starting Out

The Creative Writing programme at the University of Gloucestershire consists of the undergraduate Single Honours and Joint degrees in Creative

Writing and the taught Master's degree in Creative and Critical Writing. There is also a research MA and a PhD programme available. When I set out to design the programme, I began with two questions: what do writers need to learn? And how should they be taught? These two questions led to a third: how does one integrate these elements across a programme in such a way as to create progression for the student? This questioning approach to what we teach and how we teach proved to be a good strategy for the development of the programme because it allowed us to look at what we do from a student's perspective and ask, what is it they need to learn and how do they learn? It was a useful exercise for me as a teacher too, to interrogate everything and not to accept that just because something was traditionally part of the diet of creative writing pedagogy that it was necessarily entirely right. The approach was used to interrogate what the workshop's function was, since that was the default mode of teaching at the time. It was also used to think about what possibilities there were for large group teaching and even to look at the possibility of examinations.

One thing was clear from the start: as a team we wanted this degree to be 'writerly'. We wanted a craft-focused, student-centred and critical curriculum that focused on making writing and on reading as a writer. Above all we wanted to provide the skills and knowledge that would help young writers develop, but would also allow them to self-actualise as creative individuals and writers within a community of such individuals (Maslow, 1954; Rogers, 1961). Furthermore, we wanted to give students the opportunity to develop other transferable skills which they could use to earn money while they wrote. There were already several modules in the undergraduate subject area, which had recently emerged from English Studies, but they were not yet structured into a coherent programme. There were gaps in the provision with regard to the major genres. Neither were there enough modules to make a Single Honours degree in Creative Writing. We had a playwright, a poet and a prose writer on the full-time staff, and some part-time staff who could teach prose and poetry, so it was clear that we had the expertise to cover the major genres. Taking that as our starting point, we began to think about what types of knowledge existed in the subject area.

A Framework for Knowledge

Knowledge in creative writing takes many forms: elsewhere, I have classified such knowledge as taking the forms of poiesis, praxis, process and pedagogy (McLoughlin, 2008). That classification remains useful in that we can broadly talk about the four different types as addressing four different aspects of the knowledge base that will make adept, critically aware and reflective writers and provide skills that they can use to earn money. At the base of everything is poiesis, which can be broadly defined as the craft skills necessary to get the artifact made. Praxis involves knowledge related to the critical, editorial and reflective process of drafting the piece. Process knowledge is the reflective and theoretical knowledge surrounding the creative process and how it operates. Pedagogical knowledge involves all of the preceding knowledge types but with the addition of further reflective and theoretical knowledge that allows the knowledge related to poiesis, praxis and process to be adapted and taught to others.

In order to deliver these different types of knowledge we decided that the best framework was one that offered the maximum possible stability and sense of cohort identity. We were bound by some restrictions: the modular scheme that operated within the university at undergraduate level was built for a base 15-credit one-semester module. The possibility existed that we could double those into 30-credit, year-long modules. This created the sense of stability that we wanted. It allowed time for students to understand what they were being taught, digest it and experiment with it.

The structure created a strong sense of cohort identity and made for much more settled workshops. Under the older structure, each module changed personnel every 15 weeks, three weeks of which were inter-semester break. This meant that one had 12 weeks with the students to get them to gel as a workshop group, get them to trust each other and comment freely on work. Again, doubling the length of time they spent together was a logical approach to creating more settled groups which learned to trust each other and could then go on to work much more effectively as a workshop in the longer term. It was decided that workshops should be genre specific in order that students who really wanted to work within that genre were alongside other like-minded students. This helped to create communities of craft-focused apprentice writers.

Each of the three levels of an undergraduate degree consist of 120 credits, so we put in place a series of genre specific modules in poetry, drama and prose, of 30 credits each, where students could spend the whole year studying within their chosen genres and progress through each level of the degree following their chosen genres. The fourth strand was made up from 30-credit, year-long modules focused on critical reading skills at level one; the business of getting published at level two; and the creative process at level three. Of course, we understood that not all students would want to do all genres, so choice was built into the programme through offering selected modules at each level from the English Language and Literature programmes and screenwriting modules, which were borrowed from the Film Studies degree.

Around that basic structure some dedicated modules on autobiographical writing and the novel offered additional choice particularly in the third year, where some students preferred to specialise in a single genre. We wanted the programme to be flexible enough to accommodate those students as well as those who wanted to continue writing in several genres or who wished to experiment with mixed genres. An undergraduate module on creativity and the creative process was added in order to provide a formal structure for students interested in the creative process as a subject for study in its own right. The Master's course built on the undergraduate structure and offered focused modules on genre, theory, translation and adaptation, the creative process, editing and pedagogy. These were built around a core Master's workshop that was genre specific. The modules were designed to hone the students' critical skills, provide knowledge of various relevant theoretical perspectives and models and to allow the student to receive hands-on training in areas that would be useful for their future employability.

Again we had to make some compromises regarding the structure of the programme since MA degrees were expected to fit a pattern of six, 20-credit modules, topped off with a 60-credit dissertation. This was not overly problematic for poets, who could produce a chapbook sized collection, or for short story writers who could produce between two and four short stories, but the dissertation was quite short in terms of possible word count available for novelists and allowed them only to present a small portion of their novel. In practice, this has not proved to be a problem. Students have been happy to select the portion of the novel they feel best represents the quality of their writing and include a synopsis of the rest for context.

Teaching Methods

At the time we set out to design the programme, the workshop was the default mode of teaching, and after we had a base structure in place, we set about examining in detail the teaching methodologies we employed. Under the old system we had a number of duplicate runs of modules for each set of 18 students who chose to undertake them. This made sense if the runs were in different semesters, but could be problematic as staff numbers grew, in that if there were two runs taught by two different lecturers. Students would often seek out the run of a favourite lecturer, and be unhappy if they had to go to another (perhaps less favoured) lecturer. It also meant that there were possibilities of lecturers teaching different syllabi within the broad framework of the module structure. One possible way around this was to separate the knowledge which was 'received' or 'procedural' from the knowledge which was 'constructed' (Belenky et al., 1986).

For instance, in poetry, I might talk about the sonnet for an hour, looking at the history of the sonnet, the structure of various different types of sonnet and, basically, it does not matter if there are 10 students or 50 in the room, the knowledge is largely being transferred one way and is received by the students. Poems might be given out and students offered a procedure or method for analysis of the poems. This may then be carried out among groups of students and a plenary discussion could take place as to what each group's findings were. This is a much more dialogic way of imparting knowledge through offering a procedure by which the students can find knowledge for themselves. It uses and builds upon the knowledge already in the room and, again, larger group teaching becomes possible. The workshop is different in nature. It is the place where small group criticism of student work really comes into its own. It is a testing ground for work, where students can gauge and engage likely reader response. It is a place where work may be improved through the criticism and suggestions for improvements received. It can also be a place for creative play, through the exercises given. It is a place where reading strategies can be observed and discussions on craft, influence and process can occur; and it is a place where new knowledge about these can be constructed.

One of the most invaluable resources I found when thinking about programme design was the literature related to creativity. This provided insights into the way creative processes operate at a cognitive and social level, and what may promote truly creative outcomes or inhibit them. For instance, research into creativity undertaken by Teresa Amabile and her various collaborators (Amabile, 1996) implies that supervised free-writes tend not to produce really creative responses, since they combine factors such as surveillance, deadlines and expectation of assessment – all of which are factors that were found to inhibit creativity. Under conditions of surveillance, deadline and expected assessment, students tend to resort to satisficing and to using an algorithmic approach to writing, which they know will generate something, rather than taking a more risky and time-consuming strategy that may produce something more creative. The other problem is that there is often considerable time given over in workshops to listening to this raw work. It is often in such a raw state that it is pointless making comment on the work other than to offer encouragement to continue to work on it. Given this information, it was felt that writing exercises would be much more productive if they were undertaken in the students' own time and they could be given at the end of the lecture, seminar or workshop for the students to attempt on their own or in collaboration later. The students can hone these exercises through several drafts before the work in progress is brought back to workshop. This frees up workshop time for critique-based discussion of work in progress. The students spend more time having their work in progress analysed and taking on board opinions and suggestions related to the work. They also spend more time looking at the work of others and honing their critical faculties.

Reflexive Poetics

We wanted the programme to build student knowledge from key skills and technical knowledge and vocabulary towards more specialist knowledge later as the student chose areas which interested them, and where they felt their talents best lay. In designing the actual modules taught, the team felt that a broad structure which proceeded from basic skills, such as set form in poetry or looking at characterisation, plot and dialogue in prose, would provide a good base for the first years to work from both in terms of getting to practice the basics of writing, and also in offering them the critical vocabulary to discuss work in those terms. This structure was built upon at second year, which concentrated on particular aspects of trope in poetry such as metaphor, allegory and irony; drama focused on elements of stagecraft and use of physical space. The third year modules built on this again, looking at more theoretical aspects of poetry such as projective verse; taking a more politicised view of drama; and in prose, a transgressive approach to writing. Particular care was taken to ensure that the teaching methods, syllabi, learning outcomes and assessment criteria of the modules were constructively aligned (Biggs, 1999).

The supplementary critical discourse that accompanies the writing at all levels is generally referred to as a responsive critical understanding (RCU) in order to highlight the fact that it is intended to be a critical response to the work, and to the creative processes of writing the work in so far as the writer can understand them. This may include discussion of context, influences, inspiration, praxis and poetics. This focus on analysis of process, praxis and poetics is an important part of building a reflective and writerly ethos across the degree. The RCU is one way to ensure that this is inherent in teaching methods, and explicit in learning outcomes and assessment criteria. However, the RCU is also supplementary to the creative work and this is clearly signalled by the percentage of marks awarded to it. At undergraduate level it is given 20% of the total mark, at postgraduate level 30%. This difference is due to the expectation of greater analysis and theoretical integration at postgraduate level.

Assessment

In many cases, under the old system, we were assessing students after six weeks. The time required to assimilate the craft knowledge adequately;

to experiment with it to produce initial writing; to edit and hone the resulting writing, meant that assessing at six weeks only assessed either very raw writing or in some cases the knowledge they already had. It was decided that if assessment points were placed at the ends of the semesters, then greater development time was allowed and the writing portfolios assessed would be more polished and more developed as a result. Our experience is that this has proved to be the case.

In order to create a varied and well-balanced diet of assessment, some assessments are done through oral presentations; others include book reviews, formal essays on writers or groups of writers, or comparative analyses of two books or writers; discursive and more theoretical essay questions are also set. During the design phase, we felt it was important to ensure that reading and analysis of other writers' work was seen as an integral aspect of the programme in order to prevent students' writing becoming too inward looking. Previous experience had shown that many students at undergraduate level did not see the connection between reading other writers' work and producing work of their own and it was felt that this critical element would encourage greater engagement with literature more widely. This is particularly true of the first year cohort, many of whom have been more attuned to film as the main medium through which they engage with plot and character. Many other students when they arrive are used to reading novels for pleasure. However these are often narrow in range and read for entertainment only, rather than analytically and critically.

Conclusion

The programme has been running since 2006. It includes elements of large group teaching as well as workshop-based teaching. This has raised the staff-student ratio so that it is in line with other subjects in the wider humanities in the university, without adversely affecting small group contact time. Basically, the design removed duplication and ensured that appropriate methods of delivery were deployed which were suitable to either the knowledge transfer function or the practice-led workshop-based elements of the programme. We have worked smarter rather than harder, and by decreasing the assessment points, neither the staff nor the students feel as though they are in a constant assessment cycle. This was a significant problem when we were assessing every six weeks. Given the prevailing financial situation regarding the funding of universities at the current time and the likely conditions that will prevail in the medium term, this structure has placed the degree programme on a good financial footing and means that we continue to be efficient in our use of staff time and resources.

We have made further changes over the last five years in order to improve the provision, but the basic structure remains. Because we tend to teach in self-contained fortnightly cells where knowledge transfer elements lead to workshopped work, the structure is very flexible and mirrors the natural creative cycle of inspiration, motivation and inputs to the creative process followed by writing, editing and workshopping outputs of the creative process. It allows students to focus on a topic and build their knowledge organically through relating the topics to each other as they learn about them. It also facilitates a direct relation of what they learn and how it may be applied in practice in their own writing. This process can be mapped directly onto Kolb's cycle of experiential learning (Kolb, 1984).

Given the prevailing economic conditions and likely higher education funding model in the medium term, it will no longer be sufficient to design a programme that replicates unthinkingly the Iowa Workshop model, or to replicate what has been standard practice. Universities are demanding more distinctive programmes in an era of student choice. Bespoke programmes that fit niche markets will be in demand. The advent of modules teaching the pedagogy of writing, and their spread throughout the academy, will have an impact also. Programme design in the future will be much more informed by theories of how students learn and what research tells us about how the creative process works. It is certain that there will also be further economic pressures to find new ways of teaching which respond to funding cuts and efficiency drives but also maintain the quality of the teaching and learning experience. However, these new teachers may well have to draw heavily on the literature not just to design innovative courses, but also to defend small group teaching methodologies where appropriate.

References

Amabile, T. (1996) *Creativity in Context*. Oxford: Westview.

Belenky, M., Clinchy, B., Goldberger, N. and Tarule, J. (1986) *Women's Ways of Knowing*. New York: Basic Books.

Biggs, J. (1999) *Teaching for Quality Learning at University*. Buckingham: SRHE and Open University Press.

Kolb, D. (1984) *Experiential Learning*. Englewood Cliffs, NJ: Prentice Hall.

Maslow, A. (1954) *Motivation and Personality*. New York: Harper and Row.

McLoughlin, N. (2008) Creating an integrated model for teaching creative writing – one approach. In G. Harper and J. Kroll (eds) *Creative Writing Studies: Practice, Research, Pedagogy* (pp. 88–100). Clevedon: Multilingual Matters.

Rogers, C. (1961) *On Becoming a Person: A Therapist's View of Psychotherapy*. London: Constable.

The Future of Graduate Studies in Creative Writing: Institutionalizing Literary Writing

Patrick Bizzaro

This part of the chapter postulates that the confusion in English Studies between poetry as we historically have thought of it and the poetic func-tion of language as James Britton articulates it, as exemplified in essays by Donald Hall and Art Young, has resulted in the institutionalization of creative writing. The dramatic increase in the number of students who take creative writing suggests that the field has undergone a democrati-zation that brings into the creative writing classroom students unlike those Donald Hall had in mind but students capable of doing the kind of writing Young advocates in advocating poetry to learn. Creative writing is firmly entrenched in English departments and Young's efforts have made it possible for us to see creative writing as a subject of use in grad-uate courses across the disciplines as new professionals attempt to articulate new findings.

If Donald Hall (1998) had his way 30 years ago, those of us concerned with the future of graduate studies in creative writing would be marching in a very different direction right now than the one recent scholarship has led us in. In his lecture-turned-essay, 'Poetry and ambition', Hall spoke against the benefits of graduate education in creative writing and argued instead for creative writing's deinstitutionalization. The problem as he saw it was the democratization of creative writing and the concomitant decline in literary ambition among writers. Hall's solution: 'Abolish the M.F.A' (p. 4). Why? 'The workshop schools us to produce the McPoem ...'.

By contrast, Art Young (1982) in 'Considering values: The poetic func-tion of language', written a year later, argues:

Somewhere along the line, I think about sixth grade, our system of mass education gives up on creative writing as a useful learning experience. The rationale seems to be that true proficiency in creative writing is a gift from the gods given to the inspired few who are predestined to become great artists no matter what their educational experience, and that further opportunities for everyone else to write poetically serves no useful purpose. (p. 77)

What Young refers to in this passage is not poetry as Hall uses the term, but more importantly in the institutionalization of creative writing, the poetic function of language. Young defends the poetic function as a mode of learning: '. . . poetic language helps students assess knowledge in terms of their own systems of belief' (p. 78). He is not talking about the works of Dante, as Hall does. Rather, he explains, 'Poetic writing in its most familiar and completed forms is what most of us would recognize as, among other things, poetry, stories, plays and parables'.

Thus far, no one has directly attributed ongoing conflicts in creative writing in the academy to the split between creative writers who, like Hall, advocate deinstitutionalizing or at least further isolating creative writing from other subjects and compositionists who, like Young, plan to further institutionalize it and help it merge with the other tasks typically undertaken in American universities. Nonetheless, the conflict between those who would deinstitutionalize creative writing and those who advocate further developing it as an academic subject connected to other subjects must be at the center of our reflections on what we have done in university creative writing programs in the United States and are yet to do. What's more, whatever the future holds for graduate studies in creative writing – and it could hold a great many things, some unimaginable to us right now – I believe the future direction of creative writing will be a product of an evolutionary process that is already underway and reflected in current scholarship in the field: creative writing studies.

(Com)positioning Creative Writing: Recent Views

In 'Out of the margins: The expanding role of creative writing in today's college curriculum', Chad Davidson and Gregory Fraser (2009: 76) ask a question important to the future of graduate studies in creative writing: '. . . where do creative-writing workshops fit into students' broader curricula?' Moving beyond the dominant concern of most people who have theorized creative writing's connection with composition – that it ceases to be creative writing at all and instead becomes a subdiscipline of composition studies – Davidson and Fraser continue: '. . . how do workshops interact with other college courses – philosophy, history, biology, foreign language, literature?' Thus, Davidson and Fraser ask questions focused on *institutionalizing* creative writing, as I use the term. My perspective slightly inverts theirs because I want to know how creative writing might evolve to help philosophers, historians, scientists, and others trained in the university learn to describe their own new discoveries. That is, my interest is not in how philosophy, history, science and other subjects might be used in a creative writing classroom, but in how creative writing might be taught in philosophy, history, science and other academic courses to help future professionals in those fields better describe new discoveries. In short, creative writing must eventually teach writing *skills that are not currently being taught* generally in the university, skills we currently do not know how to teach in any other way right now except as 'creative writing'.

I want to stress my belief that whatever graduate studies in creative writing eventually becomes, it will be a product of an evolutionary process that has begun with the kind of thinking Davidson and Fraser have done. But it must not end there. In any case, it is clear that the line of inquiry one must trace to survey recent scholarship in the field, creative writing studies, is one that follows the further institutionalization of creative writing. So woven is creative writing into the fabric of most universities, the plan Hall called for to evict creative writing entirely from the university seems a distant and almost laughable recollection. Clearly, Hall seemed to have thought of creative writing in terms very different from the way it has been theorized these past 30 years by composition scholars such as Art Young. Indeed, most would agree that the traditional view of creative writing as an effort to develop the next generation's writing talent is no longer the single and paramount concern in creative writing programs, not with the recent rage for creative writing pedagogy. Davidson and Fraser call for a 'cross-fertilization' which actually began several years earlier.[1] All information I can find makes me hold to my belief that creative writing will not be deinstitutionalized or even isolated in the academy. Rather, given the rapid institutionalization of creative writing since 1981 and its growth in popularity ever since, creative writing has been used in the university in increasingly innovative ways. *This* – that is, the various scholarly discussions of ways creative writing might be used – is the process that is already underway.

Curricular Institutionalization: Poetry as a Mode of Learning

As a past writing program administrator and director of writing across the curriculum myself, I am especially impressed by recent work done at Clemson University, work spearheaded by Art Young, where writing across the curriculum has developed a subdiscipline, poetry across the curriculum. This particular use of the poetic function of language to help students learn has had positive results. In it, 'teachers from across campus assigned students to write a poem in response to material being taught' (Connor-Greene *et al.,* 2006: 5). There seems to have been little, if any, instruction in writing poems; to paraphrase Elbow (1998) from *Writing with Power,* it's really okay to write poetry 'as a non-poet', as Elbow has. Emphasis at Clemson was placed on writing to learn, not on the writing of great poems. Results as they are reported in *Teaching and Learning Creatively: Inspirations and Reflections* are likewise informal and anecdotal, lacking scientific rigor, which no one has asked for or come to expect in creative writing anyway: teachers 'found indications that students were bringing together material from across a course, or from more than one course, or combining lessons from the course with insights gathered elsewhere' (Connor-Greene *et al.,* 2006: 5). In a sense, Poetry Across the Curriculum answers Dianne Donnelly's (2010: 21) call for 'more interdisciplinary activity' and provides an excellent example of how creative writing has become institutionalized in the academy.

What is the significance, then, of Young's work at Clemson? It asserts the belief not only that writing poetry helps students learn, but that it brings the descriptive power of poetic language into contact with difficult concepts in other fields. Until now, philosophers, historians and scientists, among others have long made claims about the inadequacy of language: our understandings are defined and thus limited by our powers of discourse, which depend on perception and our ability to describe those perceptions. While it is true that my argument about language might have been made in the 17th century, I make this assertion now with a different emphasis entirely because I believe that something important is about to happen or, at least, should: the rhetorician and the poet will soon need to help those in the professions who are working at the cutting edge with difficult concepts generally unavailable through language to lay persons. I call this writing *quantum rhetoric* and find it already being published widely.[2]

I believe the teaching of Quantum Rhetoric, which combines training in creative writing at the graduate level with graduate study in a professional/ technical field, constitutes the future of graduate studies in creative writing. This option may come to exist alongside more conventional instruction for those who study to become part of the next generation of writers and those, more recently, who plan to teach creative writing in the academy. My position here is based on my belief that we are already making a call for such collaborative efforts and that much creative work we find most difficult to interpret really partakes of Quantum Rhetoric and has been incorrectly read.

Thus, my point about the future of graduate studies in creative writing is that institutionalization of creative writing means that creative writing will soon do the work of various kinds of *writing we are not now teaching in the university*. And I see a need for such writing instruction.

Quantum Rhetoric and the Hybridity Model in Creative Writing Instruction

In keeping with my sense that creative writing is evolving toward something this essay wants to name, I have paid particular attention to those scholars who have begun to articulate the terms of hybrid classes as well as contemporary published works that reveal Quantum Rhetoric as writers already employ it.

Katherine Haake (2010) for one envisions this institutionalized or global usefulness of creative writing in the university in compelling terms: 'the struggle continues as we seek to convince not just ourselves, but all our English colleagues, that what creative writing has to offer in the classroom goes beyond the familiar production of student poems and stories to an enriched experience of the various activities that we engage in, in general, throughout English studies' (p. 15). We have long known but have not had courage enough to say that though writing in genres is a time-tested approach to teaching creative writing, the production of poems, plays, stories and creative essays is not our only (or maybe even our chief) outcome and has not been for nearly 20 years. Clearly, from the perspective Haake gives us, the folks at Clemson have begun to respond to Tim Mayers' (2007: 3) plea that program developers of the future 'consider how creative writing might fit into a larger writing curriculum'. Indeed, as Mayers has posited, 'creative writing can offer unique perspectives on where English departments have come from, and *where they might go*' (p. 5, my emphasis). No doubt, and quite importantly, the work at Clemson characterizes the continued democratization of creative writing in the American academy and thus its further institutionalization. As a field of study, creative writing is much more than an avenue for expressing understandings, though it expresses understandings too: 'One cannot be taught to be a genius, but one can learn to imitate some of the techniques in which geniuses are expert' (Ritter & Vanderslice, 2007: 3). From this perspective, we may see that creative writing is already treated as a democratic endeavor in some of its uses in the academy. This is an exciting proclamation because, by claiming that creative writing is a democratic pursuit, we open the possibility for uses of the techniques of poetry and fiction in ways that include not only the making of publishable works of art but much more than that. And this view requires that we reconsider what we mean when we use the term 'creative' in a course title and what we construe 'writing' to be in that course and elsewhere. I appreciate and concur with what Katharine Haake has to say in this regard:

As we entertain new possibilities for our own writing workshops, it's worth at least acknowledging that every occasion is an occasion for writing, that it is all 'creative,' and that this particular discussion should be part of a larger project of re-configuring English studies itself as an inter-disciplinary site where, valued for difference as well as sameness, all the strands of scholarship and creativity intersect and commingle to enrich one another without losing their discrete autonomy. (pp. 182–183)

The Pedagogy of Intersecting and Commingling: Hybrid Graduate Classes

Hybrid classes are an emerging pedagogy whose potential for the teaching of creative writing is only beginning to be understood. Some discussion of them has appeared in our scholarly writing. The cross-fertilization they enable us to envision makes the hybrid class an excellent model for graduate creative writing courses of the future, as I envision them in this essay as an outgrowth of current scholarly thinking.

Increasingly we hear calls to further investigate hybrid classes in creative writing. Some hybrids are more easily managed than others. For instance, not long ago and without an awful lot of forethought I co-taught a course in 'Writing Poems and Making Drawings' with a colleague from the School of Art. He wanted to learn how to write poems, and I wanted to learn how to draw. Our students earnestly wanted to learn how to do both. Apart from the administrative concern over how we would get credited for teaching that semester (in the end, we each got credited generously with one three-hour course), this course was relatively easy to teach. The teachers got along, had fun, and did things that seemed sensible to them. Both teachers attended all classes. One day each week (we met three times per week) was dedicated to instruction and acquisition of skills related to producing poems, one day to making drawings, and the third for workshop or critique. My colleague from art and I became each other's student. Students taking the class for credit decided upon what and how much they would do and for what grade; predictably, they were more demanding than we would have been. In keeping with that approach, their first assignment was to draw up contracts. The art teacher critiqued the drawings and I, as poet, workshopped the poetry. We decided on final grades together. Everyone in class agreed that the final project for the course would be a poem/painting that everyone had to do. That project, by agreement with the instructors, could be individual or collaborative. The art teacher and I collaborated on the making of a poem/painting that took up most of one wall and was critiqued by the class. We were young, exuberant, and fearless then and during the subsequent year worked on a book that would include my poems accompanied by his drawings.

This seems a reasonable effort at a hybrid class, if not a model for other such collaborative efforts. Much of what we learned was from trial and error and serendipity. What did I learn from running such an experiment that might work as well in Quantum Rhetoric classes of the future? I learned that both teachers should attend all classes, even if they are not teaching that day; they should write and draw with their students and be open to the same critique (this ended up being one of the fun parts of class though not everyone might be willing to undergo such playful scrutiny); they should share the space, perhaps taking turns teaching or planning connected instruction on a given day; the use of a contract method for purposes of grading ended up being a very good decision; critiques and workshops were led by the teacher who specializes in that area; grading was done jointly. These insights are the results of one informal effort.

Some years later, while I was serving as Director of the University Writing Program at the same university, the Vice Chancellor for Graduate Studies and Research asked me to design a graduate program in writing across the curriculum. Because of the nature of requirements in graduate studies, a model different from the one we used in developing the under-graduate program in WAC had to be invented. The need was clear at that university, as at most others: students entering graduate school with a thesis or dissertation ahead of them, need instruction in writing. The hybrid model seemed best suited then for that purpose. In it, a writing teacher shared space with a faculty member from the major department, be it busi-ness, education, health sciences, natural sciences, medicine, whatever. In addition to having two teachers there, the program necessitated bringing in experts to run what we might call mini-lessons, focusing on the uses of writing in those particular professions. Upon reflection, I think a poet and an artist who had collaborated on a project such as the culminating poem/painting we assigned in our undergraduate poetry and drawing class would have been an excellent addition. We selected these outside consultants from among past graduates of programs and that worked out nicely on many levels. Donnelly has suggested a format such as this for hybrid courses: 'coordinated carefully, a program that includes a series of mini-lectures on relevant topics might interest a large number of students, could defray costs, and might be managed over shorter six to eight week semesters' (p. 22). Donnelly thus has thought through many of the details of hybrid courses.

Donnelly envisions an entire program as having two tracks, and that idea will sustain creative writing graduate programs into the future because it will accommodate further institutionalization. My view here requires adding a third track in Quantum Rhetoric. Donnelly's model for graduate studies in creative writing is dynamic and inclusive, which is its strength. By having the two tracks Donnelly envisions, spaces will be made for writers who want to advance their genre writing and those in Donnelly's words 'who are also interested in the pedagogy of creative writing' (p. 22). She adds to this a 'complimentary and overlapping track' with 'a concentration on creativity in the marketplace'.

My plan would be to add to Donnelly's dual curriculum by including a track focusing on 'Quantum Rhetorics'. However it might shape up at an individual university, this track must meet institutional needs. In any format, I would recommend that the program require a seminar in rhetorical traditions. In such a course, students would have an opportunity to study a 'minor voice' in rhetorical history such as Longinus and contemplate what the world of writing instruction would look like if Longinus's ideas instead of Aristotle's had been passed forward. Other courses could focus simultaneously on a genre – for the sake of providing a familiar example, let's say poetry – and a disciplinary subject area, let's say physics. The goal would be to employ the poetic function of language 'to help create more adaptable and rhetorically aware student writers, writers whose knowledge of different genres and contexts allows them to succeed at multiple writing tasks' (Mayers, 2007: 12).

Conclusion

Current scholarship has moved toward a view of creative writing as best taught in hybrid classes. The needs of professionals in fields such as physics, who need to be given better tools for articulating new findings, suggest that learning to describe deep imaginings may help us describe matters as complicated as the deep universe or any other insight we have never before described. And as Pound has urged, by doing so we 'Make it new!' Hybrid courses give us the opportunity to teach techniques of writing – usually employed in poetry writing classes, for instance – to professionals from departments around campus. While our methods of delivery will continue to evolve and are outside the scope of this essay, there are no doubt discoveries ahead of us that will need to be described in techniques previously isolated in the academy but that need to be further institutionalized.

Notes

(1) A look at the uses of creative writing in the Progressive Education of the late twenties and early thirties suggests that 'cross-fertilization' has already been implemented. Additionally, Art Young and his colleagues at Clemson University had already implemented a Poetry Across the Curriculum program, which I discuss below. And Peter Elbow in *Writing with Power* probably was not thinking of Dante when he entitled his chapter 'Poetry as No Big Deal'.

(2) In spite of literary history's insistence that poetry and science are incompatible partners (see Poe, 'Sonnet: To Science' and Whitman, 'When I Heard the Learn'd Astronomer', for instance), contemporary poets like Ernesto Cardenal (2009) and Coleman Barks (2008) have written poems that employ deep imaginings in describing the deep universe. Note as well the proliferation of 'medical poetry' as well as the highly successful *Quantum Lyrics* by A. Van Jordan (2007).

References

Barks, C. (2008) *Winter Sky: New and Selected Poems, 1968–2008*. Athens: The University of Georgia Press.

Cardenal, E. (2009) *Pluriverse: New and Selected Poems*. J. Cohen (ed.) NY: New Directions.

Connor-Greene, P.A., Mobley, C., Paul, C.E., Waldvogel, J.A., Wright, L. and Young, A. (2006) *Teaching and Learning Creatively: Inspirations and Reflections*. West Lafayette, IN: Parlor Press.

Davidson, C. and Fraser, G. (2009) Out of the margins: The expanding role of creative writing in today's college curriculum. *The Writer's Chronicle* 42.3 (December), 76–81.

Donnelly, D. (2010) If it ain't broke, don't fix it or change is inevitable except from a vending machine. In D. Donnelly (ed.) *Does the Writing Workshop Still Work?* (pp. 1–27). Bristol: Multilingual Matters.

Elbow, P. (1998) *Writing with Power*. New York: Oxford University Press.

Haake, K. (2010) Re-envisioning the workshop: Hybrid classrooms, hybrid texts. In D. Donnelly (ed.) *Does the Writing Workshop Still Work?* (pp. 182–193). Bristol: Multilingual Matters.

Hall, D. (1998) Poetry and ambition. *Poetry and Ambition: Essays 1982–88* (pp. 154–170). Ann Arbor: University of Michigan Press.

Jordan, A.V. (2007) *Quantum Lyrics*. New York: Norton.

Mayers, T. (2007) Figuring the future: Lore and/in creative writing. In K. Ritter and S. Vanderslice (eds) *Can it Really be Taught? Resisting Lore in Creative Writing Pedagogy* (pp. 1–13). Portsmouth, NH: Boynton/Cook.

Ritter, K. and Vanderslice, S. (2007) Introduction. In K. Ritter and S. Vanderslice (eds) *Can it Really be Taught? Resisting Lore in Creative Writing Pedagogy* (pp. xi–xx). Portsmouth, NH: Boynton/Cook.

Young, A. (1982) Considering values: The poetic function of language. *Language Connections: Writing and Reading Across the Curriculum* (pp. 77–98). Urbana: NCTE.

Conclusion: Investigating Key Issues in Creative Writing

Dianne Donnelly and Graeme Harper

Our aim in this book has been to explore what *we* consider key issues in the undertaking, exploration and teaching of creative writing. To do this we have drawn together a range of writers, from different parts of the world. We also realize that to entitle a book *Key Issues in Creative Writing* will potentially be a challenge to others to ask: are those really the key issues? We haven't covered every part of the world, and we haven't asked everyone we might have asked to contribute to this book. There are gaps here and that is entirely intentional, as well as natural.

In addition, our particular focus has been on creative writing as it occurs in and around universities and colleges. For some readers, that might be one of the first points of contention, because one additional key issue that some might say needs addressing is the issue of whether creative writing, as we have come to know it around our higher education institutions, is different in activity, attitudes and/or outcomes to creative writing undertaken outside of our higher education institutions. Authors in this book have not greatly addressed this issue, focusing primarily on the environment and activities around our contemporary universities.

Other missing issues might include those relating to the writing of specific genres, or those focused on the interactions between creative writing and other art forms, or those connected with creative writing as a therapeutic tool, or issues associated with creative writing as a leisure activity unconnected with the academy and those things around it, or issues of creative writing at different levels of education, or issues of creative writing as the human enterprise behind the creation of literary or media culture. Some readers might consider *these* to be key issues, and thus feel we have left them plenty of room for their own investigations. Here's to that!

Key Issues in Creative Writing is not meant as a guide to all that should be considered and discussed. Rather, it is an exploration of some of the issues that can be addressed, and it is an indication that there are creative writers and creative writing researchers, many of whom are one and the same, working in universities around the world and increasingly exploring exactly the kinds of issues we have included here. Needless to say, to be unquestioning would hardly be productive and, as we come to the end of writing and editing this book, we are even more questioning than we were when we started it. It's hoped readers will react in the same way.

Given these concluding comments, we should also declare that as editors of this book we orchestrated (to medium extent) the kinds of topics the writers explored, and we suggested (in our orchestration) the kinds of directions the writers might like to take. In some cases – most notably the Bizzaro-McLoughlin chapter – we went about structuring the book to place alternative viewpoints in very close proximity. In that case, one writer from the UK and one from the USA independently exploring the same topic, while more or less aware of the other. We did not, of course, write the pieces for any of the writers, and we did not, of course, control what was said. So this can be seen as a book with an editorial core and around it, lava-like, is flowing the magma of writerly interest and expression!

With this in mind, and leaving behind the planetary metaphor, what readers could well find exceedingly interesting are the individual voices that have emerged by the time they begin reading this conclusion. None of the writers here appear so similar to those beside them that someone could comment 'those people who deal with key issues in creative writing all seem like the same kind of people'. Indeed, it is indicative of the individuality of creative writing practice that our contributors bring to these discussions their own sense of how creative writing happens, why it happens, and what the results are of it happening.

Therefore, if there is another key issue on which we have touched, but which we have not declared, it is the key issue of how to bring together a community of people with a shared interest but one which locates itself so readily in the role and disposition of the individual, a practice that assumes there is a culture, a society, indeed a shared sense of learning too, but that always returns us to the often personal actions of individuals, to their thoughts but also to their feelings and emotions. Creative writing does this, and the exploration of creative writing should rightly do this too. There is a rule of thumb with any activity concerned with seeking new knowledge, and that is that if you begin in the wrong place you rarely end up with the right answers. With this in mind, beginning with the nature of creative writing and with the activities and understandings of creative writers is the *only* way to ever get closer to understanding creative writing itself. Other starting places might produce interesting asides, even useful information on other things, but they will never address key issues in creative writing.

As we stand today in universities around the world with a considerable community of creative writers and creative writing researchers around us, we are continuing rapidly forward through an era in which the open exchange of the activities and artefacts of creative writing grows more possible and thus far more common. No longer is it necessary for creative writers to work only through a relatively narrow range of distribution channels, whether we talk in terms of these being publishers or distributors, companies or agents. Huge technological changes have occurred that now make the distribution of works of creative writing possible through what sometimes seems a limitless number of avenues, and certainly these are more in the control of the individual than anyone else. Further to that – and as the great many online creative writing discussions make plain – it is now exceedingly possible to regularly talk about creative writing *as it happens* as well as creative writing works when they are complete or near complete. Creative writing therefore is very well represented today by writing-in-progress, and this focuses us very well on how much human time, knowledge and energy is devoted to that very progress.

All of these things need to be incorporated into how we are thinking about, and evolving, the learning and teaching of creative writing in universities and colleges. We're not alone in this: much of 21st century higher education is faced with questions considering the future of its disciplines, its disciplinary expertise, and its development and maintenance of relationships between teachers and learners. How is the academy dealing with its leadership role in this regard? How might we improve the ways in which we develop creative writing within the academy and the many new cultural, societal and economic developments we see going on in the world at large? What might our future roles as creative writers in higher education be? Unsurprisingly, knowing what we can explore, why we might explore it, and how we might go about doing these explorations, seems fundamental to us, as we indicate here in *Key Issues in Creative Writing*.

Index

Artist communities, 20
Arts and Humanities Research (AHRC), xx, 109, 128
Association of Writers and Writing Programs (AWP), xiii, xxi, 6, 12, 18, 19, 23, 26, 100
Australasian Association of Writing Program (AAWP), 23, 26
Australian Council for the Arts (ACR), 18
Australian Research Council (ARC), 21
Authorship, 68, 69

Bachelor of Arts, 36, 37, 38
British Council, 18

Collaboration, 138
Community, 17
Composition, 73, 74, 108, 139
    see also Conference on College Composition and Communication (CCCC),
Conference on College Composition and Communication (CCCC), 6, 82
Creative Industries, 15–16, 65–66
Creative Literacy, xxiii, 63–64, 72, 75, 77
Creative writing *as* research, xxiii, 104–107, 131
    see also Practice-Led Research
Creative writing *in* research, 113–114
Creative Writing Benchmark Statement (UK), 41, 44

Creativity, xvi, 7, 8, 14, 21, 61, 65–66, 70, 117, 118, 146, 158, 165
    see also Creative Literacy
Cross-pollination, 8–9, 129, 171

Digital Competency, 141
    see also Technology
Doctoral programmes, xiii, xv, xvii, xvii, 11, 13, 43, 44, 45, 110, 117, 152, 161

Emotions, 112, 179
English Studies, 32–34, 148, 162, 173
Environments, 147, 151, 155
European Association of Creative Writing Programs (EACWP), 24
Excellence in Research for Australia (ERA), xix–xx, 21

Foucault, Michel, 5, 35
Funding, xvi
    see also Arts and Humanities Research Council
        Australian Research Council (ARC)
        Excellence in Research for Australia (ERA)
        Research Excellence Framework (REF)
        Research Councils
        National Endowment for the Arts (NEA)

Genre, xxiii, 85–86, 89, 94, 153, 156
Great Writing International Creative Writing Conference, 24, 28

Habitation, 49–50, 54, 58–59
Habitats, xxii, 48–60
    see also Environments
    Habitation
Hybridization,   4, 5– 9, 86, 91, 96,
    173–174, 175
    see also Cross-pollination

International Center for Creative
    Writing Research, 24, 28
Internationalization, 24
Interstitial,   93, 97–98, 99,

Knowledge,   xv, xviii, xxi, xxiii, 9, 17,
    22–23, 38–40, 92, 103, 105, 108,
    116–131, 147, 157, 162–164
    see also Propositional Knowledge
    Situational Knowledge
    Procedural Knowledge

Literary Intelligibility,   85, 91

Master of Arts (MA),   xv, 17, 36, 164
Master of Fine Arts (MFA),   xvii, 11,
    13, 62, 73, 76, 169
Methodologies,   xvi, 7, 23, 126, 127

National Association of Writers in
    Education (NAWE), 23, 28, 115
National Endowment for the Arts
    (NEA),   4, 20, 67
*New Writing: the International Journal for
    the Practice and Theory of Creative
    Writing,* 23, 24

People-centred,   52–53, 56, 58–59
Power, 5, 69, 93
    see also Foucault, Michel
Practice-led research,   xv, 104, 109–
    113, 117, 130, 158
Procedural knowledge,   121

Programme design,   xxiv, 11–12, 17,
    19, 60, 150, 159–176
Propositional knowledge,   121

Quantum Rhetoric,   xxiv, 172–176
Questioning,   103

Reflection,   112
Reflexivity,   112, 166
Responsiveness,   111–112, 166
Research Assessment Exercise (UK),
    21, 29
    see also Research Excellence
        Framework
Research Councils (UK), xix
    see also Arts and Humanities
        Research Council (AHRC)
    Australian Research Council (ARC)
Research Excellence Framework (UK),
    xviii

Situational Knowledge,   107, 114, 115
STEM subjects,   10
Story,   80, 83, 95

Technologies,   64, 138, 139
TEXT,   23
Therapeutic practice,   35, 178
Time,   52, 53
Translation,   9, 164
Transparent Approach to Costing
    Teaching (TRAC),   104, 105

Universities,   xiv, xv, xvi, xviii, xix,
    xxi, xxii, xxv, 3–5, 8, 10, 11, 13, 14,
    20, 22, 25, 30–46, 62, 72–75, 107,
    149, 178

Workshops,   41–42, 86, 149, 154, 155,
    165, 168, 170
Writers' Chronicle, The,   23
Writing in Education,   23